DATE DUE

LEBANON
Death of a Nation

SANDRA MACKEY

CONGDON & WEED, INC.
New York • Chicago

Library of Congress Cataloging-in-Publication Data

Mackey, Sandra, 1937–
    Lebanon : the death of a nation / Sandra Mackey.
      p.   cm.
    Includes index.
    ISBN 0-86553-204-4
    1. Lebanon—Politics and government—1975–   I. Title.
DS87.M28   1989
956.9204′4—dc20   89-7404
                                       CIP

Published by Congdon & Weed, Inc.
A subsidiary of Contemporary Books, Inc.
298 Fifth Avenue, New York, New York 10001
Distributed by Contemporary Books, Inc.
180 North Michigan Avenue, Chicago, Illinois 60601

Published simultaneously in Canada by Beaverbooks, Ltd.
195 Allstate Parkway, Valleywood Business Park
Markham, Ontario L3R 4T8 Canada

To Colin.

"Here am I, the wretched city, lying in ruins, my citizens dead . . . you who pass me by bewail my fate, and shed a tear in honour of Berytus that is no more."

—*Unknown sixth-century poet*

CONTENTS

AUTHOR'S NOTE

When using a limited number of words to write about a subject as complex as Lebanon it is critical to establish exactly what the author intends to accomplish. This is not a history of the Lebanese civil war. I feel that task is better left to the historians. Rather, this book explores the agonizing divisions within Lebanon between its Arab soul and its Western veneer. In approaching the war in this manner, I seek to explain to nonspecialist Western readers why the Lebanon of the 1960s and early 1970s, which they perceived as a magical playground proudly touting its Western ways, is now a caldron of ugly hostilities that have effectively sealed off the country from Westerners. Thus the narrative emphasizes those conditions and events that have contributed to the anti-Western aspect of the war.

In this context, I emphasize Israel's treachery in Lebanon more than Syria's, because Israel is central to the Arabs' virulent anti-Western passions. The wartime role of the Soviet Union as an arms supplier to various Muslim forces has only been touched on since its impact on Arab perceptions of the West is minor. I have chosen to discuss only a select number from the galaxy of men who competed with each other within the communal politics of prewar Lebanon. Each of these men represents the attitudes of a faction or a confessional about Lebanon's place in the Arab world. Other factors that play an important part in the carnage in Lebanon are similarly treated within the context of Lebanon's cultural divisions.

One further note. The transliteration of Arabic to English is problematic at best. There is no standard system recognized for either academic or general audiences. Since no method of transliteration is without its critics, I have chosen to use the simplified forms of Arabic words, names, and locations commonly used by newspapers in the United States. The diacritical marks, glotal stops, consonant sounds unique to Arabic, and marks for long vowels have been omitted. Quotations from other writers are retained in their original form.

ix

ACKNOWLEDGMENTS

Authors know more than anyone else that books are never written alone. And during the process of producing a book, the person who contributed that perfect little vignette or that memorable quote sometimes fades into the overall fabric of the book. But the contributions of others are too important to recede. Very special thanks go to Dr. Donald M. Reid of Georgia State University, who graciously reviewed the manuscript along the way. I am most grateful to him for his insights and suggestions and most of all for so readily understanding what I was about in this project. As always, I must thank my husband, Dan, for his unflagging support, keen editing skills, and endless patience without which my writing projects probably would never reach fruition.

I also wish to thank the many people in the Middle East, the United States, and elsewhere who offered their time and often their hospitality during the research phase of the book. I would like to particularly thank certain officials of the Lebanese government, several people in Syria who must remain unnamed, Clinton Bailey and Daniel Gavron in Israel, Ibrahim Dakkar in Jerusalem, Elizabeth Bonkovsky in Frankfurt, and Jim Muir in Cyprus. In the United States, my thanks go to Dr. R. K. Ramazani for his clear analysis of Iranian goals in Lebanon and even more for being such an inspiration to a young graduate student many years ago; to Dr. C. Michael York of the Georgia Institute of Technology for his advice on interview techniques; to Anthony E. DiResta for his counsel concerning U.S. travel restrictions to Lebanon; to Norman McKenzie and Bettye Sue Wright for their poetic musical references; and to Ginny Perkinson for her prodigious memory of the popular songs of the 1970s.

My heartfelt appreciation goes to Helen Rees, who is both a wonderful literary agent and a terrific traveling companion. My time in Israel would have been far less memorable without her. Appreciation also goes to my editor, Bernard Shir-Cliff, who gave me such free rein in writing this book. His enthusiasm for the project from start to finish did much to keep me going through all the frustrations.

And who could ever write a book without the support of friends? To Lynne and A. J. Land, who so generously made their mountain house available to me; to Carolyn Robinson of the Georgia State University library, who smoothed my access to research materials; to Cheryll Tobin for her help with the manuscript; to Boyd and Daphne Eaton for their unfailing interest; and to Clay and Barbara Moore for just being there—thanks!

MAP 1—LEBANON BY GEOGRAPHIC REGION

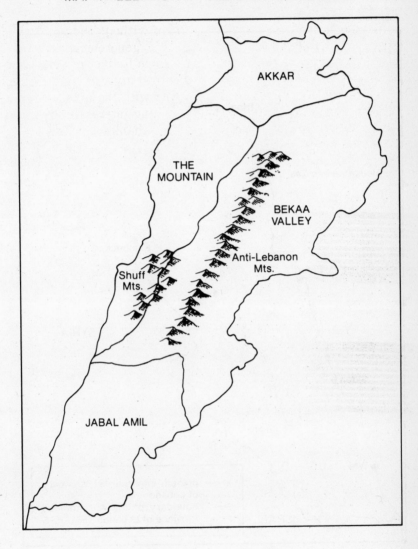

MAP 2—SMALLER AND GREATER LEBANON

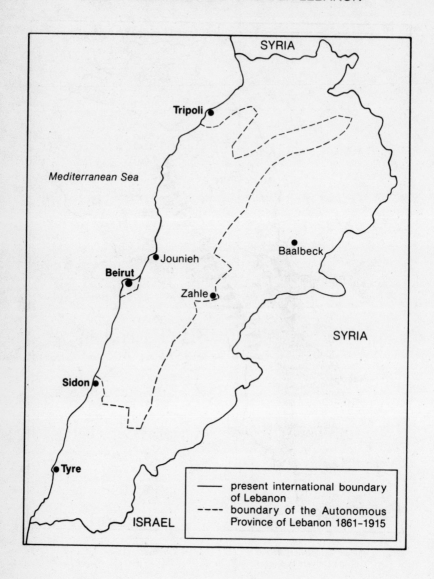

SYRIA

Tripoli

Mediterranean Sea

Jounieh

Beirut

Baalbeck

Zahle

SYRIA

Sidon

Tyre

ISRAEL

——— present international boundary
of Lebanon
– – – boundary of the Autonomous
Province of Lebanon 1861–1915

MAP 3—GEOGRAPHIC CONCENTRATION OF MAJOR COMMUNITIES

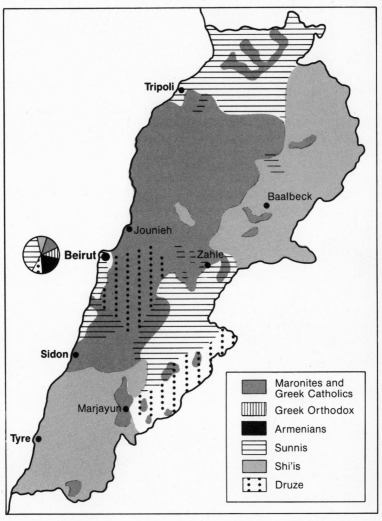

Tripoli

Baalbeck

Jounieh

Beirut

Zahle

Sidon

Marjayun

Tyre

Maronites and Greek Catholics

Greek Orthodox

Armenians

Sunnis

Shi'is

Druze

Source: Itamar Rabinovich, *The War for Lebanon, 1970–1985*, rev. ed. (Ithaca, N. Y.: Cornell University Press, 1985), 23.

MAP 4—LEBANON, 1989

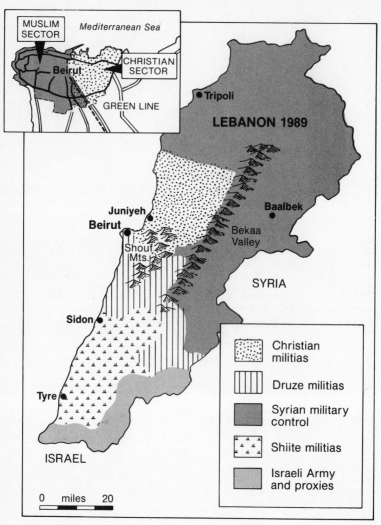

Source: Based on a map by Joan Forbes in the *Christian Science Monitor*.
© 1988 TCSPS

CHRONOLOGY

1861	The "Mountain" declared an autonomous province within the Ottoman Empire.
1920, August 31	Establishment of Greater Lebanon under the French Mandate.
1943	The National Pact.
1946	Final withdrawal of French forces, leading to an independent Lebanese republic; Bishara Khoury elected president.
1947	War for Palestine sends first influx of Palestinians into Lebanon.
1952	Camille Chamoun becomes Lebanon's second president.
1958	First Lebanese war; Fuad Shihab begins his term as president.
1964	Charles Helou elected president.
1968, December	Israel raids Beirut Airport; marks beginning of conflict within Lebanon over the Palestinian issue.
1969, November	Lebanese government grants certain concessions to PLO in Cairo Agreement.
1970	Suleiman Franjieh becomes president; PLO transfers its main base to Lebanon following defeat in Jordanian civil war.
1975, April	Opening phase of the Lebanese civil war.
1976, June	Syrian army intervenes in Lebanon.
1978, March	Israel launches Litani operation in southern Lebanon.
August 31	Musa al Sadr disappears.
1980, January	Second Syrian deployment in Lebanon.
1982, April 6	Israel invades Lebanon in Operation Big Pines.
June–August	Israeli siege of Beirut.
August 8	United States negotiates agreement for the withdrawal of the PLO from Beirut.

August 23	Bashir Gemayel elected president.
August 25	U.S. Marines land in Beirut as part of the Multi-National Force; evacuation of PLO begins.
September 10	Troops of MNF withdraw from Lebanon.
September 14	Bashir Gemayel assassinated.
September 16	Massacre of residents of Sabra and Shatilla begins.
September 20	U.S. Marines ordered back into Lebanon.
1983, April 18	U.S. embassy in Beirut bombed.
September 19	U.S. naval vessels shell Souq al Gharb.
October 23	U.S. Marines barracks bombed; quarters of French contingent of MNF attacked.
1984, February	Shiites take control of West Beirut; United States and other nations of MNF withdraw from Lebanon.
March	Militant Islamic groups pursue hostage taking as a tool in their war against the West.
September 20	Temporary quarters of U.S. embassy in Beirut bombed.
1985, January	Israel announces three-stage withdrawal from Lebanon.
May	Beginning of "Camp Wars" between Amal and the Palestinians.
June 14	Hijacking of TWA flight 847.
1987, February	Fighting between Amal and pro-Arafat factions of PLO in West Beirut; Syrians increase their military presence.
1988, May	Amal and Hizbollah battle for control of Beirut's southern suburbs; more Syrian army troops are deployed.
September 23	Lebanon fails to elect a new president; rival Christian and Muslim governments established.

LEBANON
Death of a Nation

West Went Thataway, East
Life *magazine*
January 7, 1966

ONE

BEIRUT: PARIS OF THE EAST

It was early April 1975 in Beirut, the capital and epicenter of Lebanon. Around Martyrs' Square, the center of the city, traffic snarled into tight, noisy knots that crept through the streets at a frustrating pace. Hurried pedestrians heading toward unknown but purposeful destinations dodged and jockeyed for position on the congested sidewalks. Along the fashionable Rue Hamra, Western tourists off the cruise ships anchored in the harbor crowded the boutiques and bars while shrewd Lebanese entrepreneurs huddled in offices and coffeehouses, consummating lucrative deals with the world's newly rich—the Arabs of the Arabian peninsula. Everywhere it seemed life was pulsating to Beirut's own special tempo.

But beyond the bustle of the city, on the seaward-facing bluff that supported the neo-Arabesque buildings of the American University, tranquility reigned. In all directions, the graceful panorama of Lebanon unfolded. A snow-capped mountain peak loomed in the distance like a mighty sentinel over the rugged coastal plain at its feet. On that plain, a series of low hills supporting colorful multistoried buildings dropped down to a white beach. Bisecting the beach was a ribbon of highway carrying cars north to Tripoli

1

and south to Sidon. Far out from shore, a lone water-skier seemed to be smoothly pursuing the ghosts of the ancient Phoenicians across the Mediterranean. For someone gazing out on the turquoise sea reaching up to meet the limitless blue of the sky, the view created a feeling of boundless freedom, a perfect peace.

Eight Aprils later, on a similar pristine afternoon in 1983, black smoke billowed from ground-level fires roaring through the ruins of the American embassy on Bliss Street. At the entrance to the diplomatic compound, a Marine dressed in battle fatigues loosely grasped an M-16 in one hand and furiously directed rescue vehicles with the other. Inside, television crews lugging heavy equipment on their shoulders pointed their wide-angle lenses at a medical team loading an unconscious victim into a white van identified as an ambulance only by the red Arabic lettering on its side. The noise, the smell, the excitement were all centered on the six floors of the middle section of the three-wing embassy building, which had collapsed like a layer cake that had fallen on one side. Between two upper floors, a body, its head crushed by the buckling cement, hung out with arms dangling toward the ground. Below, red-bereted French soldiers of the Western powers' Multi-National Peace Keeping Force picked through the rubble looking for more casualties. Just in front of them, a member of the Palestinian Red Crescent, the PLO-linked rescue squad, emerged from the wreckage carrying a clear plastic bag filled with human hands. With his grisly cargo, he passed a lone traffic light that, although its glass circles of red and green were blown away, somehow still flashed its commands to stop and go.

Amid the destruction the American ambassador, John Dillon, dressed in an immaculate blue shirt that set off his handsome head of gray hair, stood stunned but unscathed. Others were not so fortunate. The Central Intelligence Agency's chief Middle East analyst, Robert Ames, was dead, as were fifty-seven other people, seventeen of them Americans. With the world press clamoring for answers, the embassy's public affairs officer, John Reid, head swathed in bandages and right eye swollen shut, tried to field reporters' questions.

At 1:05 that afternoon, a large van had hurtled past a Lebanese police checkpoint and accelerated up the circular driveway of the embassy. It halted in front of the Consular Section, crowded with Lebanese pleading for visas to the United States and a way out of the hell of Lebanon. Within seconds, an explosion equal in power to five hundred pounds of TNT blew away the van and its kamikaze driver and collapsed the building on top of its occupants. The force was so powerful that it shook the windows of a house seven miles away and caused the *U.S.S. Guadalcanal,* cruising five miles off Lebanon's coast, to shudder.

Word of the explosion raced through war-weary Beirut and across the world. Before sunset Amin Gemayel, the Christian president of Lebanon, had appeared at the site and proclaimed, "Those responsible for this crime have united in death innocent Lebanese and Americans and strengthened the determination of our two countries to continue to work together." And an anonymous voice claiming to represent the Iranian-inspired Islamic Jihad had called the *Agence France Presse* to proclaim the bombing as "part of the Iranian revolution's campaign against imperialist targets throughout the world."

In the confusion of that terrible afternoon, someone had remembered to lower the American flag to half-staff. It was a portentous gesture: In another six months, 241 U.S. Marines sent to restore order to war-torn Lebanon would be blown away by another suicide bomber, another martyr whom Islamic Jihad would claim as its own. After the United States removed its remaining Marines in February 1984, ordinary American citizens, along with nationals of other Western countries, began to be snatched off the streets, victims of a bitter, clandestine war against the West and all that it represented. Finally, in February 1987, an order of the U.S. government that all Americans leave Lebanon, coupled with a series of kidnappings of well-known Westerners, sealed Lebanon off from the West. Today a skeletal staff ensconced in an embassy guarded like a fort, a few transient journalists, and a handful of U.S. citizens granted special permission by the State Department are all that remain of America's presence in Lebanon.

In the years since the Lebanese civil war began, Lebanon has emerged as the place where centuries of Arab resentment toward the West found voice and direction, where the ideology of Iran's Ayatollah Khomeini took root and bore its bitter fruit. As a result, the long conflict in Lebanon has moved beyond mere civil war. Lebanon has come to represent all the myths Americans once held about the Middle East and to capsulize all the problems American interests face in an area where emotion often overrules reason and East struggles against West. Lebanon, once the West's gracious gateway to the Arab East, is in danger of becoming a barricade at the door to the Arab world, repelling Western entry into a region of one hundred million people sitting at the crossroads of Europe and Asia who control one-third of the world's proven oil reserves.

For nearly a decade and a half, the Western world has been baffled and tormented by the carnage in Lebanon. Much of the confusion about Lebanon and the West's interests in it stems from the fact that before the war Lebanon was more an illusion than a reality. Americans, particularly, saw this tiny Mediterranean country only through the eyes of slick travel brochures, media personalities, and even many reporters, who were as seduced as their audiences by Lebanon's charm. Lebanon was Rita Hayworth posing beside the pool of the Hotel St. Georges. Lebanon was Beirut, a chic port of call for Mediterranean cruises. Lebanon was casinos, elegant shops, and French cuisine presided over by the urbane and cosmopolitan Beirutites. The inconsistency between Lebanon's prewar image and the reality of its society was seldom recognized, leaving the real Lebanon buried under the allure of that magic time from 1955 to 1975 nostalgically called the "Golden Age."

During this Golden Age, Beirut was a caldron of boundless vitality. It stood as the visceral center of Lebanon, a country only slightly larger than the state of Delaware that harbored adherents of seventeen religious groups, Christian and Muslim, in artificial harmony.

In late 1947, Beirut was little more than a sleepy village whose only claim to fame was the notable American University. But by the mid-1960s, Beirut had become a glitzy Mediterranean metropolis, a mecca for the international set, a haven for exiles of the world's political wars, and the one taste many Westerners ever had of the Middle East. In 1966, *Life* magazine, that quintessential American eye on the world, described Beirut as "a kind of Las Vegas–Riviera–St. Moritz flavored with spices of Araby." *Life* was there covering the tourist boom that had hit after Greek, Italian, and Turkish cruise lines discovered Beirut's Arab character and Western amenities, making it an ideal port of call. Even the stately *Queen Elizabeth II* once joined the stampede to "Arabia" by steaming into Beirut's harbor for a day.

What Western tourists wanted in Beirut was to snatch a taste of the Middle East without having to endure the dirt and clamor of Damascus and Cairo. Erupting from their ships, well-heeled travelers stormed colorful *souqs* (markets) created expressly for the tourist trade. There they bought *narghiles*, the old brass "hubbly-bubblys," as proof that they really had been to the Middle East, or at least what they thought was the Middle East. These forays into the *souqs* were followed by stops at *shwarma* stands to sample the succulent strips of meat layered on tall standing skewers and roasted as they rotated around flaming jets of gas. Armed with the requisite souvenirs and authentic samples of Arabic food, the tourists pushed on to the gold shops and clothing stores to indulge themselves in products designed for Western tastes. They topped off the day with French pastries eaten at sidewalk cafés reminiscent of Paris. And they whiled away the night in the small clubs scattered throughout the tourist section of Beirut, where plump Egyptian belly dancers shared the floor with lithe Western show girls while the orchestra shifted between Arabic music and Western disco tunes.

Despite the tourists' brush with its Arab side, Beirut was not an Arab city. It was a city caught in a cataclysmic division between its Arab roots and its Western patina. That facade was maintained by Beirut's political and economic establishment, who themselves had consciously rejected their Arab roots, choosing instead to copy the West. Consequently, a city geared to present Lebanon's Arab side in a Western showcase curiously mirrored the leadership's own split identity.

The seasoned travelers of the international set, unlike the cruise ship tourists, were attracted to Beirut's Western aura rather than its Arab character. Flying into Beirut's international airport, they headquartered in the Hotel St. Georges, which rose from a peninsula jutting out into a quiet cove of the Mediterranean. On warm afternoons, near-nude sunbathers slumbered under a garden of umbrellas in blue, yellow, orange, and pink scattered across the sand. Or they sampled the superb cuisine served on a graceful terrace overlooking the bay. The St. Georges was a favorite rendezvous for journalists and diplomats, for it offered an unparalleled listening post on the Middle East.

Across the street was the Phoenicia Hotel, the newest, poshest, and most westernized hotel in the city. Rather than a minibeach, the Phoenicia boasted a huge, round swimming pool tiled in three shades of Mediterranean blue. One end of the pool was an expanse of glass that formed the backdrop of the elaborately stocked downstairs bar, where customers sat in the dark and watched the swimmers glide past. The Phoenicia was an oasis for Western businessmen and employees of the Arabian-American Oil Company (ARAMCO) on vacation from the heat and alcohol-parched landscape of Saudi Arabia.

There was also an old, charming hotel down by the waterfront called the Normandy. With its mirrored walls and chrome-railed staircase, the Normandy might have served as the set for a vintage MGM musical. Yet it had its regular clientele just as did its newer competitors. Kim Philby, the infamous British spy, made the Normandy his headquarters until he defected to Moscow in 1963. True to its tradition of service, the Normandy was still faithfully holding Philby's mail in 1965.

Beirut was able to create and maintain its flashy facade because of a series of post–World War II developments that occurred outside Lebanon's own borders but that economically transformed the country and Beirut in particular.

As its bountiful oil fields went into production following the war, Saudi Arabia prepared to build the Trans-Arabian Pipeline to carry crude oil from the fields on the Persian Gulf to the Mediterranean, where it would be refined and shipped onward to Europe. Known as the "Tapline," the pipeline originally was slated to terminate in British-held northern Palestine. But by the time construction began the British were gone, Israel was a reality, and control of the ports of Haifa and Jaffa had fallen from Arab into Jewish hands. Consequently, the Saudis rerouted the Tapline to terminate in the southern Lebanese city of Sidon. Similarly, Iraq's pipeline, originally destined for Haifa, went instead to Tripoli in northern Lebanon. Almost overnight, Lebanon found itself the major way station on the oil route between the Persian Gulf and Europe.

While much of the Middle East was trapped in the Arab-Israeli struggle or convulsed by movements fueled by Arab nationalism, Lebanon stayed aloof, reaping benefits from the disorder of others. The ability of the Lebanese establishment to play on Lebanon's Western image and to establish their country as a haven from the apparent chaos of the surrounding Arab countries contributed greatly to Lebanon's economic allure.

The 1948 Arab-Israeli war that delivered the Tapline to Sidon also brought to Beirut's protective environment a cadre of upper-class Palestinians, armed with money and skills. Unlike the poor, uneducated Palestinians who went to the refugee camps, the well-to-do plugged their capital into Lebanon's expanding economy and joined Lebanon's aggressive entrepreneurial class.

In 1952 another infusion of monied political exiles arrived in Lebanon after Egypt's overweight and corrupt king, Farouk, was toppled in a military coup led by the young Gamal Abdel Nasser. When Nasser began to trumpet a new economic order, summoning all Egyptians to unite under an arabized version of socialism, a sizable number of Egypt's foremost businessmen, industrialists, and bankers fled. They too went to Beirut, where Lebanon's stability and laissez-faire economy provided a safe harbor for their capital.

Finally, Lebanon benefited from Europe's post–World War II "economic miracle." The European nations, particularly Britain and France, had long-standing interests in the Middle East. After the disruption of the war, Europe, bolstered by its strengthening economies, began to reactivate those ties. It was joined by the Americans, who had come out of World War II with global interests. With Arab oil constituting an increasing share of U.S. oil consumption and, in the process, creating for the Gulf countries sizable national incomes, the Middle East commanded American attention. And like the Europeans, the American diplomats, bankers, sales representatives, geophysicists, educators, and airline pilots headed for Beirut, where they reinforced the city's Western ambience.

The 1950s economic boom, although stimulated by events outside Lebanon, was maximized in the 1960s by the Lebanese people's own energy and commercial aptitudes. There existed in the Lebanese psyche a drive that demanded hard work and commercial success. The Lebanese enjoyed a literacy rate of 88 percent, far above that of most other Arab societies. But above all the Lebanese were true descendants of the Phoenicians, traders in every sense of the word. There was nothing a Lebanese would not trade—and trade at a profit. Profit was the supreme value of commercial life, underscored by a government committed to a flexible, freewheeling form of laissez-faire capitalism. In fact, the profit motive was so imbedded in the Lebanese culture that when an American reporter asked a kindergarten child, "How much is two and two?" The child replied without pausing, "Are you buying or selling?"

If Beirut was pulsating in the 1960s, it was vibrating by early 1975. With the 1973 oil boom in the Arabian peninsula, every source of Lebanon's income had ballooned. Once more Lebanon's economy reaped the benefits of events beyond its borders. But this time the infusion of capital was Arab money—money from the Arabian peninsula, where the Arabic language was revered and where Islam was all but untouched by westernization.

The components of the Lebanese economy dovetailed with the wildly escalating demands of the Gulf economies. Lebanon sat at the crossroads of the movement of capital and goods between East and West. Inexperienced Arab investors from the Gulf arrived to pour copious amounts of money into both sound and shady investments put together by worldly Beirutite businessmen. Ships in the port of Beirut off-loaded cargoes destined for the markets of the Arab hinterland. Lebanese farmers sent their produce via truck to the Arabian peninsula, where it would feed the cadres of foreign workers flooding in to pump the oil. And the Lebanese themselves, with their high literacy rate and prodigious language skills, flocked to the Gulf countries, where they became managers, contractors, doctors, and clerks. The emigrés, in turn, sent a large percentage of their high salaries back into the economy of Lebanon.

With thirty international carriers serving Beirut's international airport, more and more Western businessmen made Beirut their headquarters, an oasis to which they could retreat after their incursions into the heat, disorder, and restrictions of the Gulf states. Attracting both Westerners and high-rolling Arabs, the Casino du Liban, Lebanon's major tourist attraction, was doing a booming business. In its 1975 sequin-and-feather extravaganza, scantily clad Western show girls lacquered in gold and silver stepped off the petals of a giant flower that descended from the casino's ceiling. Although it was spectacular show business, everyone agreed that the new show fell far short of the 1970 production. Packaged in Paris for a cost of $1.5 million, that show lasted three hours and employed a cast of 110, not including the stallions that galloped across the stage or the elephant that was led through the audience during the finale.

Life for the affluent Lebanese, foreign diplomats, Western

businesspeople, and journalists revolved around "Ras Beirut," a hilly, sun-drenched peninsula spread out around the American University of Beirut. Ras Beirut was the closest the Arab world ever came to possessing its own Greenwich Village. In apartments that rented for as much as $1,000 a month, avant-garde literary circles met to discuss the little magazines that abounded and to critique the latest productions at the experimental theaters. Colonies of artists, poets, popular writers, and intellectuals clustered in the coffeehouses, where ideas swirled around and among tables, often appearing the next day in a column in one of the dozens of daily newspapers published in Arabic, French, and English. It was in this milieu that most of the books the Arab world read were published, under the protection of the only Arab government that allowed freedom of the press.

Ras Beirut was a safe haven for those periodically out of favor with the political regimes in the adjacent Arab states. It served as a test ground for innovative ideas and modes of life and as a forum for articulating public dissent and collective grievances. The atmosphere of Ras Beirut was instrumental in shaping the ideological movements that rocked the Middle East between the mid-1950s and mid-1960s. Pan-Arabism, Arab nationalism, progressive socialism, and Baathism were all either initiated or vented in Ras Beirut.

In some ways, Ras Beirut was little more than a village where clusters of old stone houses with walled gardens still nestled among tall, stuccoed apartment houses. For nine months of the year, life in Ras Beirut was lived in the outdoors. Most people spent hours on their balconies or patios. There they read the morning newspapers over Turkish coffee, tended their pot gardens of flowers and herbs, yelled at the children in the street, or simply sat watching the world go by. At sunset, they hit the streets. The old men who had spent the afternoon at the sidewalk café smoking their narghiles and clicking their backgammon pieces over inlaid tables moved over for the evening crowd in search of a Western movie and an American hamburger.

The residents of Ras Beirut whirled through an unending round of parties, receptions, and dances—all faithfully, if not always accurately, reported for the *Daily Star* by social columnists Genevieve Maxwell and Peggy Johnson. These parties were not mindless social events but provided a quick and efficient way for newcomers to penetrate Beirut's commercial and government circles. After one of *Time* magazine's famous receptions at the Phoenicia, its newly arrived correspondent marveled, "In one night I met half the people I needed to know in Beirut for the next three years."

It was Ras Beirut with all its glitz and glitter that most symbolized the "Golden Age" of Lebanon, the period when the good life was the birthright of the privileged among the Lebanese and when Beirut's foreign guests dipped in the pool of grace, ease, and plenty. Ras Beirut was truly multicultural, smoothly blending timeless Arab traditions with the tempo and technology of the West. For a poignantly short time, Ras Beirut's diverse, dynamic, multinational society came to represent the illusion that Westerners believed was Lebanon. Yet in this charming amalgam of Arab character and Western patina lay the roots of Lebanon's destruction.

The reality beyond Ras Beirut was that for every Rue Hamra there were dozens of Rue Ghalghouls. Little more than alleyways, these streets twisted through Naba, Burj al Barajneh, and Beirut's other poor areas where those cut off from Lebanon's prosperity eked out their livings. Unlike the privileged residents of Ras Beirut, here the people lived in cement-block houses patched together with surplus building supplies purchased at bargain prices. They shopped in the traditional vegetable *souqs* wedged into narrow intersections and shaded from the Mediterranean sun by faded, tattered awnings strung from adjacent buildings. They bought their meat from the local butcher, who hung his lamb carcasses in the open, unprotected from the swarming fly population. They competed for living space in an area too small for the numbers dumped there by economic dictate. And unlike the political and economic elite who frequented Ras Beirut's restaurants, here those who huddled in the coffeehouses often were plotting the destruction of the power structure.

Nothing illustrated the economic division within Lebanon more starkly than the infamous "Belt of Misery" that encircled prosperous Beirut in a great swath of slums, squatter areas, and Palestinian refugee camps. Here employment was unpredictable and menial and the death rate ran two to three times higher than the national average. By the living standards of the Middle East, these slum dwellers were not destitute. Yet when contrasted with the lifestyle of those who controlled Lebanon's government and economy, the quality of their life was impoverished.

The bidonvilles, or slums, originally were identified with the Armenians, Kurds, and other minorities. But after the first wave of Palestinians arrived in Lebanon in 1948, the bidonvilles became synonymous with Palestinian deprivation. Although many merged into Lebanese society, most were relegated to fragile, wooden lean-tos clustered in camps on the edge of Beirut. By 1970, ninety thousand Palestinians were crammed into camps and neighborhoods running south from the racetrack to the airport and west to the Presidential Palace and the insane asylum. Burj al Barajneh was among the largest. It was a jumble of crudely constructed cement-block hovels roofed with corrugated tin, where the only greenery was the scraggly bushes that pushed their way up through any ground not covered by a house or pathway. Adding to the squalor were the pall of smoke and the stench of burning rubber that perpetually hung over the rambling camp. Burj al Barajneh's lone symbol of Lebanon's prosperity was the forest of TV antennas that stretched from the patched roofs through the smoke to grab the same signals that reached Ras Beirut. By the time the Lebanese civil war began, the Shiite Muslims, the great Lebanese underclass, had pushed into the already crowded bidonvilles.

The crucial fact of Lebanese life missed by Westerners of the time was that the population of Lebanon was a pluralistic pot of nationalities made up of Armenians, Syrians, Kurds, and Palestinians, plus Lebanese who themselves were bitterly split by malignant religious and communal divisions. Within its cramped borders, Lebanon packed a population of two million people, all fiercely attached to their own nationalistic or communal group. Lebanese society, often spoken of as "pluralistic," actually was a mosaic of many groups, none of them committed to the common good of Lebanon; rather, each looked solely to its own special interests in a rigidly hierarchical political and economic structure. Thus, the Lebanese and the migrants coexisted within Lebanon's borders, isolated within the boundaries of their individual communal identifications.

Immigrant groups not only were alienated from Lebanese society but suffered from their precarious legal status. Most were not lawful residents of Lebanon, and even those who were were denied the right to participate fully in Lebanon's economic and political systems. They suffered discrimination in employment. Their legal rights were marginal, and, under Lebanon's curious political system, most were denied representation. Except for the elite among the Armenians and Palestinians, the minorities lived beyond Lebanese society. Closed out of the clannish communality of Lebanese life, the Kurds, the Syrians, and others falling into the category of "immigrant" clung to their jobs and their housing areas and stayed out of overt political activities that might threaten their continued residence in Lebanon. Only the Palestinians refused to bend.

After the Arab-Israeli war of 1967, the Palestinians established themselves as a separate force in the carefully constructed balance of the Lebanese political system. Few desired to be merged and lost within the Lebanese collage. Instead they constantly affirmed their own nationality and dreamed of and planned for their return to Palestine. It was the Palestinians who would become the catalyst for civil war among the Lebanese, fatally split by religion, frozen in a political system bequeathed by a European colonial power, and embittered by economic inequalities and regional disparities.

In its simplest form, native Lebanese society was split into four broad communal groups that conformed to religious confessionals. The Christians, including Roman Catholics, Maronites, Greek Orthodox, Greek Catholics, and a smattering of Protestants, made up an estimated 40 percent of the 1975 population. The Druze, standing apart from the other Muslim communities, claimed a 6 percent share of the population. Another 22 percent was composed of Sunni Muslims, the mainstream of Islam. The Shiite community, the members of the other main branch of Islam, commanded a rapidly rising 32 percent of the Lebanese population.

Lebanese society, fatally divided along communal lines, seemed to pattern itself neatly according to religion. But in reality religious identification was further subdivided by family loyalties, regional differences, economic rivalries, or simple hatred generated from past disputes and ongoing vendettas. A Lebanese was first a member of his family, then his village, then his religious group, and finally he was a Lebanese.

Government was structured according to a precise formula that reserved the office of president for a Christian, the premiership for a Sunni Muslim, and the speakership of the parliament for a Shiite Muslim. In this formula, established under French colonial rule, seats in the legislative body were portioned out to Christians and Muslims at a ratio of six to five. The public school system, attended almost exclusively by the poor, competed with religious schools for students and funding. Even the legal system was emasculated by the existence of religious courts that claimed jurisdiction over disputes among members of that particular confessional.

The Maronite Christians dominated the economic system as well as the political structure. Although Lebanon's laissez-faire economy and Western-oriented business class pulled in foreign capital and nurtured the bonds between the economic and political establishment of the various religions, the institutional structure in place created gross inequalities both in the distribution of wealth among the Lebanese and in economic development between Beirut and the rest of Lebanon. While the Lebanese' kinetic quest for profit cut across religious and class lines to unite the successful, it also gravely alienated those who did not succeed economically. In a profound way, the economic triumph of the Golden Age exacerbated the carefully masked communal tensions that the Lebanese tried so hard to ignore and the Westerners refused to acknowledge.

The divisions within the country that the economic realities reflected were stark. As Lebanon divided religiously and geographically, it also divided economically. Greater Beirut, including the mountainous areas north and south of the city, was like a prosperous city-state. But the Akkar region in the north, Jabal Amil in the south, and the Bekaa Valley in the east, all largely populated by Sunni and Shiite Muslims, were forgotten zones of economic stagnation. In 1960, per capita income in Beirut was $803 compared with only $151 in the south. By 1975, the gap was even wider. The overwhelming Christian area north of Beirut claimed 29 percent of the population but possessed 38.2 percent of Lebanon's schools, while the south, with 19 percent of the population—primarily Shiite Muslim—has only 14.8 percent of the schools. An even starker statistic: In the Akkar, there was not a single doctor available for a population of two hundred thousand.

During much of the Golden Age, an estimated 4 percent of Lebanon's population disposed of 32 percent of the country's gross national product (GNP) while only 18 percent of the country's wealth filtered down to the bottom half of the population. This disparity in wealth cut across all religious sects. There were Christian poor and Muslim poor. But the prevailing difference was that the Christian poor were fewer in number and, although impoverished, few suffered the abject living conditions of the Muslim poor. Perhaps even more important, the Christians psychologically cherished the self-assumed attitude, reaffirmed by the political system, that they were superior to the Muslims. Some would argue, with good grounds, that the Christians' claim of preeminence was defensive, a protective mechanism adopted by a minority sensing itself endangered. Nevertheless, the Christians' sense of superiority and their pride in the veneer of their Western ways were what divided them so severely from the Muslims.

In the myth of prewar Lebanon, the Lebanese seemed to easily blend the many facets of their society, but the reality was as close as the nearest café.

It was nearing the eve of the war. Beneath the shade of three sycamore trees growing out of ragged holes cut in the cement sidewalk, a small café located just off Martyrs' Square in central Beirut was serving the afternoon crowd. Conversation drifted over the street noise created by the horns of sleek Mercedes Benz clearing their path of peddlers' donkeys and by the peal of church bells competing with the calls of the *muezzin* from the nearby mosque. At one of the white circular tables, students from the nearby Jesuit University of St. Joseph chattered over their coffee and Coca-Colas. Heavy gold crucifixes lay beneath the open collars of the Western-style shirts they wore above American blue jeans. Around the table conversation moved freely from French to English, punctuated only occasionally by an Arabic phrase. There was about the group the unmistakable aura of the elite. It was obvious that here sat the holders and beneficiaries of power in Lebanon.

Sitting apart from everyone else were two elderly Druze, each wearing a red fez wrapped with a wide white band, hunched over small cups of coffee. Appearing to have all the time in the world, one pulled on the wooden mouthpiece of a narghile allowing the thin smoke to escape from the corners of his mouth. His companion fingered his prayer beads between slow sips of his thick, black coffee. Neither acknowledged the presence of anyone else in the café.

Next to the curb, four men in business suits huddled around their own tiny table covered with papers containing jumbles of numbers. Upper-class members of the Sunni sect of Islam, they were hammering out the terms under which they would accept a job subcontracted by a company owned by one of the wealthy Christian families north of Beirut. Although dressed in Western-style clothes, their rapid-fire conversation was entirely in Arabic.

One other person was on the sidewalk of the café. Between the two empty tables near the door, a small, thin man in his early twenties maneuvered his broom around the unoccupied chairs. Periodically he bent to sweep the dust and cigarette butts into a makeshift dustpan that he listlessly emptied into a garbage can. He lived in Beirut's slums. He spoke only Arabic, wore worn clothes, and worked at menial jobs. He swept the floor while his fellow Lebanese sat at the tables primarily because he was a Shiite Muslim, a descendant of those Muslims who split with the mainstream Sunnis in A.D. 680. As a Shiite, he lived in Lebanon as a second-class citizen. He was discriminated against in education, housing, and employment. His community was the poorest and least represented of all the Lebanese communities, condemning him to life as one of Beirut's hewers of wood and drawers of water. His slow movements with broom and dustpan symbolized the waiting game Lebanon's Shiite community was playing. It was a deadly serious game whose object was not only political power but the affirmation of Lebanon's Arab character and the authority of Islamic society.

As the Golden Age moved to its unforeseen end, Lebanon's compartmentalized society appeared to be the world's prime example of divergent groups with conflicting interests living and working together in a veritable utopia. The unique ability of Lebanon's Christians and Muslims to live in apparent tranquillity amid the tumult of the Middle East was a frequent topic of Western journalists and television news shows. For more than a quarter of a century, while war raged between Israel and her neighbors, Gamal Abdel Nasser railed against the Western imperialists, the Baathist regimes of Syria and Iraq hurled invectives at each other, and the Palestinians took up arms to regain Palestine, Lebanon, except for one ugly incident in 1958, appeared to float placidly along like a little Switzerland.

By the time the Western world began to concentrate on the

perilous tensions between the Lebanese themselves and with the Palestinians, the oil boom had arrived. Most observers believed that the Lebanese love of making money would hold things together indefinitely. Western diplomats, while aware of the problems, looked on Lebanon as some kind of charmed political entity that somehow would survive its internal divisions and the enmity on its borders. No one, least of all the Lebanese, wanted the good life to end. But everyone was blissfully deceived.

Observed from the outside, Lebanon did appear to fulfill the idyllic illusions, so cherished by the West, about the little country hugging the eastern end of the Mediterranean. For at this time the Lebanese were struggling not on the street but only within themselves. Their internal struggle was more profound than any political movement or economic philosophy. Lebanon was tragically split in its very soul. At the crossroads of West and East, the Lebanese for centuries had agonized over whether their identity lay in the philosophy and mores of the West or in the traditions of the Arab world. In April 1975, the "Paris of the East" exploded. Lebanon started down the long road of civil war, a war that eventually would become a war against the West.

American Board of Foreign Missions Establishes Syrian Presbyterian College in Beirut
Missionary Advocate
June 18, 1866

TWO

THE LEVANT

I n the cool early morning hours, the mountains cast their purple shadows over the coastal highway running north from Beirut to Tripoli. It is quiet. Only the noise of the car engine and the air brushing over the top of the partially opened window break the stillness. To the left, the escarpment falls away toward the Mediterranean, where the soft waves lick the shoreline. The mountains, like everything else in Lebanon, appear to point inexorably toward the sea. For Lebanon, unlike its Arab neighbors, clings to the Mediterranean, an intermediary between the deserts of the Middle East and the Western world beyond. Early in the morning, along that road, the beauty and tranquillity suggest that no man would dare mar this perfect place.

Suddenly the highway narrows perceptibly to bridge a chasm where the mountains plunge to the ocean. Beneath, the waters of the Dog River eat away at a gorge dug deep through measureless time. Along the ravine's gray face of pockmarked limestone, the history of Lebanon is carved in the alphabets and languages of those who came to trade or to master. It is at Nahr al Kalb that Egypt's Ramses II (reigned 1304–1237 B.C.), buying cedar to scaffold the great Abu Simbel, left his sign. It is here that those

17

who conquered—the Hittites and the Assyrians, the Greeks and the
Romans, the Crusaders and the Ottomans—carved their marks.
And it is here that an inscription left during the French withdrawal in 1946 weathers alongside the marks of others who tried to
possess Lebanon.

For centuries the mighty and the feeble, foreigners and Lebanese, have fought over Lebanon, an area so small that it could fit
into a corner of Switzerland. At its maximum, the country is only
135 miles long and less than 50 miles wide. It is dramatically
divided by the Lebanon mountains, which run spectacularly along
the coast north and south of Beirut, and the parallel Anti-Lebanon
mountains along the Syrian border. Between the two ranges lies
the Bekaa valley, the northeasternmost part of the Great Rift
valley. Lebanon's landscape is so diverse that before the civil war
anyone living in Beirut could, in an hour's drive, lay out a picnic by
an icy waterfall in the Damour valley, swim secreted away in a
hidden inlet near Sidon, or race down the ski slopes around Faraya.
It took only two hours to reach the famous cedar forest at Barouk
or the spectacular Roman ruins at Baalbek, the farthest reaches of
Lebanon.

Lebanon is cursed by its size. Its population of disparate
identities, each harboring conflicting aspirations and fears, is
trapped within the country's scant four thousand square miles. As
a result, the intensity with which each group senses its own interests is magnified by the close proximity of its rivals. It is almost as
if conflicts concentrate to fit the space in which they must ultimately be resolved. Consequently, the civil war in Lebanon, unlike
most modern conflicts, is fought not with armies facing each other
over battle areas ranging many square miles but by armed militias
engaged in combat from urban block to urban block.

Lebanon has always been a battleground for someone. And
each conqueror has deposited something of itself with a segment of
the population, creating a people fragmented into groups possessing no common identity with the whole. Throughout their history
the Lebanese, buffeted by the forces of cultural diversity, ethnicity,
religion, and ideology, have marched toward some tragic confrontation whose final outcome would define Lebanon's character or
destroy its very being. This is the essence of Lebanon's current
trauma—the ultimate battle to determine its own identity.

Lebanon, together with Syria and Palestine, is part of the
Levant, the territory lying at the eastern end of the Mediterranean.

Lebanon shared the historical events that created the dappled character of the Levant. As a result, Syria is a mosaic of Alawites, Druze, and Christian minorities overlaying a Sunni Muslim base. The State of Israel, now occupying the old British mandate of Palestine, is dominated by Judaism but is bedeviled by the Eastern and Western cultural biases of its Jewish population and challenged by its Arab population. Yet of the three, Lebanon most closely represents the true complexity of the Levant.

Lebanon is literally the bridge between East and West. At the crossroads of the great land and sea routes that link Europe, Asia, and Africa, Lebanon through the centuries benefited from trade in times of peace and, as part of the principal invasion routes, suffered in times of war. Most often trade and war were waged by Eastern empires pushing West or Western empires pushing East. As a result, during peacetime Lebanon became in intricate montage of the best that competing cultures had to offer. But Lebanon also periodically became trapped between warring armies, which in pursuit of their own territorial and economic interests inflicted aspects of their culture on Lebanon. In Lebanon, Phoenician was besieged by Greek; Christian was martyred by Muslim; and, in the nineteenth century, East was occupied by West. Today, in the unfinished struggle for cultural dominance, Lebanese murder Lebanese in a bloody contest for the nation's identity.

This disjunctive intermingling of cultures began with the extraordinary Phoenicians, early settlers along Lebanon's coast. Their origins remain a mystery. They called themselves Canaanites, but the Greeks dubbed them Phoenicians after the purple dye they sold from the port of Tyre. Herodotus, that diligent chronicler of the ancient world, claimed they migrated from the Persian Gulf and settled in the Levant around 2800 B.C. Wherever they came from, the shrewd, ambitious Phoenicians claimed a narrow coastal strip of the Levant between the sea and the mountains and set out to become history's slickest salespeople.

By 1400 B.C., the Phoenicians held a monopoly on the cedar forests that covered the mountains behind the port of Byblos. Thus, emissaries of Egypt's great pharaohs trekked north to buy wood to embellish their grand public buildings, and oil and resin to preserve their dead. In time, every Egyptian death meant money in a Phoenician pocket.

The Phoenicians were manufacturers of glass and metal objects, but their real wealth came from carrying the cargoes of others. Their square-rigged triremes were larger, faster, and easier to handle than any other ships in existence, and on these the Phoenicians built their fleet. Sailing up the Nile, the Phoenicians loaded the products of Egypt from the busy wharves of Thebes and set sail for the ports of the ancient world. By 1100 B.C., they controlled the commercial sea lanes and positioned their trade routes, which eventually would reach from the Black Sea to Spain.

The secrets of the Phoenicians' success were daring, cunning, and an incredible talent for business. From the towering Pigeon Rocks, which still jut dramatically from the water within sight of Beirut's Hotel St. Georges, the Phoenicians launched their corps of carrier pigeons to fly messages back and forth between far-flung business associates, maximizing their ability to buy low and sell high. They developed double-entry bookkeeping to track their profits. They took the phonetic alphabet, perhaps developed in Egypt or Crete, imported it piecemeal to Tyre, Sidon, and Byblos, and exported it through their bills of lading to every city in the Mediterranean.

Profit, not ethics, was the Phoenicians' stock in trade. They made little distinction between trade and treachery, commerce and robbery. To their rivals, they stole from the weak, cheated the stupid, and were honest with the rest. The Greeks became so frustrated in bargaining with the wily Phoenicians that they gave the name "Phoenician" to anyone who engaged in sharp business practices. Perhaps the Greek historian Polybius best captured the true spirit of the Phoenicians when he reported that they regarded nothing that resulted in profit as disgraceful.

In the name of commerce, the Phoenician traders reigned as cultural synthesizers. The ships of Phoenicia took the arts and sciences of Egypt, Crete, and the Near East and spread them to Greece, Italy, North Africa, and Spain. From the crossroads of the Levant, they bound together East and West in a commercial and cultural web. Even today, segments of Lebanon's population who reject arabization regard themselves as Phoenicians—and, with a certain degree of mythological reasoning, look to the Phoenicians as their true fathers.

The Phoenicians stayed out of war through skilled diplomacy, but they could not always elude the grip of those more powerful than they. Phoenicia's city-states were at times independent and at times absorbed into empires. Periodically they were conquered by the Egyptians, the Assyrians, and the Persians from the East. By 335 B.C., the Phoenician city-states faced their first great threat from the West when Alexander the Great laid siege to Tyre. After massacring eight thousand Tyrians and selling thirty thousand into slavery, Alexander imposed Hellenistic culture on the Phoenician cities lining the coast. Phoenicia absorbed from the Greeks what it chose but remained deeply and inexorably itself.

By the time the Romans arrived Byblos, Tyre, and Sidon were still ports of trade. But Tyre showed decay and stank from purple dye. Phoenicia, no longer the jewel of the Levant, unmistakably had become part of the Roman province of Syria.

Physical evidence of Rome's presence has survived centuries of conflict and even the last years of civil war. On Mount Lebanon, among five windswept, leafless walnut trees huddled at the edge of a gorge, a badly weathered marker declares "Boundary of the Forest of the Emperor Hadrian Augustus." Rome put the stamp of the West not only on Lebanon's resources but on its culture. For the first time, a conqueror of Phoenicia moved off the coast. Although the Romans traded off the cedars of Lebanon, their real interest lay in the Bekaa valley. Throughout the days of glory of the Roman Empire, the Bekaa provided imperial Rome with a sizable portion of its grain. And it was in the Bekaa that the Romans established their presence.

Baalbek, rising over the plain of the Bekaa, stands on a site previously dedicated to the Canaanite god Baal. Construction of the city bridged three centuries and the reigns of eight emperors. Best approached from the West when the late afternoon sun plays on all its magnificent colors and shapes, Baalbek bespeaks the Roman presence in the Eastern world. The cobblestone road that emperors traversed is still there, and the triumphant gate to the city stands ruined but unbowed. The orange light of approaching sunset sets ablaze the six remaining columns of the Temple of Jupiter, and shadows soften the mass of what was once the largest temple in the Roman Empire. The remaining walls of the adjacent Temple of Bacchus support massive doorways crowned by heavy stone lintels of a structure larger than the Parthenon in Athens. It was here, before the Lebanese embarked on the road to self-destruction, that modern Lebanon so perfectly blended the East and West. Yearly the Festival of Baalbek offered the best of the two cultures. Umm Kalthum, the most famous Arab singer of modern times, and

Lebanon's own magnificent vocalist Fayrauz rotated performances with such international greats as Dame Margot Fonteyn and Rudolf Nureyev. And on one unforgettable evening, the velvet voice of Ella Fitzgerald sent the sounds of George Gershwin shimmering off the ruins left by Lebanon's early Western conquerors.

The Western part of the Roman Empire fell, and for a brief period between the fourth and seventh centuries A.D., interest in the Levant shifted back to the coastal plains. The territories of the now forgotten Phoenicians became part of the Eastern or Byzantine Empire. With its strange amalgam of Western culture and Eastern rulers, Byzantium endeavored to reestablish the Roman Empire. From their capital at Constantinople, the Byzantine emperors forged an empire with Christianity at its core. Large segments of the Lebanese population accepted Greek literature and philosophy, continued to observe Roman law, and practiced the Christian religion within their great churches rich in gold and mosaics. At the same time, they proudly defended their Semitic culture and speech. But for Lebanon, the Byzantine Empire was only an interim before the arrival of the next and most enduring conqueror—Islam.

Muslim armies erupted out of the Arabian peninsula early in the seventh century, swept northward to Damascus, then turned west toward the Mediterranean. By 640 they possessed what is now Lebanon. The conquerors carried on their swords a burning ideology unadulterated by Western ideas and mores. In this sense, Islam was a new power. Unlike previous conquerors, the Muslims' objective was not only territory and resources but the propagation of a religion with pure Arab roots. And unlike previous conquerors, the invaders brought with them settlers. Arab immigrants from the western and southern parts of the Arabian peninsula followed the path of victorious armies and located in the south, then expanded into the old Phoenician coastal cities. While the city dwellers largely stayed within the mainstream of Islam, those in the rural south would by 681 participate in Islam's great schism to become the predecessors of modern Lebanon's Shiite population.

The rapid establishment of the Islamic Empire in Lebanon was aided by the presence of large numbers of Arabs already in the population who easily had accepted the rule and then the faith of the Arab invaders. For the rest of the population, conversion usually was not by the sword; instead the Muslim invaders gave the conquered a choice of Islam or tribute. Christians, who made up the vast majority of the population at the time, were permitted to keep their churches, rites, and beliefs in exchange for *jizya*, a head tax on non-Muslims. Gradually large numbers of Christians converted to Islam both to further their own political advancement and to escape taxation. But over the years, Muslim tolerance of the Christians oscillated. By the mid-eighth century, the Muslim rulers were confiscating churches and turning the Christians into an oppressed minority. By the time the Crusaders arrived, Lebanon's Christian population had shrunk to less than half the total, and Arabic had replaced Aramaic as the first language. Phoenicia was, at last, truly dead.

Feeding on the cross-pollination with Byzantine culture, Islam's fanatical warriors quickly gave way to thinkers and scientists. For the next four hundred years, the Islamic Empire dominated from Persia in the east to the Pyrenees in the west. While Europe wallowed in darkness and ignorance, the Muslims astounded the world with their architecture, mathematics, and medicine. The glory days of the Islamic Empire that built the great mosque of Cordova, produced the first medical treatise on smallpox, nurtured legal reasoning, and devised algebra remained for the Arabs proof of the East's superiority over the West. The Arabs, including those of Lebanon, came to see their history in terms of the Islamic Empire. And, in a profound sense, the Arabs of Lebanon believed that Islam's halcyon days were somehow part of a divine plan to recover the Levant from the domination of Western culture.

Yet the West would not stay out of Lebanon forever. In 1095, Pope Urban II proclaimed the first crusade. Setting off on the Via Dei, or Road of God, the Crusaders marched the tortuous route to Jerusalem to recapture the holy places from the hands of the Muslim infidels. It was history's first mass movement of Europeans toward the East since the armies of Alexander the Great pushed into Asia Minor. Between 1099 and 1291, as the righteous and the greedy arrived on foot or resplendent on horseback, Lebanon was opened once again to Western influence. On the stones of Phoenicia's decayed ports, the Crusaders built their castles, incorporating part of Lebanon into the Crusader states. Westerners turned into Easterners as the crusading citizens of Rouen and Chartres became residents of Tyre and Beyrouth (now Beirut).

For two hundred years, the Western invaders remained divided from their Arab subjects. The chasm was more cultural than religious. Recovering from the initial shock of discovering large numbers of Christian faithful in the very heartland of the Muslim heathen, the Crusaders came to distrust the Arab Christians as much as they did the Muslims. With their non-Western dress and non-Latin religious rites, more than a few Christians were mistaken for Muslims and killed by zealous Crusaders. Partly as a result of this European arrogance, the majority of Arab Christians remained forever alien to the European Christians.

In the end, the Crusades proved an ill-fated venture. Plagued by disease, impossibly long supply lines, greedy internal feuding over land and booty, a rebellious populace, and persistent attack by their Muslim adversaries, the Crusaders gave up their mission. But their legacy remains in Lebanon. One group of Arab Christians wholly embraced the Crusaders. The Maronites, ensconced in their enclave on Mount Lebanon, quickly discovered that allying themselves with Western military powers gave them a way to survive in an area dominated by Muslims. When the Crusaders were driven out, the Maronites clung to their mountain strongholds, nurtured their Christian religion, and maintained their links to the West. Because of their strong ties to the West, Lebanon's Maronites were destined to stand unique among the Christians of the Middle East. And through the Maronites, Lebanon became bound to Europe to a degree never achieved by other Middle Eastern countries. For them, the Maronites, Lebanon was not the Levant, the western edge of the Arab Middle East. To them, Lebanon was and always would be the eastern edge of Christendom.

The Crusaders' two-century-long presence in the Arab East also left the Arabs with a lasting legacy. In the eyes of the Arabs, the Crusaders were never pious men in quest of the Holy Grail; they were Westerners who had come to conquer territory, to occupy Arab land. With passion undimmed by the centuries, the Arabs still regard the Crusaders as nothing more than Western imperialists. They were simply the precursors of the imperialism of France after World War I and the imperialism of Israel after 1948. For the Arabs, the Crusades have been neither forgotten nor forgiven.

The buffeting between the cultures of the West and Arab East that the Lebanese had experienced for centuries took a new turn in 1866, when a soft-spoken Presbyterian missionary persuaded the American Board of Commission for Foreign Missions to build a university on a deserted stretch of sand dunes that served as Beirut's garbage dump. In 1871, from his office at the Syrian Protestant College (SPU), the Reverend Daniel Bliss proclaimed, "This college is for all conditions and classes of men without regard to color, nationality, race, or religion. A man, while black or yellow, Christian, Jew, Mohammedan, or heathen, may enter and enjoy all of the advantages of this institution . . . and go out believing in one God, in many Gods, or in no God. But it will be impossible for anyone to continue with us long without knowing what we believe to be the truth and our reasons for that belief."

So began the mission of the American University of Beirut (AUB) to the Levant, one that eventually made the university the most prominent venue from which the Lebanese wrestled with their Western and Arab identities.

The Lebanese Arabs welcomed the missionaries' medical and teaching skills, but few converted. What the Arabs wanted from the missionaries was Western knowledge, not Christian ethics. Remarkably, Bliss and others understood this. Over time, American Protestants developed an institution that gave the Levantine Arabs a Western education while instilling in them an appreciation of their own language and culture.

In 1920, SPU dropped its religious name to become the American University of Beirut. Up until 1975, when it was all but fatally disrupted by the civil war, AUB was a true Levantine institution, a conduit through which Eastern and Western culture flowed. While teaching the science and technology of the West, the school made important contributions to the revival of classical Arabic. Its Arabic press actively disseminated secular as well as religious educational materials. In 1924, the university admitted its first female student. (An Egyptian, she arrived veiled and accompanied by her husband, who was allowed to enroll as a special student to keep an eye on his wife.) The medical school educated Middle Eastern doctors to the same standards as in the West. Through the 1920s, 1930s, and 1940s, AUB trained much of the political leadership of the Middle East. At least nineteen of those who signed the United Nations charter in 1945 were AUB graduates. In short, AUB proved to be in the best tradition of what the West had to offer the Arabs.

Throughout Lebanon's golden years in the 1950s and 1960s, AUB appeared to be the perfect Levantine combination of East and West. Its arabesque gates enclosed seventy acres of semitropical gardens, fifty-odd buff stone buildings, and "Uncle Sam's Snack Shop." Its students crossed the campus dressed in jeans or flowing robes, equally comfortable in either. Arabic poetry stood juxtaposed against Western political thought. And always, the challenge the university posed to its Arab students was to grapple with what it meant to be Arab in the twentieth century.

Much of the open political and intellectual atmosphere that distinguished Beirut from the rest of the Arab world was due to a significant degree to the presence of AUB. To be at AUB meant to try various lifestyles, to challenge unexamined belief systems, and to benefit from association with men and women who demonstrated in their lives the values of a liberal education. Lebanese students at AUB particularly confronted Arabism, Syrianism, and dozens of other "isms" both relevant and irrelevant to their own lives. And unlike those educated in the close confines of St. Joseph University, AUB's students appreciated what was at stake in Lebanon and what opponents of westernization had in store for them. As a result, they were more sensitive to Lebanon's vulnerability as well as to its value.

The university was notorious for controversial and highly charged political activities. Lebanon's first generation of secularists, buttressed by successive groups of gifted scholars, writers, and public figures, were instrumental in articulating and popularizing ideas and values that would transform the lives and visions of millions of Arabs. Its political clubs offered tutelage to successive generations of Arab nationalists and left-leaning political activists. Both Wadi Haddad, a pan-Arabist of the 1930s, and George Haddad, currently the radical leader of the National Front for the Liberation of Palestine, were products of AUB's student political organizations. It was over coffee in nearby cafés or within tumultuous student council meetings that they and other students argued the future direction of Arab nationalism through the decades.

During the 1960s, AUB suddenly found itself at odds with the very nationalist sentiments it had done so much to foster. To many Arab nationalists, AUB had become a force for alienation. They charged that its educational system, based on Western values and the English language, was producing graduates divided from their own culture. To the extreme nationalists, AUB was little more than an outpost of neocolonialism and its American sponsor nothing but a representative of the imperialist West bent on insuring the survival of its interests in Lebanon.

AUB had become symbolic of the Lebanese people's internal struggle. To its supporters, its presence testified to Lebanon's value as a model of what the Arabs could gain from the West. To its detractors, it was evidence of Lebanon's lack of an Arab character and its isolation from its own world.

By 1984, nine years after the civil war began, many of AUB's classrooms were empty. Its Western faculty was all but gone. Malcolm Kerr, a highly respected American Arabist, stayed on as president, keeping alive a small flame of optimism for the future of AUB and his beloved Lebanon. On January 18, Kerr left the president's house and walked across the quiet, tree-shaded campus, passing under the old stone archway bearing the inscription "May They Have Life and Have It Abundantly." He entered College Hall and went to his office on the second floor. Outside the door, two young men stepped out of an adjacent hall, raised their pistols, and fired. Kerr died instantly.

Malcolm Kerr was killed because he was a symbol. He was killed for issues of the moment. And he was killed for much that had gone before in Lebanon—the tug-of-war between whose culture and whose values would define the society; the nineteenth-century mission of the French to save Lebanon's Christians from brutal communal war that turned into a pretext for occupation; the legacy of that colonialism, which created within Lebanon two classes, one Christian and one Muslim; the displacement of the Arab Palestinians by Israel that thrust on Lebanon a problem it could not handle; the years of abundance that turned cheap materialism into a false god and glorified Lebanon's pseudowesternization to the detriment of its Arab character; the years of civil war in which the embattled Maronites reached out first to Syria and then to the Arabs' most hated enemy, Israel, to save them from political compromise.

But most of all, Malcolm Kerr was killed because he was a symbol of the West. Just as the American University of Beirut had unlocked the Arabs' search for themselves, the image of the West portrayed by AUB also unleashed the Arabs' fury against their own perceived impotence. That impotence had been mirrored in Lebanon since the country's founding by the political and economic preeminence of the Christians.

Lebanon, Little Bible Land in the Crossfire of History
National Geographic
February 1970

THREE
THE CHRISTIANS

The groaning ferry working its way through the turquoise Mediterranean waters from Larnaca to Jounieh is still well out to sea when the outline of a 2,500-foot-high mountain rising above the bay begins to materialize in the pink haze of early morning. Poised at its very top, facing out on the shimmering expanse of the bay, is the towering statue of the Virgin Mary, arms outstretched to her supplicants. The serene look on the Virgin's face is in stark contrast to her message. "Our Lady of Lebanon" is the emblem of the Maronites, and her presence boldly announces, "This is Christian land."

Jounieh, an eccentric combination of low, red-roofed stone houses abutting a high bluff overrun with theaters, restaurants, and the infamous Casino du Liban, is the gateway to Christian Lebanon. Beyond its bay looms the Mountain, once the cradle of the Maronite Christians and now their bastion against the swelling tide of Muslim Lebanon.

Within the Mountain's hills and valleys, the Maronite Christians over the centuries burrowed into a self-made world and generated a singular ideology. That ideology came to dwell in the University of the Holy Ghost. The university, located at Kaslik, just

28

off the express highway to Beirut, comprises an impressive array of mock Gothic buildings constructed of the pale buff stone of Lebanon. Inside, its halls emit an aura of wealth, the assurance of righteousness. As an educational institution, Kaslik ranks several steps below the French-supported St. Joseph University in Beirut, where the Maronite elite receive what the monks at Kaslik would consider a secular, cosmopolitan education designed to merge its graduates into Lebanon's eclectic society. Kaslik's students come out of the mountains instead of the cities. They are largely unsophisticated, unscathed by the glitz and glitter of prewar Beirut, and unspoiled by the complexities of life beyond their villages. At the feet of the monks, Kaslik's students learn Maronite history, a legacy punctuated by persecution and glorified by survival, "history evoked in ballads of martyrology, surely more bloody and tragic, of a long oppressed nation, who for centuries, lived the liturgy of Good Friday." In prewar Lebanon, the University of the Holy Ghost represented to the Maronite establishment a fundamentalism that was embarrassingly out of step with Lebanese sophistication. But over the years of civil war it would be the hardcore Maronites, many educated at Kaslik, who would dominate the Christian side of the war.

Coming from the urbanity of Beirut, one was invariably jarred by the militancy that spewed forth from the monks, who still wear the medieval cassock. One memorable priest—chubby, with a round face and only a fringe of hair—evoked Robin Hood's Friar Tuck. But when he spoke, he did so with the cold reality of his cause: "We know how to be terrorists if we have to."

And terrorists they became. For it was the monks of Kaslik, with their wealth from vast land holdings, who before the war participated in arming the Maronites for the defense of Christian Lebanon. More important, it was the ideology the monks espoused that sent young men into battle against the Muslims and alien Palestinians, wearing heavy wooden crosses around their necks and carrying rifles with decals of the Virgin Mary glued on their stocks. And it is the monks who still speak in the apocalyptic terms of the Maronite Christian cause. Gripping a much-used M-16 rifle, a grizzled Maronite mountain man stands beside his priest and declares, "We know the bear is in the vineyards, but they will have to kill all of us for the Muslims to take over."

The Maronites are the dominant group among Lebanon's

Christians. Since the late nineteenth century, they have commanded the political and economic power of Lebanon. Therefore,
when the political prerogatives of the Christians are stated, they
are Maronite prerogatives. And when the Christian militias wage
battle, they are most often Maronite militias.

Lebanon's Christians, including the Maronites, are not a monolith but a collection of distinctive groups possessing marked diver-
sities. They broadly divide into three major denominational
groups—the Maronites and the Melkites, both Roman Catholic, and
the Greek Orthodox, who are part of the Eastern Orthodox church.
In addition, there are small Christian groups such as the Syrian
Orthodox, Syrian Catholics, Nestorians, Chaldeans, and Latin
Catholics, as well as a small Protestant presence that runs the
gamut from Presbyterian to Seventh Day Adventist. In 1975, when
the war began, the Maronites probably comprised 59 percent of the
total Lebanese Christian population; the Greek Orthodox 16 percent; the Melkites 10 percent; the Protestants and others 3 percent.

Another distinction among Lebanon's mosaic of Christian
groups is their perception of themselves in relation to the West—
that is, how they define their own Arabness. The dilemma of the
Christians of Lebanon is their internal conflict between their
centuries-old desire to deny all things Arab and their powerful and
inescapable need to forge links with the Arab world. The three
Lebanese Christian groups large enough to be politically relevant—the Maronites, Greek Orthodox, and Melkites—differ in the
degree of Arab cultural identity they accept. The Maronites reject
inclusion in the Arab world outright; the Greek Orthodox accept
their status as part of that world; and the Melkites vacillate between the two attitudes. However, all Lebanese Christians per-
ceive as imperiled their survival as a religious minority trapped in
a sea of Islam.

It is this pervasive fear that causes most Christians to mistrust
political movements that push Arab nationalism. In the Christians'
minds, Arab nationalism conjures a limitless Arab state devoid of
national boundaries in which Islam rules. Rightly or wrongly,
Christians assume that Muslims understand the concept of nation
only in terms of *umma*—the Islamic community. This thrusts the
Muslim image of the nation into direct conflict with the Western
idea of the nation-state that most Christians embrace. The way in
which Muslims and Christians view Lebanon as either a part of the

total Arab world or distinctly separate from it underlies the divisions not only among the Christians but among most of those involved in the war in Lebanon.

Before the seventh-century birth of Islam, Christians were the major religious group in Lebanon. Jesus himself preached in Lebanon, where in the vicinity of Sidon and Tyre he made whole the daughter of a Syro-Phoenician woman "grievously vexed with a devil." Early in the apostolic age, after the death of St. Stephen, followers of Christ returned to southern Lebanon and established a church at Tyre. In the first centuries of the church's existence, Christian converts in Lebanon, as elsewhere in the Roman Empire, suffered persecution. The most renowned of the martyrs was St. George, who, legend tells, slew the dragon near present-day Beirut where the bay still bears his name. The Christian community survived, and by the mid-fourth century most of Beirut's population had embraced Christianity. When a destructive earthquake struck in 349, most of those who still clung to their heathenism converted to Christianity, interpreting the death and destruction as a sign of divine wrath.

During this period, political as well as religious changes altered the character of Lebanon. The Roman Empire in the West crumbled, but the Eastern half stayed alive as the Byzantine Empire—Christian in faith, Greek in language, and Eastern in orientation. Lebanon was part of that empire.

As a Semitic area overlaid with a thin veneer of Hellenism, Lebanon became enmeshed in the struggle for control of Christendom that dominated the politics of the Christian Church in the fourth and fifth centuries. Rome and the church in the West were too far from the Levant to embroil the Levantine Christians in the grand contest between Rome and Constantinople; rather, the encounter in Lebanon was between Constantinople and the Christian churches centered around Damascus.

These Syrian groups claimed to predate both the Greek and Latin churches. In theory, their roots trace to the Last Supper to St. James, the cousin of Christ, and their church in Jerusalem is recognized as one of the earliest in the history of Christianity. Still, these Eastern churches were not themselves united but split into factions over theological issues. Although they waged their theological battles among themselves with the passion of true believers, it was their opposition to the religious and political rule of the Byzantine emperor that gave them a degree of unity. In some ways, the nature of Christianity rising out of Syria was in reality a form of Semitic nationalism.

The other major group of Lebanese Christians was called the Melkites, a name derived from the Aramaic word *melk*, or "king." The Melkites adhered to the theology of the Byzantine Church and fell under the patriarch of Antioch in Syria. Many were descendants of Greek colonists who followed the Greek traditions. The remainder came from the coastal cities. As followers of the Byzantine Church, the Melkites benefited from the protection of the state church. But over time Greek influence waned, and the Melkites drew nearer to their own patriarch at Antioch. No longer the "king's men," the Melkites became known as the Greek Orthodox, although separated from the authority of Constantinople.

When the Muslims mastered Lebanon in the seventh century, they found a population united in opposition to the rule of Byzantium. The Christians, largely of Semitic stock, regarded the invading Arabs as nearer of kin to them than the hated Greek Byzantines who ruled over them from Constantinople. In that it brought an end to alien rule, the Christians welcomed the Muslim invasion. As a result, Beirut quickly dropped into the hands of the Muslim armies in 635. Tyre and Sidon followed in 636.

The Muslim conquest was easy, because the Arabs were seen as waging as much an ethnic war as a religious war. The Christians appreciated the significance of Semites freeing their Semitic cousins from foreign rule. Thus, "the victory of Moslem arms in the Eastern Mediterranean strip . . . was in reality the victory of Arab nationalism, of Islam the state."

Until 685, the Christians fared reasonably well under Muslim rule. Given the status of *dhimmis*, or "people of the book," the Christians were left alone, their land and right to worship protected. Although the *jizya*, a special tax, was levied on non-Muslims, non-Muslims also escaped military duty. But the Christians, left without military or political power, soon felt the heavy hand of the Muslim authorities.

The *dhimmi* system eroded. New decrees forbade Christians to build more churches, and many of the existing churches were appropriated by the state and turned into mosques. Christian religious groups were forbidden to seek new members, even among non-Muslims. And apostasy from Islam was punishable by death.

Under these rules, the Christians faced a slow but inevitable decline.

The reign of Caliph Abd al Malik (685–705) energized a profound fear of extinction in the Christian community. The caliph threw open Christian lands to Muslim settlement, allowing waves of immigrants from the Arabian Peninsula to settle in southern Lebanon, thus reducing Christians in the area to a minority. The caliph further moved to classify Christians as second-class citizens, often barring them from public office. By the middle of the eighth century, the Christians bitterly recognized that Muslim rule, which had seemed so attractive a century earlier, was in fact "a rigid prison from which there was no escape other than apostasy or flight."

The place of flight became the Mountain. As the Arab warriors, government officials, and bedouins flocked into Lebanon from the Arabian peninsula, they settled on the coastal plain. Sons of the desert, they possessed no skills as mountain warriors, abhorred snow, and regarded the pursuit of agriculture, the economic life of the mountains, as beneath their dignity. That left the mountains to the Christians.

As different in character as in topography from the coastal plain, Mount Lebanon developed its own distinctive culture. The society that took root there was defined by the landscape. Today, as in earlier centuries, the farmers, herders, quarrymen, and foresters struggle against the harsh terrain, a terrain that changes drastically in altitude and vegetation over amazingly short distances. Within forty minutes, one can climb five thousand feet, passing through the palm, banana, and citrus trees of the coast; the olive, almond, peach, and apricot groves of the foothills; and the cherry, pear, and apple orchards of the upper elevations, all knitted together by stately pines. In the high mountain villages, the smoke of the shish kebab brazier drifts lazily over the landscape, one reminder of the Mountain's Arab side. In the highest reaches of the steep hills, a battered sign points to the old Ksara wine cellars, a legacy of the French presence on the Mountain. Outsiders have influenced the Mountain, but none have ever really owned it without the acceptance of the people themselves. This is why the Mountain is the refuge of minority groups. Few governments are willing to make the sacrifice to conquer its rugged terrain to either possess it or control it.

The tempo of Christian flight to the security of the Mountain escalated with the repressions of succeeding caliphs. During his rule (847–861), Caliph al Mutawakkil decreed that Christians and Jews affix wooden images of devils to the exteriors of their houses, level the graves of their dead to the ground, wear belittling colored patches on their sleeves, and suffer the humiliation of riding only on mules. As more Christians fled, the Mountain became an island of refuge for the oppressed and discontented from inner Syria and the Lebanese plain. "Lebanon set out on its traditional course as a citadel of minorities and dissidents and as a home for the lost cause." It was from one group of Christians from Syria seeking sanctuary on the Mountain that the Maronites emerged to politically and economically dominate modern Lebanon.

The conglomeration of people who came to be designated as Maronites owe their name to Maron, a monk who lived in the wilderness of Syria between Antioch and Cyrrhus in the latter half of the fourth century. A priest in the Uniate Church of Syria, Maron broke with his own order and founded an order of ascetics. Shortly after his death, his followers became embroiled in controversy with the church of Antioch. Seizing the saint's relics, Maron's flock fled to the mountains of Lebanon, where they erected a monastery at Qalat al Madiq on the Orontes River. There they grew in number.

Because of their flight from Syria, the Maronites already had begun to see themselves as persecuted. Then in 517 their rivals, the Jacobite Christians, assaulted the Maronite monastery and slaughtered 350 monks. The survivors fled deeper into the mountains of Lebanon. Gouging caves out of the craggy rocks of the rugged Qadisha valley, Joannes Maro, the first patriarch, drew the Maronites together and nurtured a new nation. "[S]ettled . . . on the outskirts of the wild cedars, . . . in hostile climate and barren nature, the Maronites led a life of disconcerting austerity without any provisions for the next day; this provisional life of a man who about to set sail to the infinite, had not a permanent city down below."

While the Maronites clung to the slopes of Mount Lebanon, jealously guarding their separate identity, the Greek Orthodox lived in the coastal cities surrounded and outnumbered by the Muslims. By the tenth century, the Christian population of what is now Lebanon had shrunk to less than half of what it was before the Islamic invasion. Thus, as a decreasing minority, the Christians of the Middle East met the Christians of Europe.

Europe established contact with Lebanon's Christians during the first Crusade. In 1097 Tancred, a Norman commander, landed on the eastern shore of the Mediterranean. His army, commanded by armored knights mounted on swift chargers, moved down the coast. When they entered Tripoli, Tancred allowed the city to escape the horror of siege only at a price of fifteen thousand pieces of gold, fine silks, and the population's best horses and mules. Loaded with booty, the Crusaders marched along the old coastal invasion route to Byblos and on to al Batrun, where the jubilant Maronites came forth to meet them. After generations holed up in the mountains living from hand to mouth, the Maronites welcomed the Crusaders as heroes come to deliver them from the Muslim menace. Using the Maronites as guides, the crusading Normans moved on to Beirut, Sidon, and Tyre, plundering for foodstuffs and booty and battling a plague of poisonous snakes along the way. At last they reached Jerusalem, laying claim to the city on June 7, 1099. Inspired by the triumph of religious war, other European Crusaders came and conquered, creating along the Lebanese coast a string of fragile fortresses that they ordained as states.

From the beginning, there was little likelihood that the Crusader states could survive. Populated at most by a few hundred Europeans, a Crusader state was seldom more than a small enclave of transplanted Christians standing against a vast and dark background of Islam. Increasingly the Crusaders faced the opposition of Christians loyal to the Byzantine Empire. The arrogance, greed, and rivalry of the Crusaders made the Byzantines regret their original invitation to the Europeans seeking to wrest control of the Holy Land from the Muslims. The widening political division between Rome and Constantinople expressed itself in bitterness and recrimination between Roman Catholics and Greek Orthodox across the region. By 1302, the Crusaders had lost their last foothold on the islet of Arwad and the West retreated once again from the Levant.

Still, the Crusaders left behind a lasting legacy—the bond between Europe and the Christians of the Middle East. During the Crusades, the Roman Catholic Church was as interested in reclaiming Christendom's Eastern Christians as it was in recapturing the holy sites. When the Crusades were called, Pope Urban II and his advisers assumed that the harsh conditions the Muslims inflicted on the Christians would make the Christians receptive to overtures from the Western church. Yet when the Roman Catholic

Church attempted to join the Eastern churches with the Church of Rome, it was rebuffed. The Syrian churches were still of the East, distrustful and wary of the West.

But the Maronites were different. The Maronites sensed in the West a powerful ally not only against the Muslims but against their Christian rivals. The Maronites eagerly gave and the Roman Catholic Church enthusiastically accepted assignment as protector of the Maronites. With hardheaded realism, Rome recognized the Maronites as the Roman Catholic Church's best opportunity for establishing itself in the East. Thus, the seduction began with the Maronites and Rome each playing the role of seducer. In 1213 the Maronite patriarch was invited to Rome, the first Maronite clergyman to establish personal contact with the Papal See. On his return to Lebanon, the patriarch instituted reforms in the Maronite mass that incorporated significant parts of the Latin liturgy, a development Rome noted with gratitude. In 1521, the romance between the Roman Catholic Church and the Maronites had advanced to the point where Pope Leo X designated the Maronites "a rose among the thorns." And in 1584, the Maronite college in Rome opened its doors to students from the Middle East seeking training in Western languages and ideas. In 1736, the Maronites at last succumbed to the wooing of the Roman Catholic Church and accepted a qualified union with Rome. While recognizing the authority of the Pope, the Maronites have preserved their identity by retaining their own Syriac liturgy, their own saints' and feast days, and their own patriarch, who is confirmed rather than appointed by the Pope.

While wooing the Maronites, the Holy See toiled with equal vigor among the Greek Orthodox. Ignoring earlier rebuffs, Roman Catholic missionaries attempted with painstaking patience to separate the Greek Orthodox from their Eastern roots. The effort was partially successful. In 1717 a segment of the Greek Orthodox surrendered, assuming the name *Greek Catholics* or *Melkites*, another misnomer in the lexicon of Christian labels. Today's Melkites, like the Maronites, are of the Roman Church yet apart from it. While classifying themselves as Roman Catholics and professing allegiance to the Pope in Rome, the Melkites have retained their oriental rites and rituals.

It was midnight, the dawn of Easter Sunday. While the Lebanese civil war flashed around them, small knots of people moved through the narrow streets of Zahle toward the small, white stucco church whose bells were pealing out the call to mass. One by one, they climbed the steep stone steps of the Melkite church and entered through the thick cedar door hung on weathered brass hinges. Once inside, the symbols of that intricate crossing of East and West that characterizes Christianity in Lebanon were obvious.

The sweet, heavy essence of incense permeated the church. Iconlike representations of saints adorned the walls between the windows, reflecting the bright blues and purples of the stained glass. Above the chancel, the one-dimensional mosaic figures of the Last Supper gazed down upon the worshipers. Just in front of the tableau, an ornate lamp crafted of red glass and gold leaf hung from heavy gold chains. All spoke of the traditions of the Eastern fringes of the Christian church.

Latecomers, many carrying or dragging small children, hurriedly genuflected, completing the sign of the cross by touching their fingers to their lips. They crowded into their seats as the service began. The priest stepped before the altar. He wore the robes of the Roman Catholic Church, but a large, red, Eastern-style cross adorned the back of his vestments. Before him on the altar, an ornate gold and silver cross in the style of the Eastern Orthodox Church dominated the collection of bejeweled vessels and simple Roman prayer books carefully laid out for the mass. While the priest chanted the liturgy, a large man with thick glasses and a white fringe of beard sat in the back of the cramped church pumping a small organ whose keys barely accommodated his thick fingers. Behind him, a nine-member choir chanted in response to the priest. Eventually the service broke for the annual message from the Melkite patriarch of Antioch. But this year—perhaps because of the war, the priest mused—the message had not arrived. In its place, this priest of the local church capsulized his patriarch's messages of previous years. All conveyed the same theme—the perilous conditions facing the Christians of the Middle East.

Basically leaning toward the West in culture and political orientation, the Melkites are the bridge between the Maronites, the Lebanese Christians most closely tied to the West, and the Greek Orthodox, who, though Christians, see themselves as an integral part of the larger Arab world and feel the least threatened by Lebanon's Muslims.

The Greek Orthodox have always been rooted more deeply in

the East than in the West. During the Crusades, those who became known as Greek Orthodox remained identified with the Arabs. So vigorously did they reject contact with the Europeans that one group actually prayed openly in Jerusalem for a Muslim victory while the remaining Christians valiantly fought to stave off Saladin's siege in 1187. Ignoring the Maronites' pursuit of the West, the Greek Orthodox were content to remain part of Greater Syria.

Lebanon's Greek Orthodox Church always stayed centered in geography and theology in Syria with its patriarch, and its members accepted themselves as Arabs. As a result, today's Greek Orthodox relate to the Muslims and adopt ideologies of the Arab world and pan-Arabism itself more readily than either the Maronites or the Melkites.

The Greek Orthodox are the most urbanized, best educated, and perhaps the most universally liked of Lebanon's religious groups. A Palestinian said of them, "They are the rightful citizens of the land. They can live with any group." Maronites and Sunnis "find no problems with them," and a Druze believes they could be mediators among the Lebanese. Although the most nonthreatening group in Lebanon, the Greek Orthodox are among the most politically complex. Their community includes many members of the financial elite as well as some of the most radical political thinkers.

Early in the twentieth century, Greek Orthodox intellectuals argued that "Greater Syria" and a distinct Syrian national identity existed. The theory was not new. For centuries "Syria" included Jordan, Palestine, Syria, and Lebanon. But it was not until 1932, during the French colonial period, that a political party articulating this uniquely Syrian philosophy emerged.

The Parti Populaire Syrien (PPS), or Syrian National Party, was founded by Antoun Saadeh, a thirty-year-old Greek Orthodox teacher. The PPS advanced the concept of a Syrian national identity among the original inhabitants of present-day Syria, Lebanon, Jordan, Israel, Iraq, Cyprus, and part of Turkey. Party ideologues, primarily Greek Orthodox intellectuals, argued that this Syrian nationality should be expressed in a single Syrian state rather than as a state embracing all Arab people, as the Arab nationalists demanded.

The central theme of the Syrian state was that it would be based not on the religious solidarity of Islam but on the idea of Syria as a distinct historical, cultural, and geographical entity. To escape the threat of Islam, PPS's Greek Orthodox ideologues postulated that the people living in the geographical area of Syria constituted an ethnic unity that had existed since prehistory, one that was independent of racial origin or religion. Adhering to the concept of this nation with near reverence, PPS members sought to subordinate all other interests to that of the political realization of Greater Syria.

The PPS embodied as closely as any party the attitude of the Greek Orthodox to the Lebanese dilemma of their crossed cultures. But the PPS never commanded the loyalty of more than a small percentage of the Greek Orthodox community. And after 1946, as the party moved leftward economically and Lebanon joined the ranks of independent nations, the appeal of the PPS's ritualistic greeting "Long Live Syria" waned and many of its Greek Orthodox supporters chose the political mainstream.

The chronicle of the PPS is important only insofar as it demonstrates the difference among the Christians of Lebanon in attitude toward their identity with and commitment to the Arab world. The idea of a Syrian nation particularly appealed to the Greek Orthodox because it promised the possibility of creating a state larger and stronger than Lebanon and one free of the Maronites' stranglehold on the state's economic and political apparatus. It also gave Lebanon the option to merge with Syria and other countries of the Levant without subjecting the Christians to the overwhelming numerical power of the Muslims of the entire Arab world.

Within a decade of the end of World War II, most Greek Orthodox had ended their quest for an alternative to independent Lebanon. But they remained the least committed of the Christians to an independent Lebanese state. During the early 1970s, just before the war broke out, fewer than 50 percent of the Greek Orthodox supported the idea of an independent Lebanon over another type of political entity. An independent Lebanon was less crucial to the Greek Orthodox's perception of their survival than it was to the Maronites. While the Maronites conceptualized Lebanon as a country *in* but not *of* the Middle East, the Greek Orthodox accepted themselves as an Arab people living in an Arab state.

The Greek Orthodox, though complex and interesting, represent only a small minority of Lebanon's Christian population. The dominant group among the Christians is the Maronites, that reclusive group that trekked west from Syria in the fourth century seeking escape from religious persecution and that so eagerly embraced the West during the Crusades. It is the Maronites who politically and economically controlled Lebanon before the civil war. And it is the Maronites who are most often "the Christians" in the political jargon of that war.

From its inception, the Maronite Church was alienated from Arab culture and religion. Although contacts with the West had been tenuous and intermittent over the centuries, the Maronites nonetheless developed a deep sense of affinity with Christian Europe. This pull toward the West was deliberately fed by France, as it had been by Rome, from the beginning of French contact with the Christians of Lebanon. When Louis IX of France landed at Akka in the Seventh Crusade, he responded to the Maronite offer of a contingent of archers by declaring the Maronites a part of the French nation. From the seventeenth century onward, France, first through the Jesuits and later through its own imperialists, assumed protective responsibility for the Maronites of Lebanon. But even with their French protectors, the Maronites clung to the Mountain, fearful of conquest or assimilation. Their worst anxieties were realized in the dreadful war of 1860 between the Druze and the Maronites.

The war that had begun in 1840 as an economic revolution against the Mountain's feudal system collapsed almost immediately into a communal war. Although the Maronites were hardened mountain people, it was the Druze who warred with a viciousness that would forever brand them as dreaded fighters. Twelve thousand Druze routed sixty thousand armed Christians in what the Maronites called ". . . a dark design . . . to throw their whole race into a state of abject servitude by letting loose upon them the ferocious passions of the Druze. . . ."

As the war unfolded, the mountains rang with warnings of Druze attacks, sending Christians from isolated towns fleeing to larger towns for protection. Those who straggled behind were intercepted and slain, their ears severed from their heads and nailed to the nearest barn wall. Druze fighters entered the abandoned towns to plunder and burn the deserted houses and drive off the stock of fleeing farmers. Not even the church provided refuge. Rampaging Druze broke into the Maronite convent of Ameek and murdered the superior in his bed, while other priests were slain at the foot of their altars.

For weeks after the initial skirmishes, the Druze sold their spoils in public bazaars where people haggled over Maronite watches, jewelry, lace shawls, silver church vessels, and richly embroidered priests' robes.

Still, Christian towns such as Hasbeya, Zahle, and Dayr al Qamar refused to surrender. Zahle finally fell to the Druze onslaught, and the residents of Dayr al Qamar were starved into surrender. Herding Dayr al Qamar's twelve thousand resisters into the town center, the Druze massacred them over a period of six hours. In the interest of its Christian wards France intervened, tightening the bonds between the Maronites and the French. While the war resulted in the establishment of European political interests within a division of the Ottoman Empire, changing the economic and social structure of the Mountain, the enduring result of the conflict was the incurable trauma it inflicted on the Christians. Today it is the single event on which the Maronites focus their collective consciousness of all Christian persecutions in the Middle East since the advent of Islam. Although great numbers of Greek Catholics and Greek Orthodox also were killed by the Druze, only the Maronites dwell on the war of 1860 as a never-ending wrong. "[T]he events of 1860 became the touchstone of Maronite psychology, and when the question of security from 'the Muslim threat' arose in Maronite minds as it did increasingly with the rise of nationalism throughout the Arab world, 1860 became a potent symbol of what could not be allowed to happen again."

While the war of 1860 is its touchstone, the Maronite psyche is propelled by three factors: the Maronites' determination to separate themselves from their cultural environment; their innate sense of superiority in relation to the Muslims and other Lebanese Christians; and their visceral fear as a Christian minority in the Muslim Middle East.

The Maronites suffer enormous inner tension because they are enmeshed in contradictory emotions between their Western facade and their Arab roots. The very nature of the Maronites' relationship to the Church of Rome indicates their near schizophrenia about the West and their own fragile westernization. Because they are Arab at the core, the Maronites harbor nagging suspicions about Western Christianity. Only through several centuries of close contact with the West and a concerted effort to embrace Western

culture have the Maronites emerged with a thin veneer of westernization. But that veneer is neither deep enough nor bonded enough
for the Maronites to avoid the searing conflicts between their Arab
nature and their Western patina. They deny all things Arab, yet
they cannot escape the fact that they are, in their culture, Arab.
Thus, the Maronites play a game of acceptance and disavowal with
studied determination. During the 1950s, two Maronite professors
at the American University of Beirut hotly challenged their department's decision to list Lebanese students in a statistical study
under the rubric of "Arab students." The whole department was
paralyzed for weeks before an ingenious professor, Greek by nationality, proposed that the classification be changed to "Arabic
speaking" thereby assuaging the objection of the Maronites.

In searching for an avenue of escape from their tense ambivalence about their identity, the Maronites have created a mystical
"Mediterranean civilization" that combines Western and Arab
affinities. The Maronite economic and intellectual elite are the
foremost proponents of the theory that Lebanon possesses a "Mediterranean culture." Typical of their spokespeople is the prosperous
businessman who, fastidiously attired in a three-piece suit, sat
behind his ebony desk in the office of his successful import-export
firm. Flowing smoothly through three languages, he explained to
this writer the Maronite view of Lebanon, ending with a matter-of-
fact statement delivered with absolute conviction: "Maronites, you
know, are Phoenicians." With this one statement, the Maronites
escape their dualism.

The first to introduce the idea that the Maronites were the
direct heirs of the Phoenicians was Tannus al Shidyaq, who died in
1861, just after the cataclysmic massacre of 1860. In the 1920s, the
writings of the Christian intellectual Michel Chiha embellished
Lebanon's image as the successor to the ancient Phoenician states,
a merchant republic, a bearer of a Mediterranean culture, an
illuminator of its environment, and an interpreter between East
and West. The disconcerting facts that Phoenicia included many
city-states outside Lebanon's borders and that the Maronites were
migrants from Syria rather than descendants of the populace of
Lebanon's coast have been conveniently brushed aside by the disci-
ples of al Shidyaq and Chiha in favor of their own romanticism. The
Maronites are so caught up in defending their own myths that
unsavory facts about the Phoenicians transform into slurs against

the Maronites. In 1965, a group of well-heeled Maronites attending a National Museum lecture on the Phoenicians were grievously offended when the lecturer matter-of-factly stated that the Phoenicians practiced child sacrifice.

Being Phoenicians is a fable the Maronites work to perpetuate. During the Golden Age, members of the French-educated Maronite intelligentsia poured articles into the literary magazine *La Revue Phenicienne* and pushed other vehicles of the cultural life that glorified Lebanon's non-Arab aspects. For the Maronite population as a whole, the acceptance of their Phoenician heritage is an article of faith in their ideology. For the Phoenician illusion is critical not only to the Maronites' thinking about themselves but to their perception of the whole character of Lebanon. Through their Phoenician myth, the Maronites justify a concept of Lebanon's identity entirely different from that held by the Sunni Muslims or Greek Orthodox. It is because of its Mediterranean culture that the Maronites claim Lebanon is above and apart from the Arabs who surround it.

Yet the mythology goes a step further: Lebanon is not only the heir of Phoenicia, it is a child of the Christian church nurtured by French culture. Thus, the illusion of being Phoenicians is also entangled with the Maronites' other dominant perception: that they are French. Spawned during their early contacts with the French Crusaders, missionaries, and envoys, identification with France became a striking phenomenon in Maronite society. The charade of being French reached full flower during the French Mandate (1920–1946) and added yet another dimension to the Maronite identity. "So successful was [France's] *la mission civilisatrice . . .* that many Maronites not only assumed French as their first language . . . but also conceived a hopeless love of French civilization."

The Maronites' attachment to their French character is obvious the moment one crosses the threshold of an upper-class Maronite's apartment. Maurice, attired in his impeccable, continental-cut suit, welcomes his guests in flawless French and with exaggerated European mannerisms. He is followed by his wife, Claudette, who sweeps across the marble of the entryway, which is dominated by two enormous Sevres vases heavily painted with bouquets of flowers against a cobalt background. She is wearing a flowing hostess gown purchased on her most recent trip to Paris. The greetings completed, she gently presses the arm of a guest and steers her into the spacious living room furnished in gilded Louis XVI and accessorized with more Sevres and heavy crystal. The Limoges tea and coffee cups are filled while the hostess passes ornate porcelain bowls overflowing with French chocolates bought in one of Beirut's many shops that cater to French tastes. The overall effect is crowned by the French language. Through the entire evening, not one word of Arabic will be spoken.

Arabic is for the bazaars and the servants. A poet who writes in French once related how he hated to read anything in Arabic, that it sounded "heavy, rigid, and fanatical." Some Maronites will even apologize to other Arabic-speaking people about their lack of facility with their mother tongue. English, the third language of Lebanon, spread rapidly among educated Lebanese after World War II. But English is the language of commerce. It is a useful tool, but it remains external to those who learn and use it. French, on the other hand, is part of the inner man.

Before independence, the Maronites, although beginning to split with France politically, clung to French culture. For this appropriation of French culture was for the Maronites another form of identification, a way to further demonstrate their divorce from Arabs and Islam. But when free Lebanon with its large Arabic-speaking population emerged in 1946, it was no more possible for the Maronites to turn their French illusion into reality than it had been for them to verify their Phoenician illusion. Yet they tried. While the Maronites lived in an Arab country, their cultural orientation remained geared to France. "They wanted to be what they were not and what they could not be—Frenchmen. They acquired and used the trappings of French civilization (language, clothing, food, social forms) without ever acquiring the feeling that they were integrated into French life. The *evolue* did not become a Frenchman, he became an *evolue* Arab."

Just as the Maronites use their Phoenician roots and French culture to distance themselves from the Arab world, so do they use religion to distinguish themselves from the Muslims. The Maronite Christians defend their privileged status in Lebanon as part of some divinely inspired mission to the Muslims. It is a position that the Maronites readily articulate. Waiting for the traffic light to change on a busy street corner, a Maronite store owner turned and said, "Muslims and Druzes can't receive the love of God as we can." As blunt as that statement is, it is when the teacups are circulating and the conversation is relaxed and flowing that the Maronites' attitude about their superiority really surfaces. A tall, bewhiskered Anglican minister, newly arrived in Beirut, sat uncomfortably poised on the edge of a red brocade sofa listening aghast to Maronite women describing the Shiite Muslims as less than human. And a Frenchman subjected to a similar discourse on the Muslims exclaimed, "My god, they talk just like the colons in Algeria did about the Arabs."

Still, beneath the bravado lurks the Maronites' paranoia about their survival. Their status as a minority, their long history of persecution, their great trauma of 1860, their perpetual search for Western alliances are all part of the Maronite psyche. Though accused by other Lebanese of believing they are a bit more than first among equals, the Maronites' basic fear is that stripping them of their economic and political prerogatives is the prelude to driving them from Lebanon. As it did when the Maronite community took root on the Mountain, Lebanon today represents to the Maronites the survival of the Christians in the Middle East. Symbolically Maronite villages in the mountains are little stone fortresses waiting to receive Christianity's last defenders. Any mention of true Muslim equality in Lebanon releases all their old fears of the Islamic *umma*—state and church as one. Thus, the Maronites reject all forms of pan-Arabism as nothing more than a mask for pan-Islamism. The Maronites are not only the Lebanese minority most devoted to Lebanon's sovereignty and least likely to allow themselves to be absorbed into a larger Arab unity; they are also willing to bring their whole world crashing down on their heads rather than yield anything to the Muslims.

In describing Maronite behavior, one always must return to fear. Fear consumes the Maronites. It is the dominant factor in their behavior. Because of it the Maronites possess a Masadalike complex that makes them ready to separate Lebanon from the rest of the Arab world and, if necessary, defend the Mountain as a Christian enclave. Maronite ideologue Fuad Ephrem Boustany, long before the civil war began, prophetically said, "You don't know what a mountain people with six thousand years of history behind it is capable of doing when faced with the choice of suicide or fighting against the enemy."

In the 1970s the Maronite religious establishment, in response to the escalating Muslim demands for political equity, embraced extremist politics. Led by Father Sharbal Qassis, the extremists among the clerics advocated a "pure Lebanon" and rejected the notion that Lebanon had what the moderates were willing to concede— an "Arab face." After years of warfare, others still carry on Qassis's philosophy. With a passion verging on hysteria, a young spokesperson for the fathers of the University of Kaslik, his finger jabbing the air for emphasis and spittle collecting in the corners of his mouth from the forceful delivery of his words, leaned forward and declared, "The Maronites are a body of the land and people. They have to have some privileges. Without them the Maronites will vanish. The church protects the land, the people, and their privileges. Freedom does not exist without a piece of land. The amount of freedom we have depends on the amount of land."

As owners of a sizable portion of Lebanon's agricultural land, the monastic orders provided financing for developing Maronite militias with such illustrative names as Defenders of the Cedars, The Phalange (phalanx) of Fear, The Wood of the Cross, Youth of St. Maron, and Knights of the Virgin. Before he was replaced by his moderate patriarch, Qassis stored weapons and ammunition in his monasteries for the burgeoning Christian militias.

Extremist groups with no clerical ties were also swelling as war approached. The Guardians of the Cedars drew inspiration from Said Aql, who set to poetry Michel Chiha's theory of the Christians' Phoenician roots. Tanzim, a small, secretive organization of professional men, was ready to go to war for Christian Lebanon. The Maronite League, a militia headed by Sahker Abu Suleiman, vowed to take any action necessary to protect the Maronites' place in Lebanon. All of these groups struck a clear distinction between "Lebanonism" and "Arabism." In other words, the role of Islam and the Arabs in the development of Lebanon was minimized, if not ignored.

These were the fanatics of prewar Lebanon. They were but one facet of the Maronite collage. Just as the Lebanese Christians are not a monolith, neither are the Maronites. Some Maronite leaders are willing to concede a large share of their power in the Lebanese system to other Christians and to the Muslims if for no other reason than to preserve the framework of the Lebanese state. While the Christian militias were arming themselves before the war, Raymond Edde and other moderates were attempting to devise a formula that would allow non-Christians a place in Christian

Lebanon. To the moderates, the worst situation the Christians could create for themselves would be to become isolated within a Christian ghetto. The moderates recognized, albeit grudgingly, that the Maronites' economic interests lay with the Arabs. They further argued that the Maronites could survive only by reaching an accommodation with the Muslims, for Western powers no longer could be counted on to guarantee the protection of Lebanon's Christians.

Although the moderates were an important voice in the years before the war, the Maronites' precarious situation during the war years deadened the voices of reason. Raymond Edde himself was forced into exile in Paris in 1981 by the radicals within the Maronite community. But during the prewar years, neither of these groups spoke for the Maronites.

Between the fanatics and the moderates was the third group— the real politicians, the clan chieftains who traded and connived, charmed and intimidated to protect their own interests along with those of their clients. The names Camille Chamoun, Suleiman Franjieh, and Pierre Gemayel echoed through the hills like those of ancient tribal lords. From the time of the French Mandate in 1920, each of these men headed quasi-political parties, weak on ideology and strong on personality. They played on the Lebanese' responsiveness to personal relationships with men perceived as commanding power and competed with one another over political patronage and the division of spoils in Lebanon.

Chamoun, Franjieh, and Gemayel headed powerful clans and performed like a hybrid of ward politician and feudal chieftain. Chamoun was the patrician, the consummate French-educated Maronite, whose power rested on his ability to float like an aristocrat through the drawing rooms of Lebanese society, seeming to forge coalitions on the spot without dropping one ash from his thin cigar on the carpet of his host. Suleiman Franjieh, the quintessential tribal chief, reigned from the Mountain, executed vendettas, and protected his clients' interests with paternal devotion. And the hawk-faced Pierre Gemayel began organizing for the preservation of Christian Lebanon forty years before the outbreak of the civil war. He drew to him those who were intimidated by the sophistication of Chamoun and who were closed out of the traditional power structure of the Mountain represented by Franjieh. He developed among his followers the singular mentality of survivors. Thus, each

of these men entered the civil war as a powerful master of a
segment of the Maronite community. Only Franjieh still survives.
Chamoun was unable to pass on his legacy. The political heirs of
the paramilitary organization Gemayel founded now speak more
than anyone else for the Lebanese Christian community.

A superbly talented politician, Camille Chamoun created his
own power base without the benefit of an entrenched ancestry.
Born in 1900 in Dayr al Qamar in the Shuf, that part of the
Mountain south of Beirut, he was the son of a finance officer in the
Ottoman administration. Like many in his community, Chamoun
grew up on the stories of the 1860 massacre and the deaths of
hundreds of Dayr al Qamar's unarmed Christian citizens. Fitted
with his heritage, he went to Beirut in pursuit of the typical French
education of the Maronite elite, emerging from the law school of St.
Joseph University as an ardent Francophile.

After practicing law for six years, Chamoun entered parliament in 1934 as a deputy from the Shuf. He served the French
Mandate as minister of finance, was appointed the Lebanese representative to the United Nations after independence, moved on to
become ambassador to London, and in 1952 was elected Lebanon's
second president.

Chamoun radiated the image of a president, especially a president the West would admire. Elegant, silver haired, always impec-
cably dressed with a small cigar delicately balanced between his
fingers, he looked like he belonged in the Quai D'Orsay. In political
orientation, perhaps he did. Chamoun always looked West, to
France, to the United States.

During his presidency, Chamoun became an object of virtual
idolatry among the Maronite masses because of his staunch defense of the Christian Lebanon ideal. During the crisis of 1958,
Maronite villages were papered with pictures showing Christ
pointing an approving finger toward the image of Camille Chamoun framed within a heart on the Savior's bosom. Not even
Chamoun's forced withdrawal from the presidency in 1958 failed
to dampen the aura. In 1963, the visage of Camille Chamoun was
still plastered across the Mountain, often depicted next to the
Madonna, her arm draped protectively over his shoulder.

Throughout his political career, Camille Chamoun operated
from the Shuf region south and east of Beirut, where he was
trapped between Franjieh's territory to the north and Gemayel's to

the south. Unlike his rivals, he had no geographically distinct and undisputed home turf.

Chamoun functioned as the nominal head of the patrician National Liberal Party, which promoted no coherent doctrine but supported a militia with the unlikely title "the Tigers." The National Liberal Party was neither national nor liberal—in fact, in any real sense it was not even a party. It had little organization, lacked a program, and thought nothing of operating for years at a time without issuing a single policy statement. In reality, the National Liberal Party was little more than a collection of the most westernized Maronite families grouped around the most charismatic of all the Maronite leaders. Chamoun succeeded in the game of Maronite politics because he was a consummate pragmatist who derived power largely by adroitly playing his rivals against each other.

If Camille Chamoun was the most Western of the Maronite leaders, Suleiman Franjieh was, if not the most pro-Arab, the most personally tied to Syria. Born in the Zghorta region of northern Lebanon, Suleiman Franjieh was the scion of one of the Mountain's principal families. The Franjiehs claimed direct descent from the Crusaders, insisting that "Franjieh" actually means "Frank." As head of an old, established family, Suleiman's father served as a member of parliament from 1922 until his death in 1932, when Hamid, Suleiman's older brother, inherited his seat. For the next twenty-five years, Suleiman stood in his brother's shadow as Hamid climbed to national prominence as a leader of the Independence Movement, then minister of finance, and finally minister of foreign affairs.

This was one side of the Franjieh dynasty. The other side was the mountain clan Franjiehs, protective of their turf and all the benefits that went along with it.

In early summer of 1957, Camille Chamoun, preparing to grab a second term as president, used the Dwayhi clan to move in on Franjieh territory. Their rivals for generations, the Franjiehs struck back. The Dwayhis, trapped at the village of Mizyara, took refuge in the church. But sanctity had no meaning in tribal war. The Franjiehs stormed the church and murdered twenty-three people hiding inside. Not only was Suleiman Franjieh on the scene; witnesses accused him of killing several of the victims. Under threat of arrest by Lebanese security forces, he fled to Syria. But when Hamid Franjieh's political career was suddenly ended by a massive stroke in October 1957, Suleiman returned from exile to assume his rightful place as head of the Franjieh family.

Suleiman Franjieh is a warlord in the traditional sense of the term. And he lives the role of warlord. His home in Zghorta is like a stone fortress. Its walls are hung with daggers, swords, and florid nineteenth-century rifles with stocks inlaid with mother-of-pearl. And like a warlord, he and his family claim the spoils of political power.

In the early 1970s Tony Franjieh, Suleiman's son and heir apparent, became synonymous with mismanagement and corruption. Stories about his alleged illicit involvement in the hashish trade abounded. As minister of post, telephone, and telegraph, he was accused of pocketing huge sums of money as fees for a major modernization scheme. So blatant was his greed that television transmission via satellite was delayed for a decade when potential customers, especially the American networks, refused to pay the exorbitant installation costs that Tony demanded as a hidden payoff.

As a warlord, Suleiman Franjieh kept an armed force. In 1969, during one of the Lebanese' early conflicts with the Palestinians, he raised the Zghorta Liberation Army, which drew its membership from the Franjiehs' following in the Zghorta region. A private army was a natural response to outside threats to Franjieh territory, for Suleiman Franjieh's power derived from his willingness to resort to violence to protect his own and his community's positions. Although the Zghorta Liberation Army would ensure that Suleiman Franjieh was president of Lebanon when the civil war erupted, once the war unfolded Franjieh's militia would prove no match for the forces of Pierre Gemayel—the Phalange.

When the tall, lank, muscular Gemayel, a devotee of athletics, attended the 1936 Olympic Games in Berlin, he was irresistibly drawn to the order and discipline of the Third Reich. Almost as a revelation, Gemayel divined that the same degree of order and discipline was the solution to welding the unruly and individualistic Lebanese into a unified force. Gemayel returned to Lebanon and founded the Phalange, which as the Lebanese Forces has become the single most important Christian group in Lebanon.

The Phalange began as a Christian youth organization modeled after those of Mussolini's Italy and other fascist organizations that dotted Europe in the 1930s. Armed with the motto "God, Family, and Nation," Gemayel set out to fulfill his vision of Lebanon as an ordered, unified Christian nation. Although they adopted a fascist salute and the flag-waving paraphernalia of fascism, the early Phalangists were less fascists than glorified Boy Scouts.

Although the Phalange ideology and structure was influenced by the ultranationalist and fascist models of the decade, it was the stress on paramilitary organization and the importance of an ever-present single, all-powerful leader that attracted Gemayel to the fascists. Fascist discipline was a natural milieu for Pierre Gemayel. He possessed intense and abundant energy that naturally channeled itself into a rigid and demanding work schedule. He was a man of habit and routine rather than intellect. Neither well read nor endowed with historical insights, Gemayel nevertheless clung tenaciously to his opinions on such topics as the link between ancient Phoenicia and modern Lebanon and the threat Lebanese capitalism faced from "international communism." True to his Maronite roots, his Arabic always remained poor, as he chose to use French instead of his native tongue. Still, he was a gifted organizer who poured his energy and singleness of purpose into building the Phalange and winning its members' fierce loyalty. Between 1937 and 1958, party ranks swelled from eight thousand to fifty thousand, making the Phalange the largest political organization in Lebanon. And with the years, its youth activities gave way to a vigilantelike militancy against the Muslim danger. Its motto, "Lebanon First," captured the core of the movement.

During its formative years, the Phalange fought to gain a place in the mainstream of Lebanese politics. In the 1930s, while the Sunni Muslims demanded that France turn Lebanon back to Syria, Pierre Gemayel ardently defended the idea of a distinct and autonomous Lebanon. With independence, Gemayel joined the ranks of the fervent believers in the National Pact, the 1948 agreement by which Lebanon's Christians and Muslims agreed to govern themselves. To the Phalange, the National Pact became "the Covenant" guaranteeing the Maronites hegemony in Lebanon and prohibiting Lebanese involvement with the affairs of other Arab states.

In the early 1950s, the Phalange succeeded in becoming a parliamentary party and an active participant in the Lebanese political game. But it also retained its militia and constructed an elaborate party hierarchy and bureaucracy that distinguished it from Lebanon's other political parties, which most often were loose affiliations cemented by one of the traditional communal or clan leaders. As organized as the Phalange was, it was contradictory in its philosophy. It advocated "Lebanonism," a nationalism that would transcend Christian-Muslim rivalries. It supported social and economic reforms, recruiting non-Christian and non-Maronite members. Yet the Phalange tenaciously remained a Maronite party—for the Lebanon for which it was willing to fight was a Christian Lebanon.

The Phalange's often-repeated motto, "God, Family, and Nation," appealed to those in the mountains who neither belonged to nor were allied with an old Maronite family. But it also appealed to Maronites who had left their villages and their traditional leaders to live in Beirut's suburbs as Lebanon swung into the Golden Age. To the uprooted Maronites, the Phalange as a party had *wasta* (influence) in the bureaucracy. To the lower class, the Phalange meant jobs, discipline, and something to which to aspire. While the Franjiehs represented the traditional clan and Chamoun's National Liberal Party the power of the elite, the Gemayels and the Phalange pulled in the outsiders and the suburbanites among the Maronites.

The Phalange's membership was basically lower middle class. The frequent charge of the Maronite establishment that the Phalangists were fascists was really a screen for the elite's basic criticism: that they were simply vulgar. As a result, no remark about the Phalangists was too low in Maronite society. Pierre Gemayel, trained as a pharmacist, ran a drugstore in Martyrs' Square close to Beirut's red-light district. To the upper class, he was "Pierre the Condom." The disdain arose from the fact that the political system was the purview of the well-to-do, who preferred to align themselves with leaders like Chamoun and Edde. What no one realized was that as Lebanon built toward war, the Phalange represented the new order.

During the early 1970s, the Phalange recruited and trained fresh recruits and acquired heavier weapons for its militia. "While some party ideologues continued to plan the reforms deemed vital for the preservation of the Lebanese political system, others were planning in great detail the defense of fortress Lebanon—that part of Mount Lebanon and the coastal plain in which the Lebanese

Christian entity could be upheld." In 1964, more than ten years
before the outbreak of the civil war, Pierre Gemayel elucidated the
motivation of the Phalange when he said, "The Christian psychosis
of fear is internalized, visceral, and tenacious. We can do nothing
about it. It is the Moslems' task to reassure us."

*Say: "Nothing will befall us except what Allah has
ordained. He is our Guardian. In Allah let the faithful put
their trust."*

Koran
9:51

FOUR

THE MUSLIMS

The small, timeworn village of Buarij grips the steep eastern
slope of the Lebanon mountains. The harsh meagerness of
its existence is softened by the clear springs that flow from
the hills and the soulful vista of the broad valley below. The short
segment of the Beirut-Damascus highway that is just visible from
a promontory on the far end of the village seems to be the only
thing that connects Buarij with the rest of Lebanon.

Buarij is a poor village. Its 235 inhabitants eke out their
livings from the rocky limestone soil that lies beyond the community's tumbled dwellings. Its population, untouched by the Christians
scattered throughout most of the neighboring villages, is all Sunni
Muslim. Like other Muslim villages—those of the Druze farther
south in the Shuf and those of the Shiites in Jabal Amil—Buarij is
the repository of its inhabitants' faith and traditions.

The war has not yet flamed across Lebanon. Life in Buarij still
moves to the ancient rhythm of its ways. Each morning the women,
balancing cinnamon-colored clay water jugs on their heads, leave
houses whose only book among the sparse contents is the Koran.
Together, they move down the rocky paths toward the village well.
On the way, their lively conversation is constantly accented with
the name of God: "*Al hamdallah* (praise be to God), Fadia is

pregnant again"; "The vines are heavy with grapes this year, *al hamdallah*"; "Ibrahim, *al hamdallah*, has returned from the market in Zahle." In the fields, the men murmur the same phrase in praise of the blessings of Allah while the long, curved blades of their scythes slash the grain.

The harvest ceases as the sheikh, the community's temporal and religious leader, raises his hand in greeting. He is plowing down the dusty road on his way to hold his weekly *majlis* (audience) where, in the dim light of his small court, he will settle the legal disputes of the community by the rules of the Sharia, the Muslim legal code. Before reaching the center of the village, he passes the door of the seamstress's shop. She ducks her head to avoid his eyes, embarrassed because buried among her bolts of cloth is a forbidden symbol of Western decadence—a tattered magazine picture of a half-naked girl in a bathing suit. Shameful as the picture is, the seamstress knows that in Buarij the bathing suit has definite commercial possibilities as an undergarment for a bride.

Ramadan, the ninth month of the Hijrah calendar, when Muslims fast from sunup to sundown, ended two weeks ago. The observance was, as usual, a mixture of piety and logic that characterizes the Sunnis of Lebanon. The prayers were called from the tower of the squat mosque five times a day during Ramadan; for the rest of the year, once a day would suffice. The women dressed even more modestly than usual. But none wore a veil, not even during Ramadan. And since it was summer and the men labored in the fields, the exigencies of life and the demands that man fulfill his duties toward his land and his family made a little water and a bit of bread during the hours of the fast permissible.

Now that Ramadan has passed, the coffeehouse—several rickety tables scattered under the trees—has returned to its place as the center of village life for the men. Even at midmorning in the middle of the agricultural season, the tables are full. The customers are mostly young men who move between the village and their jobs in the towns. As symbols of their pretensions to a cosmopolitan lifestyle, they wear European-cut trousers, odd, ill-fitting jackets, and brightly polished, Western-style shoes. And they talk endlessly of Arab politics.

Life in Buarij was a microcosm of Muslim society. Economically and educationally, the village people were far behind the Sunni Muslims who partook of the good life in Lebanon's coastal cities. Yet as they affirmed their identity as Arabs and their certainty about the supremacy of Arab culture, their internal values were the same as those who lived in the cities. For to all Muslims Arab life, Arab history, and Arab politics meld into their society defined by Islam nearly fourteen hundred years ago. And it is in the practices and traditions of Islam that the past and the present continue to merge in a universal order Muslims readily recognize. The internal link between a Muslim Arab and Islam is so complete that Arabs are baffled by the phenomenon of an Arab Christian. For centuries, Muslims have asked what to them is the most profound question of Middle Eastern Christianity: Is a Christian Arab possible? Regardless of his or her particular denomination, a Muslim sees a Christian Arab as some undefined alien in Arab culture.

From its very inception, Islam was a religion of the Arabs. Muhammed, born in Mecca in approximately A.D. 570, was inescapably a product of the Arabian Peninsula. His teachings initially appealed to those dispossessed by the corrupt merchants of Mecca whose practices clashed with the ancient bedouin ethos of the desert. While Muhammed advanced some revolutionary ideas in his teachings, he also incorporated much of his culture into Islam. As the religion spread by word and by sword, it absorbed alien ideas and customs from its new converts. Yet it remained, at its core, Arab.

Islam is not just a religion. It is a total social system. The Koran, God's revelations to Muhammed, and the Hadith, Muhammed's sayings as recorded by his followers, explicitly instruct Muslims about everything in their lives, from the structure of society to how to wash after sexual intercourse. In Islam, there is no dispute about what belongs to Caesar and what belongs to God, for the secular and the religious are one. This idea gives rise to the Muslim concept of *umma*—the Arab state ruled by Islam—that Christians so fear. In reality, segments of the Muslims fear an Islamic state with almost the same intensity. Muslims are bitterly divided over the question of whether an Islamic state is desirable, or even possible, in a twentieth-century nation. Thus, issues involving the Islamic state's challenge to modernity, economic systems, secular and legal matters, women's rights, and individual freedoms currently rage within Islam's major sects.

The Muslims of Lebanon divide into the Sunnis and the Shiites, the predominant sects of Islam, and the Druze, a splinter group of Shiism found exclusively in the Levant.

The Sunnis are the mainstream within Islam. To be Sunni means to follow "the path" or "the way" of the Prophet. In general terms, it means to accept Muhammed's original teachings unadorned by heavy cultural variations, as happened in Persia, and largely without the injections of mysticism that characterize some of Islam's other sects.

In the Middle East, the Sunnis constitute an overwhelming 85 percent of the Muslims. Historically, the Sunnis generally have controlled the government and usually the economy in every Arab country. Before the war, Lebanon was no exception for the Sunnis' role as the Muslim establishment. But in Lebanon, unlike in most other Arab countries, the Sunnis, according to the official 1932 census, comprised only about 46 percent of the Muslim population, with the Druze and Shiites making up the rest.

Just over 10 percent of all Muslims are Shiites. Throughout the Arab world, the Shiites suffer as an oppressed minority. Rejected as heretics, downtrodden by economic and political policies imposed by the dominant Sunnis, the Shiites were relegated to the bottom of the social order. Century after century, from Lebanon to the tiny island sheikdom of Bahrain, the Shiites have struggled under the yoke of the Sunnis. The only thing different about the Shiites' situation in prewar Lebanon from that in most of the other Arab countries was that they represented roughly 40 percent of the Muslim population and 20 percent of the total population. Because the Shiites encompassed a sizable bloc in a country that was prosperous and supposedly democratic, it could be argued that they suffered proportionately more discrimination in Lebanon than in most other areas of the Middle East.

Shiism rose out of the great schism that befell Islam within fifty years of Muhammed's death. The division resulted from a rancorous dispute over who would succeed to the leadership of the faith after the Prophet himself. Muhammed's only heir was his daughter, Fatima, who was shut out of the succession because she was a woman. Therefore, her husband, Ali, a cousin of Muhammed, was the Prophet's closest eligible relative. One faction of Muhammed's followers fervently believed that the caliph, or God's representative on earth, should come out of Muhammed's family. The other faction adamantly argued that Muhammed's successor should be chosen from among his lieutenants. The second group prevailed, and the first three caliphs were elected by the leadership of Mecca from among their own. Ali finally succeeded in becoming the fourth caliph. But his tenure was short-lived. He was murdered in 661, opening the way for a new leader to emerge from the councils of Mecca.

After Ali's murder, his followers began to split from the main body of Islam. (*Shiite* in its most literal translation means "follower of Ali.") The schism became complete after the murder of Ali's son, Hussein. It was Hussein's death that infused Shiism with the tenor of martyrdom that has characterized the faith ever since.

In 680, Hussein raised an army of loyalists and set out for what is now Iraq to defend the right of the Prophet's family to hold the title of caliph. His was a lost cause from the beginning. Still, Hussein, in the gesture that has come to symbolize Shiism, declared that it was more honorable to die for his belief than to live with injustice. With this profession, Hussein and his followers met the rival caliph's army on the plain near Kerbala. "That day they fought from morning until their final breath, and the Imam . . . and the companions were all martyred. . . . The Army of the enemy, after ending the war . . . decapitated the bodies of the martyrs, denuded them, and threw them to the ground without burial." In death, Hussein left the Shiites a legacy of ultimate protest. Through his example, Shiism early attached its roots to a doctrine of selfless sacrifice in the name of God against the forces of tyranny and oppression. For this reason, martyrdom is the central theme of Shiism. In contrast to Sunni Islam, which is marked by arid legalism and a high degree of emotional detachment, Shiite Islam breathes with passion.

On Ashura—the tenth day of the month of Muharram, the anniversary of Hussein's death—the Shiites remember the martyrdom of Ali and Hussein. In every Shiite village in southern Lebanon, processions of penitence and mourning wind through the crowded streets. Ashura is a passionate rite of self-flagellation. Young men stripped to the waist rake blood from their flesh with metal hooks. Others swing leather strips connected to a wooden handle over one shoulder and then the other, rhythmically beating themselves, while the women squat beside the road and wail. It is through their blood and lamentations that the Shiites reinforce the martyrdom suffered by Ali and Hussein and the persecution their sect has endured ever since their deaths.

With the exception of Lebanon, Shiism resides at the eastern edge of the Muslim Middle East and beyond. Iran, Persian rather than Arab, is the only country in which the religion commands the overwhelming majority of the population. And in important respects, Shiism is as much Persian as Arab. Besides the doctrine of self-sacrifice, the elements that so sharply separate Shiism from the Sunni mainstream are the prominence it gives to saints and other mystical aspects and the authority it assigns to a powerful clergy. The Shiite clergy is institutionalized, which gives it property and a base of power that is political as well as religious and economic.

The organized clergy evolved out of the theology of the twelve *imams*. In Shiism, *imams* are divinely inspired, infallible spiritual leaders who possess doctrinal authority to guide believers in matters of faith. Ali was the first of the twelve Imams of Shiism. The last was Muhammed al Muntazar (the Expected), who in 878 entered a cave and disappeared. According to Shiite doctrine, al Muntazar, the vanished *imam*, continues to live in "occultation," an undefined form, and eventually will return as the *mahdi*, or savior, to rule over a perfected society. In his absence, the law and creed are to be interpreted by Shiite scholars, who act only as the agents of the hidden *imam*.

The theology of the hidden *imam* existed as a shadowy precept among the Shiites for generations. But in the mid-1970s, it took on profound religious and political importance. In Iran, the Ayatollah Ruhollah Khomeini led a successful religious revolution in the name of Islam. While making no claims himself, Khomeini is revered by many of his devoted followers as the *imam* who has returned. And in Lebanon, the Shiites cherish their own vanished *imam*, Musa al Sadr, who aroused their political consciousness before he mysteriously disappeared in 1978.

The third part of Lebanon's Muslim triad is the Druze, a highly cohesive offshoot of Shiism. The Druze congregate exclusively in the near contiguous areas of the Shuf mountains of Lebanon, in southern Syria (in the Jebel Druze), and in northern Israel. While they classify themselves as Muslims, the Druze are rejected as heretics at best and nonbelievers at worst by most other Muslims.

The Druze sect emerged from another dispute over leadership within Islam. In the eighth century, the Shiites, who already had

divided over the issue of Muhammed's successor, again split over
the question of the rightful successor to Jafar al Sadik, the sixth
Shiite *imam*. Imam Jafar had chosen his oldest son, Ismail, as his
heir. Subsequently he discovered Ismail freely imbibing wine's
forbidden pleasures. Ismail was renounced and replaced by his
younger brother, Musa. But supporters of Ismail, known as "Seveners" for the seventh and rightful *imam*, refused to accept Musa,
arguing that an *imam* was incapable of erring and therefore
Ismail's drinking could not affect his right to the succession. It is
from the Seveners, or the Ismailis, that the Druze sprang.

In the eleventh century, a splinter group of Ismailis from
Egypt settled in the protective folds of Lebanon's mountains, where
they developed an elaborate set of rituals and a distinctive pattern
of life. Through conversion, the original group multiplied among
the clannish population of the hill country, who perhaps found in
the religion a means of preserving their distinctive communal
identity. While theoretically a part of Islam, the Druze shun orthodox conformity to the five pillars of Muslim faith. They do not
pray five times a day for, as the Druze's most distinguished scholar
says, "We are in constant prayer." Nor do they make the pilgrimage
to Mecca, for "Mecca is in yourself." They adhere to their own
scriptures, codified into six volumes by the fifteenth-century
scholar Jamaluddin Abdullah Janukhi. And most offensive of all
from the traditional Muslim perspective, the Druze claim Jethro,
father-in-law of Moses, as their chief prophet.

The religion draws heavily on mysticism. Seven is a sacred and
symbolic number that underlies many facets of the faith, such as
the emergence of the world in seven steps—God, universal mind,
universal soul, matter, space, time, and earth/man. But it is the
belief in reincarnation that most causes mainstream Muslims to
consign the Druze to the occult rather than to Islam.

According to Druze belief, a new nativity occurs at the moment of death. The Druze call it simply "changing the shirt." This
instant transformation from death leads into another life that can
be either better or worse than the previous one, with reincarnation
continuing until the day of judgment. Memory of a previous life is
possible, especially if the death was a violent one.

A mother of ten, a pale yellow scarf drawn tightly around her
head accentuating her already harsh features, sat in her hilltop
house in the Shuf and related the scant details of her previous life.

She spoke with quiet animation, throwing her hands in the air and exposing her missing front tooth when she smiled with the reassurance of eternal life. Leaning forward, she ardently insisted that she remembered her past life, even the name of the village in which she had lived. So vivid were these memories that she claimed she went to the village and was able to point out her former house and call some of the villagers by name. Flinging her arms above her head, she declared with finality, "It is true!"

Despite the intriguing stories of recycling life, it is the secretiveness of the Druze faith that is perhaps its most distinguishing characteristic. The Druze are divided into two distinct groups—the initiated and the uninitiated. The initiated—about 10 percent of the Druze—are those who hold the mysteries of the faith. As one of the community elect, an initiated Druze wears a ruby fez with a wide strip of white cloth wound around the lower part, creating a turbanlike appearance. Through these men the knowledge of the faith is passed on from father to son. The secrets are not divulged to an initiate until he is forty years old, and they are never revealed to a woman. The other 90 percent of the community, the noninitiates, are important members of the community as individuals but they are relieved of the responsibility of perpetuating the religion. They have no obligation to observe the rites and demands of the religion; they need only lead a moral, upright life. The essential point is that what a Druze believes ultimately is less important than his or her acceptance of religion as the vehicle through which group cohesion is maintained, for communal identification, not religious practice, motivates the Druze.

It is this cohesiveness of the Druze and their success in remaining closely united over a thousand years of turbulent Levantine history that distinguishes them among Lebanon's minorities. Because of the very strict code of moral conduct for which they are renowned, the Druze have maintained a degree of social solidarity that few others can match and a reputation as extremely formidable adversaries. The Druze are mountain people in the same tradition as the Maronites. But their solidarity and ruthlessness in defense of their interests are legendary. For centuries the Druze have fought for their existence and their religion, a phenomenon they claim is essential for their survival.

Because of their toughness, secrecy, and strict communal living, the Druze engender suspicion and hostility among other

Lebanese religious groups. Typical of the guarded comments Lebanese make when broached about the Druze is the remark of a Greek Orthodox standing in a large pen on his chicken farm in Zahle. Speaking of his trusted Druze foreman, he lowered his voice and said, "As individuals I like the Druze, but as a group I have to say they are shifty."

Before the war, the Druze fared better in their relationship with the Christians than in their kinship with the Muslims. Generally, the Christians were more tolerant of the Druze as both a community and a religion than were the Muslims. Theologically isolated from them, the Muslims subjected the Druze to even more suspicion than did the Christians, spicing their suspicion with an element of contempt. An old saying passed on through generations among the Shiites was "Eat at a Druze house, but sleep at a Christian house." And Sunni folklore advises, "When you shake hands with a Druze, count your fingers." Traditionally Druze settlements in the Shuf invariably included Christian families but rarely Muslims.

Yet it is with the same Maronite Christians who had been their neighbors for generations that the Druze most often warred. For centuries Druze and Maronites shared the Mountain. And for centuries they periodically massacred each other. After the trauma of 1860, their disputes shifted to the political arena, with only occasional skirmishes fought in the mountains between competing militias. Only after the civil war began would the Druze-Christian violence exceed the level of 1860.

Survival defines Druze politics. For the Druze, loyalty to the community exceeds allegiance to either economic ideology or ethnic nationalism. In the interest of survival, the Druze will identify with any arrangement that promises to safeguard their community interest. In the 1830s, when they learned that Christians had been exempted from military conscription, the Druze attempted to convert to Christianity en masse. Had the move succeeded, the Druze would have found no problem in publicly becoming practicing Christians. But privately they would forever have remained Druze, reverting to their religion when the advantages of adopting an alien faith ended.

Because they are such a small minority in the Arab world the Druze, like the Maronites, are terrified of any attempt to merge them into the Sunni society of the Arab East. The frequent massacres of Druze by the Ottomans, their persecution during the administration of Muhammed Ali of Egypt, and the difficulties Syria's Druze encountered following Syrian independence have affirmed the Druze's intense distrust of Sunni authority.

At the same time they hold an equal, if not greater, dislike of the Shiites, who for centuries have been gradually encroaching from southern Lebanon into Druze territory. In the interest of their own defense, the Druze cooperated with the Christians in the first half of the twentieth century to secure the autonomy and later the independence of Lebanon. Unswayed by the appeal of Arab nationalism, the Druze before the civil war were committed to the territorial preservation of Lebanon and of their traditional lands in the Shuf. Throughout the war, Druze determination has held. A Druze commander said from behind a rocket launcher, "We either live here or we die here." It was not a threat born of the bravado of war. Deep in Druze theology lies the belief that a Druze can be buried only in the mountains of the Shuf in the vault of his family.

Constituting only 6 percent of the Lebanese population, the Druze have little interest in political reforms predicated on "one man, one vote." Throughout the war years, the Druze have fought as fiercely as some and more fiercely than others for an independent Lebanon in which some communal consensus will guarantee Druze survival and Druze interests. Beyond that, their goals are contradictory. The Druze support secularization of the political system but at the same time insist that certain rights be reserved for them. They support a socialist economic system but still adhere to a feudal structure within their own community. They recognize themselves as Arabs but resist pan-Arabism.

The contradictory strands of Druze political thought partly reflect the dichotomous nature of Kamal Jumblatt, the man who shaped Druze politics in Lebanon. Jumblatt, feudal chieftain, leftist politician, Eastern mystic, and ruthless fighter, was born in the hills of the Shuf in 1917. Like so many of Lebanon's other political leaders, he was the scion of a landowning family that had ruled its ancestral lands for generations. Kamal would have inherited his father's lands as well as his political power by natural right. But when he was four years old his father was killed by bandits, placing both Kamal's future and that of his family's interests in jeopardy. For the next two decades, Kamal's remarkable mother, Sitt (Lady) Nazira, manipulated the family's affairs to hold off rival families until Kamal reached his majority. With his family's political resources as a base, Jumblatt emerged as leader of the Druze. He was not an initiated Druze, nor was he expected to be. Nothing in Druze culture linked politics and religion. His followers accepted him as the head of Druze political affairs, and he served them well.

As a personality, Kamal Jumblatt is perhaps the most intriguing of the pantheon of prewar Lebanese political leaders—the star of Lebanon's political folklore. An impresario who caused the fat, well-established bourgeoisie to quiver with rage, he was once denounced as "psychologically unbalanced, opportunist, shameless, a merchant of the fantastic, a catastrophe for the Arabs." Lebanese politics was a game of elaborate rules and rituals that Jumblatt delighted in violating. Even his mother recognized his eccentricities. On her deathbed she told Camille Chamoun, Jumblatt's childhood friend, "I know my son is not a normal person. I beg you to treat him, in spite of this, with great patience."

Jumblatt's face was long and mournful, punctuated by dark, penetrating eyes. He was moody. He was mercurial. Most of all, he was a man of conviction and vision. In his youth, he once flirted with the idea of becoming a Christian but in the end decided to stay a Druze. He became a great admirer of Mahatma Gandhi and his nonviolent philosophy—a bizarre choice of hero for a gun-toting Druze chieftain. Gandhi's portrait hung throughout Jumblatt's home in Mukhtara. And Jumblatt, donning a dhoti and sandals, made frequent pilgrimages to India, where he spent weeks and sometimes months living in ashrams, meeting with his guru, and pondering Hindu philosophy. Back in Lebanon, he frequently received visitors while sitting in the lotus position in trancelike contemplation.

But in time of peril for the Druze, Jumblatt dropped his pacifism and retreated into the Mountain's time-honored formula of violence to protect the Druze and the Shuf. During Lebanon's 1958 political crisis, a foreign journalist asked Jumblatt why, as a pacifist, his palace was surrounded by fierce-looking Druze warriors. Without pause Jumblatt answered, "I am a pacifist, yes, but sometimes you have to get those bastards."

The contradictions in Jumblatt's character were exceeded only by those in Jumblatt's political life. As a progressive minister of interior in 1963, he tried to ban the French king of "Twist," Johnny

Hallyday, from appearing in Lebanon and attempted to clamp censorship on imported films. More enduring was the dichotomy in his political identity. Jumblatt filled the dual roles of founder of the Progressive Socialist Party, a genuine leftist party, and traditional leader of the Druze community whose tenacious social bonds maintained a relationship between landowners and peasants similar to that in European feudalism. As a leftist, Jumblatt pushed for sweeping social reforms and at times sought nationalization of large corporations, proposals that flew in the face of free enterprise politicians and reinforced the establishment's general opinion of Jumblatt as a difficult and even sinister personage. As a communal leader, he assiduously cultivated the patron-client relationship between himself and the Druze. As a socialist-landlord, Jumblatt was a contradiction that bothered his enemies more than his clients. Perhaps they saw through the apparent dichotomy. Jumblatt was one of the rare Lebanese politicians genuinely concerned about Lebanon's social and economic problems and the tenuous nature of the political system; yet he burned with personal ambition.

Jumblatt's infamous rancor in politics arose partly from his deep-seated frustrations with Lebanon's system of distributing political power by religious affiliation. As a Druze he could never become either prime minister or president. Consequently he fumed when Maronite and Sunni politicians whose talents he disdained rose to great heights on the basis of their communal identification. The 1943 National Pact that reserved the office of president for a Maronite Christian, the prime minister's post for a Sunni Muslim, and the speakership of the Chamber of Deputies for a Shiite Muslim became the main target of his venom. Jumblatt once said,

> Community sectarianism was a poison transfused by the Maronites into the body of Grand Liban from the moment it was born. This sickness may have been tolerable in the homogeneous Petit Liban of 1864, but it became a festering sore in 1922. A state cannot be organized on the basis of such an inequitable division into castes, or around a religious spirit which is not shared by other communities involved.

Beneath Jumblatt's contradictions and eccentricities lay a clear vision of Lebanon's value as an independent state and of the Druze role in it. In Jumblatt's vision of Lebanon, the Druze would not only survive but would survive as equals among the country's other religious groups. Jumblatt emphasized the local nature of politics as opposed to that of an all-encompassing state that could infringe on the lives of the highly individualistic and communalized Lebanese.

This emphasis on diversity rather than order was aimed at protecting the Druze' position in a Lebanon that was neither Christian nor Muslim. Jumblatt himself refused to cast Lebanon in the mold of a Muslim state. Instead he envisioned a state that united people of different cultures. Still, he was pro-Arab, distrustful of the corrupting influence of Western materialism and philosophy but especially of Western power. He supported Arab causes only as long as they balanced the forces of the West, which he perceived as submerging Lebanon in an ocean of foreign influence in which the Christians, like a buoy, would rise.

It was Jumblatt's defense of independent Lebanon that probably ended his life. He was murdered in March 1977 by assassins widely believed to have been either inspired by loyalty to Syria or dispatched by Syrian president Hafiz Assad. At the time, Jumblatt was writing his autobiography and contemplating retirement to an ashram in India.

Through their clear definition of themselves as part of independent Lebanon, the Druze were spared the polarizing conflicts that pan-Arabism had thrust on the Sunnis. Yet the Druze, like the Shiites, shared the pan-Arabists' commitment to Arab culture and their antagonism toward the West.

Arab hostility toward the West had germinated in the Crusades. As they had on the Christians, the Crusaders also bestowed a lasting legacy on the Muslims. The Europeans, in their search for plunder, territory, and the Holy Grail, left the Muslims forever embittered toward Western imperialism. The Crusades came to represent to the Muslims an abiding threat from the West not only to Muslim land but to Islam, the custodian of Muslim culture. In their bitterness about the Western invasion, the Arabs retreated from anything that smacked of the Western world. They rejected Western ideas and innovations, choosing instead to retreat into their own culture. After advanced Arab learning contributed to the Renaissance, the Enlightenment, and the scientific advances of the first Industrial Revolution, the Muslims stood apart from the technological innovations. Sadly, in the process, they produced their own stagnation, which became complete under the heavy rule of the Ottomans.

By the time the European colonial powers were nibbling at the Arab world, the Arabs had begun to see the West as an undifferentiated human conglomerate known as "Christians":

> The very circumstance that the people who from the nineteenth century on managed to establish themselves as the new masters of the Arabs were Christians made it almost inevitable that the Arabs should generalize their animosity and make all Christendom, or the entire West, the object of their resentment and hatred. Every individual act of aggression, every particular injustice, real or imagined, was considered as expressive of what the Christian West as a whole stood for and became an added irritant exacerbating and embittering the Arabs' attitude to the West.

By the mid-twentieth century, ambivalence toward the West replaced rejection of the West as the Muslims struggled with their internal conflict over their devotion to their own traditions versus their lust for modernization. For the upper-class Lebanese Muslims, the conflict fell short of the wrenching struggle that affected the lower classes. Well-educated Muslims were products of the Levant. As children they were educated in their own traditions while learning Western languages and ideas. What emerged was a true Levantine who harbored a profound fear of the backwardness and rigidity that incorporation into the Arab world and isolation from the West implied.

The issue for the less educated was not as clear. The Muslim lower classes never fully participated in the prosperity created by the Golden Age. Instead they were the ones who felt most exploited by Western-tainted commercial interests and most threatened by Western languages and mores.

Despite the socioeconomic variations, all Muslims to a degree equated modernization with westernization. Western scientific dominance and control of international finance after World War II dictated that modernization of Lebanon would require large infusions of Western education, Western languages, and Westerners themselves. These were the very developments that benefited Lebanon's Christians. Because they shared the same religion with the

West, knew Western languages, and cultivated close links with their Western patrons, the Christians eagerly welcomed westernization. But for the Lebanese Muslims, even educated ones, the modernization that came packaged as westernization forced them to question their own culture, their innermost beliefs. The Muslims wanted modernization, yet modernization loomed over them as an incarnation of their hated Western enemy.

The Muslims' perceptions were reinforced by the reality that so much of Lebanon's success story before and after World War II was a Christian triumph, one that ignited the innate assumption of Christian superiority, encouraged by the West's own barely hidden contempt for the Arab East. Arab distrust and animosity toward the West was something the West itself never understood as it looked at Lebanon through the myopic eyes that had created those fanciful images of Lebanon before the civil war. In the 1950s the scholar Wilfred Cantwell Smith sounded a warning when he said, "most Westerners have simply no inkling of how deep and fierce is the hate, especially of the West, that has gripped the modernizing Arab."

One answer to the Muslims' dilemma over modernization espoused by various Muslim ideologues was that the Arabs must return to the original message and initial inspiration of Islam that had once made them superior to the West. Only in Islam could the Arabs uncover the fundamental ideas and ideals that are at the heart of genuine modernization.

The religious option was one Lebanon's cosmopolitan Muslim political leaders were loath to take. They opted instead for "Arabism," the complex set of beliefs and feelings that merge in the idea that the Arabs share an identity, one they should express in some type of political unity. Popular in the 1930s, Arabism was rooted in a nineteenth-century reformist movement. Lebanese Muslims, predominantly the Sunnis, were pulled to Arab nationalism because it represented both their culture and their self-image. Arabism succeeded in forging nationalism, populism, and techniques of modernization into an ideology that made sense to the Lebanese Muslim. Arab nationalism promised not only to create a foundation for a new Lebanese political system but to bring Lebanon culturally into line with the other Arab states. The nationalists argued that the basic defect of Lebanon was that the country could not establish its authenticity as long as it rejected its place in the Arab nation as a whole.

Yet with Lebanese independence, the central theme of Muslim

demands was shunted to the rear by the issues of the moment. Muslim unrest against the Lebanese state fomented not around the most basic issue—Lebanon's identity as an Arab country—but around the economic and political issues connected with the maldistribution of power between Christians and Muslims. Political rhetoric prior to the 1950s was largely that of communal voting power, rights to public office, and access to governmental largess. None of these issues brushed the touchstone of Muslim political demands—Lebanon's need to validate its Arab culture. Instead Lebanon's National Museum continued to devote its displays entirely to Phoenician and Roman relics.

By the dawn of the Golden Age, this unbridled westernization cloaked Christian Lebanon in suspicion. The Arab nationalists denounced Lebanon's close ties with the West as a betrayal of Arabism and accused its foreign universities of acting as bastions of the West. The attitude was succinctly summed up by a Muslim professor at the American University of Beirut who bitingly remarked that the procession of the faculty at graduation, arrayed in all of its colorful academic regalia, reminded him of the Crusaders on the march.

Since Lebanese politics was so rigidly controlled by an alliance of families who crossed religious lines, the most forceful protests against Western cultural intrusion and Christian political and economic domination came from those outside the councils of power. Because these were most often of the lower classes, Arabism and socialism began to coalesce.

From 1952 until the late 1960s, Egypt's Gamal Abdel Nasser lent eloquence and voice to Arab unity and Arab socialism. Under Nasser's influence, to identify with the Arab world generally meant to identify with Arab socialism. The burning question of whether Arabism was based in language and culture or solely in Islam had yet to erupt among the Muslims. Still Islam, such an integral part of the Arab psyche, underlay much of the ideology of pan-Arabism, the union of Arab nationalism and socialist economics propagated by Gamal Abdel Nasser. An avowed secularist himself, Nasser always linked Islam to Arab identity and Arab nationalism. By closely joining Muslim values and identity with Arab nationalist goals, he denied Christians participation in his political movement, which was the overriding political movement in the Middle East of the 1950s and 1960s. And by rejecting the West and its non-Arab values, Nasser demanded a commitment to pan-Arabism that by its nature would dismantle economies dominated by Western institutions and practices.

Responding to his lead, a panoply of loosely structured leftist parties arose in Lebanon, some indigenous but most tied to one or another leader or movement outside Lebanon. Philosophically these political groupings united in the belief that the Arabs must fulfill their destiny; that Western imperialism locked with the feudal and capitalist interests of the Maronites blocked Lebanon's unification with the Arabs; that Israel was the bastion of Western imperialism in the Arab world. To all of them, Lebanon with its Western ties, capitalist economy, and isolation from its culture was an aberration, a symbol of everything they wished to eradicate.

The left was polyglot. Leftist parties succeeded in crossing communal lines to unite Muslims on economic issues. But because so much of their ideology involved pan-Arabism, the leftists attracted their largest following among the Sunnis. The importance of the left was outside government—in the street, on the campus, in the refugee camp—for the Muslim establishment was inextricably tied into the status quo.

The Sunnis concentrated in the cities along the coast, especially Tripoli, fanned out across the Akkar plain into the central Bekaa Valley, and clustered in a coastal pocket of the Shuf between Beirut and Sidon. Historically the Sunnis, as cobelievers, fared better under the Ottomans than did Lebanon's other religious groups. The Ottomans ruled loosely, leaving the Maronites alone on the Mountain but giving the Sunnis in the coastal cities a certain degree of status. This was parlayed into political and economic superiority over both the Christians and the other Muslims. But that ended with the French Mandate.

The Sunnis as a whole benefited little from the French Mandate, but the upper classes, who already dominated Tripoli, Sidon, and Tyre economically, succeeded in breaking into the power structure. The Sunni social structure was crowned by a small upper class of semifeudal families. In cooperation with the leading Maronite and Druze families, they formed the political-economic establishment that led Lebanon to independence and controlled the government until the civil war in 1975. The other components of the Sunni social structure, the commercial and professional bourgeoisie and the proletariat of the cities, possessed little power, although they were important cogs in the economy.

Sunni political leaders faced formidable problems. At most,

they spoke for only a quarter of Lebanon's population. The political concessions they sought for the Muslims lay in the hands of the Maronite Christians. Thus, to forge the alliances crucial to any increase in Sunni political power, Sunni politicians aped the French ways of the Maronites. They played the game so well that they came to believe it themselves. The daughter of an old Sunni commercial baron, speaking of the Maronite-Sunni alliance that existed at the top of the social scale, proudly stated, "I only went to the best schools. The French, you know, created a relationship between the Maronites and the Sunnis through education." But the real problem for the Sunni leadership was managing the socioeconomic splits in its own community. The political bosses, while jealously protecting their own upper-class interests, also had to represent the interests of the Muslim masses, composed of urban workers and rural peasants. To hold their own constituents, the political bosses pushed Arab nationalism and at the same time upheld their commitment to Lebanon as an independent entity in order to pacify the Christians. It was only through constant balancing of demands and possibilities that the Sunnis wielded political power.

Like the Maronites, the Sunnis were split between intensely competing families—the Karamis of Tripoli and the Salams and Solhs of Beirut. It was the Solhs who reigned over Sunni politics before independence.

Riad Solh, the most notable of all the Solhs, was a dedicated Arab nationalist. Just after France snatched Lebanon by way of a mandate from the League of Nations, Solh, accompanied by several members of the Lebanese parliament, headed toward Syria to hand Lebanon over to the rule of King Faisal. French forces rushed to the border and intercepted Solh's party before it crossed. The fiasco played itself out when the governor-general sent Solh briefly into exile. But in spite of his early grandstanding style of politics, Solh developed into a real statesman.

Under the French government, Solh buttressed the Sunnis' precarious position by building a political consensus with the Maronites. This consensus allowed Lebanon to gain independence under an agreement with the Maronites that affirmed the duality of Lebanon's Arab character and the strength of its Western ties. When Solh became Lebanon's first prime minister, Lebanese journalist George Naccache, in the euphoria of the moment, wrote in the French language daily *L'Orient*, "Mr. Riad Solh is, in the new

Lebanese equilibrium, at the center of our entire political system.
. . . His personality, his past, his domestic position, his international relationships—in fact the whole subtle play of imponderables
that crystallize around him—contribute to making him an indispensable leader." But Riad Solh would not survive the maelstrom
of Lebanese politics.

Solh was prime minister when the Parti Populaire Syrien
(PPS), or Syrian National Party, was accused of plotting against
the sovereignty of Lebanon. Under Solh's orders, some twenty-five
hundred PPS members were rounded up, forcing the party leader,
Antoun Saadeh, to flee to Syria. From Damascus, Saadeh issued a
call for an armed uprising against the Lebanese state. Extradited
back to Lebanon at the request of the Solh government, Saadeh was
tried and executed before a firing squad on July 7, 1949.

Solh emerged from this crisis enormously popular. While
remaining the champion of Sunni rights, he had proven to Lebanon's other factions the Sunni commitment to the integrity of Lebanon. But he still faced the vengeance of the PPS.

On July 16, 1951, Riad Solh, a tarboosh tilted jauntily over his
puckish, moon-shaped face, traveled to Amman to meet with Jordan's King Abdullah. After they had talked for a few hours, Solh
left the king's palace for the Amman airport in Abdullah's limousine. On a lonely stretch of road, a strange car approached from the
rear and ripped past, machine gun blazing from the window. Solh
died instantly, shot through the heart. The two assassins were
members of the PPS, avenging Antoun Saadeh's execution two
years before.

Riad Solh had wielded enormous influence because of his
ability to forge alliances with the powerful figures of Lebanese
politics while still commanding the loyalty of the Sunni masses.
The question of whether he could have continued to balance both
sides of the equation was left unanswered by his death, for Riad
Solh died on the eve of Nasser's revolution in Egypt. As Nasser's
charisma grew, the Sunnis increasingly looked toward the East
and the emerging power of Arab nationalism. Their leaders thus
became trapped between their own upper-class interests and the
passions of their lower-class clients.

After Riad Solh's death, Saeb Salam took control of Sunni
politics in Beirut. While his family was a champion of Syrian unity,
Salam himself put ideology second to his personal ambitions. At

times he cooperated with the Maronite Camille Chamoun to protect Lebanon's role as an intermediary between the Arab world and the West. At other times, he was an outspoken disciple of Gamal Abdel Nasser's pan-Arabism. Although Salam was a promising Sunni leader, his power was diminished by a string of personal conflicts, particularly with the very Christian leaders he most needed to cultivate.

Indicative of the petty personal piques that Lebanese politics often fueled, Fuad Shihab, Lebanon's highly regarded president who served between 1958 and 1964, never forgave Salam's behavior at the 1960 funeral of political boss Ahmed Assad. Prime minister at the time, Salam insisted that his position demanded that he be driven to the funeral in Shihab's presidential limousine. After traveling ten miles out of his way to pick up Salam, Shihab stiffened when the prime minister climbed into the seat next to him smoking a fat, malodorous cigar. The longer Salam talked and puffed, the more nauseated Shihab became. At the funeral Shihab, growing increasingly ill, subsequently fell victim to the flu. Shihab blamed it on all Salam and never forgave him.

Although Saeb Salam served as prime minister several times during the 1950s, his political fortunes were continually entangled in his inept relationships, personal greed, and vacillating loyalty to Arab causes. This opened the way for Rashid Karami, the most enduring of the Sunni politicians.

In 1951 Rashid Karami, son of Abdul Hamid, the Sunni leader of Tripoli, entered the government. In August 1953, at the age of thirty, he was the youngest prime minister in Lebanon's short history.

Karami was a handsome man with high-arched eyebrows and a bold mustache. During the years before the civil war, he succeeded better than any other Sunni politician in pulling together the conflicting strands of Sunni thinking. He himself was a modernist, but his father was the conservative Mufti of Tripoli, who kept his daughters veiled and largely secluded. On his death, the elder Karami bequeathed his son his conservative religious credentials, which played well in villages such as Buarij. This was one end of the Sunni political spectrum. At the other were the Sunnis inflamed with socialist ideology and Arab nationalism. Karami emerged politically just as Nasser's nationalist ideology began to sweep the Middle East. Drawn to Nasser by the power of his cause and the force of his personality, Karami regularly went to Cairo to sit at the feet of the Arabs' current hero. The symbolism rested well with most of Lebanon's Sunnis.

Karami was a successful Lebanese politician because he respected power and those who wielded it. Representing a constituency with little bargaining power, Karami deemed it crucial to his community's power as well as his own to exercise his authority among his Sunni followers. In this context, Karami occasionally slapped the face of someone who in one way or another offended him. Always careful to protect his own position, recipients of his anger usually were political underlings or suppliants who were in no position to object.

With his Islamic credentials and pan-Arabist ideology, Karami attacked the real politics of Lebanon. As a major Sunni leader, Karami rotated in and out of the prime minister's office, the highest position assigned to the Sunnis in the political system. But the ability of Karami—or any Sunni political boss—to direct Lebanon or even lead the Muslim cause was doomed from the start by the leadership's own ambivalence about their commitment to pan-Arabism, versus their commitment to their own interests, and to those of Lebanon.

Early in his political career, Karami recognized that the interests of the Sunni establishment overlapped with those of the Maronites. While Karami, like Salam, demanded more power for the Sunnis in order to protect his own position with his constituents, his efforts were halfhearted because the Sunni establishment correctly perceived that their real competition came from the left-wing politics of the Arab nationalists. Consequently there was always a dichotomy between what Sunni leaders said publicly to hold their followers' allegiance and what they did privately within the halls of power.

As Sunni demands for political parity with the Maronites grew, a process of radicalization occurred among the Sunnis that the elite refused to lead. As a result, the urban power base of the Muslim elite eroded. This wide gap in confidence between the Sunni elite and their urban following developed because the real ideological leadership of the Sunnis lay outside Lebanon—in Nasserism, in other forms of Arab nationalism, or in communism. That left the Sunnis fatally divided. The leaders talked about Arab nationalism and economic and political reform, but they acted to protect their individual interests and to prevent Arab nationalism from swamping the fragile Lebanese nation. The Sunnis as a whole held no invincible commitment to either Lebanon or the ideology of Arab nationalism. While strong opposition to the Sunni establishment existed, it was fragmented. And it confronted a political system that thwarted the emergence of any alternative leadership. So the Sunnis, rent by class divisions, drifted toward a showdown with the Maronites on one side and the forces of Arabism on the other. As the Maronites and the Druze armed themselves for the defense of their interests in Lebanon, the Sunnis foundered. When the civil war came, they were unprepared.

While the Sunnis lived and breathed politics, the Shiites stood outside of Lebanon's prewar political arena. The Shiites were the festering sore on the illusionary body that Lebanon presented to the outside world during the Golden Age. In the hype ground out by the Western media about prosperity, democracy, and intellectual freedom in Lebanon, the plight of the Shiites somehow was lost. No one, least of all the other Lebanese, cared to acknowledge that the Shiites, one-quarter of the population, were both economically and politically shut out of Lebanon. The coalition of Lebanon's Maronite and Sunni establishments, aided in this case by the Druze Kamal Jumblatt, had rendered the Shiites a disinherited subproletariat.

Most of the Shiites grouped in villages such as Bint Jbail in the green, rolling hills of southern Lebanon. Like Buarij, its Sunni counterpart in the north, Bint Jbail was far removed from the cosmopolitan prosperity and political power brokering of Beirut. Its houses were small, crude structures that bespoke of the peasant class who lived within. In the few stores huddled at the center of the village, shelves were always more empty than full. During the morning hours the women dribbled in, shopping long and haggling hard for their scant purchases. They paid for these with a few precious coins drawn from well-worn change purses stuffed into the bottom of stiff plastic shopping baskets.

Money was hard to come by in Bint Jbail. The men worked the rocky fields almost year round, their checkered headcloths protecting them from the hot sun of summer and the cold winds of winter. They raised tomatoes, zucchini, garlic, citrus fruits, and a few apples, which at harvest they loaded onto rented trucks for the trip to the markets of Sidon and Tyre, and on to Beirut. Fathers and sons, mothers and daughters picked, packed, and loaded the produce just as their ancestors had done.

Families were large, and everyone worked to sustain the household's subsistence-level income. Education was rudimentary. State schools were poor even by the standards of southern Lebanon, and no one had money for private education other than some haphazard religious instruction.

Everything about Bint Jbail reflected the poverty of its inhabitants. In the early 1970s, the average family income for the Shiites was $1,511 a year compared to $2,082 for the rest of Lebanon's population, which to a degree reflected the callousness of Lebanon's power structure. During the same period, 17 percent of Lebanon's population lived in southern Lebanon, yet the central government appropriated only 0.7 percent of state funds for government services to the area. As a result, roads were seldom more than ruts that became quagmires in the winter rains. Public transportation was sparse or nonexistent. Many villages lacked electricity. Sewage disposal was handled in the same way it had been for centuries—open trenches along the road. As if the lack of an infrastructure were not enough, thousands of Shiites, solely on the basis of their religion, were deprived through political deals and bureaucratic inefficiencies of their national identity cards and hence access to government services and the right to vote.

The French, the Maronites, and the Sunnis had all succeeded in victimizing the Shiites. Even the Shiites' own leaders were collaborators in their community's oppression. The Shiites languished under the control of feudal families whose political power stemmed from the land they had acquired as tax agents for the Ottomans during the nineteenth century. After Lebanese independence, the same landowning families of southern Lebanon filled the only position guaranteed to the Shiites: speaker of the parliament. These landowners, along with key clan leaders in the Bekaa, were granted honorary government positions, paid good salaries, and given access to Beirut's commercial riches—all in return for keeping their Shiite communities politically quiescent. The Asads, Khalils, Zains, Usairans, Haidars, and Hamadas were all families a Shiite peasant was loath to cross. Lebanese scholar Fouad Ajami, himself a Shiite, tells the story of a peasant of his village who slaughtered one of his own sheep and delivered it as tribute to the local bey (or lord). The Shiites had been beaten into such subservience by the feudal system that when the peasant returned to his village he lauded the generosity of the bey who had bestowed on him a small chunk of the meat for his own family.

This subservience was bred of need. For the Shiites of prewar Lebanon, survival meant subscribing to one of the men of power, voting in the elections as a member of his bloc, defending landowners' interests and property, and always demonstrating respect for the patron. Kamil Asad, the political boss of southern Lebanon, epitomized all that was wrong with the Lebanese political system. His connections with the power structure in Beirut gave him control over the Council of the South (established in 1970), the only real source of development funds for the Shiites. A Shiite who harbored any hope of access to those funds was compelled to hang a picture of Kamil Bey, preferably in an elaborate frame he could not afford, in his house.

Reaching for a share of Beirut's prosperity, the Shiites began to trek north during the 1960s. But once in Beirut the Shiites quickly learned that the Sunni political bosses of the capital were unwilling to integrate them into their patronage networks. Crowded in the slums of south Beirut with few prospects of escape, they fell back on their traditional leaders. This allegiance was reinforced by the electoral law that made it nearly impossible to change from one electoral constituency to another.

For many Shiites, their right to vote was valid only in southern Lebanon. At election time, Beirut's Shiites were picked up and trucked back to their villages of origin to vote for the deputies to parliament who had little knowledge or understanding of their constituents' lives. Consequently, all the move to Beirut had accomplished was to shift the Shiites from rural peasants to a disgruntled urban poor that included an increasing number of young, educated men who could find no work commensurate with their abilities. In 1975, the year the war began, an estimated 250,000 Shiites were packed into a quarter-square-mile of West Beirut. Forty percent of that population was under the age of sixteen. To the urban Shiites, the Sunnis became the enemy. Hurling his invectives against the Sunnis, a student at Beirut University College said before the war, "The Sunnis are anti-Shiite. It is not like they are even the same religion. They are bigger rivals to us than the Christians." The Sunnis, who had always claimed Beirut as their city, found themselves with a bitter rival who, though powerless, increased in number year after year.

The Shiites' political impotence translated into economic powerlessness. Lebanon's free-market economy, dominated by the
Maronite-Sunni establishment, perpetuated the Shiites' deprivation and nurtured their perception that all opportunity was closed
to those outside the boundaries of the establishment. As the poorest
and least represented of the Lebanese, the Shiites, along with the
immigrant Syrians and the Kurds, constituted Lebanon's un-
washed masses. In Shiite homes, children grew up hearing their
parents rail against discrimination in everything from education to
housing to employment. Their complaints were valid. In 1962, for
example, Shiites held only two out of every seventy senior civil
service positions. But it was rumor more than statistics that fueled
Shiite resentments. The stories of Shiite repression that circulated
through the Beirut slums reflected measures of fact. If a Shiite
wanted to join the army, he had to recruit a Christian to join at the
same time. If a Christian, Sunni, and Shiite applied for the same
job, the Sunni would be hired, the Christian would be given an even
better position, and the Shiite would become the janitor.

While Ras Beirut represented status and economic success to
its affluent residents, to the Shiites it epitomized the degradation
in which they lived. Shiites who came out of their crowded slums to
work in Ras Beirut seethed at the division between rich and poor.
One educated, underemployed young man angrily dug his fists into
the pockets of his worn jeans and described his life on the fringe of
Lebanon's golden era: "Ras Beirut was like going to a different
country. I hated the people who lived there because they were
rich."

The Shiites were angry not only over their economic status but
because they were derided by Christian and Muslim alike. Their
Beiruti compatriots often depicted them in terms that mimicked
the racism of a Jim Crow bigot. Little had changed in the general
attitude toward the Shiites since David Urquhart, the mid-nine-
teenth-century traveler, described them as listless, subservient
people reveling in squalor. The Sunnis often referred to the Shiites
as "those people," with an unmistakable disdain reserved more for
creatures than for humans. The Christians depicted the Shiites as
dirty, untrustworthy, rapacious, and sexual. A self-assured Maronite once haughtily declared, "They bring as many children as
possible. They care nothing about educating them. They just send

them to the government school."

The Shiites not only absorbed these attitudes but applied them to themselves. A young Shiite, musing about his childhood in the slum of Burj al Hamoud, said, "As a poor Shiite, I had an inferiority complex. When anyone said 'Shiite,' I thought of someone with seven or eight kids shining shoes or selling gum on the street."

The Shiites did have high birth rates, and consequently their ranks continued to swell. In the years just before the war, the Shiites were becoming the largest religious group in Lebanon. The population shift hamstrung the Sunnis in their drive for reform of the political system, because their interests as well as those of the Maronites' were under challenge. If the Sunnis succeeded in the demand that government offices reflect demographic realities, the result might well have been a Shiite rather than a Sunni president of Lebanon. But not everyone was blind to the explosive nature of Lebanon's changing demographics. A former prime minister said, "No Sunni Prime Minister can accept the changes that no Shia politician can fail to demand."

As downtrodden as they were, however, the Shiites were not totally dormant. Rising political consciousness bubbled up through the layers of Shiite repression. In the 1960s, large numbers of Shiites joined the Lebanese communist party and other antiestablishment organizations. Some Shiites, struck by the similarities between their plight and that of Lebanon's Palestinian refugees, enlisted in organizations and parties that were closely affiliated with the Palestinian resistance. Some attached themselves to various pan-Arabist movements. Others joined any group offering a salary to a member of its militia. But no single party or ideology was overwhelmingly successful in recruiting Shiite members.

In the 1960s, if the Shiites were of the left, it was only half-heartedly. Leftist politics provided the Shiites with a means of protest, but at the same time they were repelled by the pan-Arabism that was the overriding theme of all leftist parties except, perhaps, the communists. Therefore, no party provided the Shiites an escape from the Sunnis who dominated them. For pan-Arabism was a Sunni movement that if successful would plunge the Shiites into the vast Arab world, in which they would remain an oppressed minority. Ironically the Shiites, like the Maronites and the Druze, are a minority in a predominantly Sunni Arab world. For them, as for the Maronites and Druze, Lebanon provided a refuge in which they could preserve their sectarian identity and security.

The Maronites, Greek Orthodox, Sunnis, Druze, and Shiites all danced around the flame that was Lebanon. Yet to each, Lebanon meant something different. The Greek Orthodox and the Sunnis celebrated the Arab side of Lebanon and pushed it toward some destiny with the Arab world. The Maronites grasped Lebanon as their refuge on the abyss of the Muslim Middle East. The Druze dug into the Shuf mountains, prepared to defend Lebanon as the repository of their separate identity and their ancestral lands. As for the Shiites, though they lived in Lebanon, their loyalties lay east in the Shiite communities of Iraq, the Persian Gulf, and Iran. Although fiercely protective of their individual identities, each of these groups was Arab in culture and behavior. And it was within Arab culture that they would play out their destiny.

Inter-Family Feud Claims 6 Lives in Zhgarta
New York Times
October 2, 1966

FIVE
CULTURE AND CONFLICT

A well-dressed American businessman, holding his garment bag over his shoulder with one hand and gripping his sleek leather briefcase with the other, stepped out of the Beirut airport into the brilliant sunshine. He paused. Juggling the briefcase on an outstretched thumb, he managed to slip on dark sunglasses and then expose his watch from under a well-starched cuff. Amid all its gadgetry, he found the right dial for the time and date in Beirut—10:07 A.M., June 12, 1971. It was his first trip to Lebanon. He had been assured that cabs were plentiful, that every make and model of car prowled the streets. The information, it appeared, was correct. As soon as he lifted his hand, a new black Buick screeched to a stop directly in front of him, its back door already swung open. Another neophyte was about to take his first ride in a Beirut taxi.

The car sped out of the airport complex and headed due north toward Martyrs' Square in the center of Beirut. Driving like one obsessed with self-destruction, the driver accomplished with two hands what would require three of anyone exercising a modicum of caution. He steered the car with two fingers, releasing his palm to blare the horn incessantly. With the other hand, he punctuated his

81

commentary on the sorry state of Lebanese affairs, a treatise he delivered while facing his passenger in the back seat.

Reaching the square, the taxi careened around the corner and sped down a street so narrow that in any city other than Beirut it would have been restricted to one-way traffic. Leaning against his horn, the driver roared up behind a massive Oldsmobile. He started to pass on a blind curve, but the competing driver refused to yield, choosing instead to do battle. They went into the curve side by side. At that instant a wide, lumbering streetcar rocked around the bend, headed straight for the cab. The taxi driver blasted his horn, the motorman jangled his bell, and the rival driver threw obscene gestures, but none condescended to slacken his speed. At the last instant, the taxi driver took the only way out. With remarkable reflexes, he pulled the wheel almost ninety degrees to the left and hurtled into the driveway of an apartment house that was just wide enough to yield about four spare inches on each side. When the car screeched to a stop, one front wheel was on the bottom step of a short stairway. A screaming woman and her four children stood on the top step, shaking their fists and hurling invectives at the driver. Unbowed, he smiled, tossed a quick wave, and slammed the car into reverse, squealing back out into the street without looking either right or left.

The taxi driver's self-absorption in his own narrow interests at the expense of public well-being was fatefully symptomatic of Lebanese society. And the nature of Lebanese society, as much as cultural identification, religion, economics, and intervention by rapacious foreign interests, fractured the Lebanese state.

The Lebanese civil war stratifies into two distinct layers: the Lebanese' conflict with one another and the separate confrontation among the Palestine Liberation Organization, Israel, Syria, and Iran, which conduct their own agendas on Lebanese soil. It was the Lebanese' own deep, pervasive conflicts with one another that prepared the way for the aliens. Like predatory packs of animals, egocentric clans operating within an artificial political framework ran the state of Lebanon to earth, then left the carcass for its scavenging neighbors. For Lebanon never functioned as an integrated society, only as a collection of individuals united in close-knit communal groups jealously guarding their own interests. There was no social contract, no readily accepted corporate interest. Kamal Jumblatt said it all: "This society is not a society in the real sense of the word, because there is no such thing as a Lebanese community. There is no Lebanese social unit. Lebanon is a collection of sects and socio-religious communities. This . . . is not a society, not a community, not a nation."

Before 1975 the Lebanese, with a certain Levantine pomposity, described themselves as the preeminent plural society. But a pluralistic society is one that enjoys a basic consensus on fundamental principles and upholds a political system that prohibits any one group from dictating to the others. Lebanon met neither of these conditions. The Lebanese were torn apart by their very cultural identity, split into communal groups pursuing their own limited visions of Lebanon, and politically subservient to the Maronites, whose own special interests and Western orientation separated them from most other Lebanese. As a result, Lebanon was never the pluralistic society the Lebanese imagined but a mosaic society characterized by "little consensus, little free and open dialogue, and no dominance of public interests over private interests." From the time of its independence from France in 1943 until the beginning of the civil war in 1975, Lebanon functioned not as a country but as a council of tribes in which constantly shifting deals among cliques of political bosses maintained the illusion of statehood but never addressed the fundamental issues that were undercutting Lebanon's survival as a nation.

The Lebanese mosaic was partly a culmination of Lebanon's entrapment between East and West. Because they have always been at the crossroads, the Lebanese are rich in mix and essence. This is a large part of their charm. But at the same time, they are tormented by their own complexity. While 92 percent of Lebanon's population was ethnically Arab, the influence of the Levant set them apart from the inland Arabs, touched them with more sophistication than the Egyptians, and yielded them vastly different from the Saudis. Over thousands of years, the Lebanese developed a culture that perhaps only they can truly understand—a culture in which the trunk is Arab and the branches pure Lebanese.

The Lebanese, even the Muslim lower classes, express a barely perceptible grimace when called Arabs. They take pride in laying claim to being Lebanese, a claim that leads every Lebanese to insist that he or she is somehow superior to all other Arabs. Still, the Lebanese, whether Muslim or Christian, are Arab. And it is in Arab culture that the behavioral patterns of Lebanese society were bred. The wholly masculine atmosphere of the coffeehouse, with its all-male clientele hunched over smoldering cigarettes and thick cups of black coffee, has always been more authentic to the overall culture of Lebanon than the artificial Western ambience that the St. Georges and the Phoenicia hotels portrayed during Lebanon's golden years. Even though the Christians—principally the Maronites—willfully divide themselves from the Muslims, they conform just as Muslims do to most Arab cultural norms. In the ceremonies of life, the patina of the Christians' Western ways dissolves to betray the Arabness they so carefully try to mask. Christians are no different from Muslims in their emphasis on elaborate hospitality. A Christian family, like a Muslim family, exults at the birth of a son. At Christian weddings, the men and women might sit on opposite sides of the church just as they would segregate themselves at any Arab wedding. And at funerals, Christian women rock back and forth ululating just like their Muslim sisters.

These are external rituals indicative of the internal values that spring from Arab culture. Over the centuries, certain aspects of Arab culture, when subjected to the peculiar mix of Lebanon, have magnified the divisions within a society already split by religion and identity. These Arab characteristics are the concept of honor, the primacy of the family, the propensity for conflict, and the imperative of revenge. Since these are also characteristics of Mediterranean cultures, elements of them are found in Western society. And just as they are not exclusively Arab, neither are they inherently destructive to society. It is simply that these particular traits within the Lebanese culture, combined with the uniqueness of Lebanon itself, have produced a climate in which the Lebanese' skills at negotiation and compromise have labored against enormous odds.

Nothing characterizes Arab culture more than the concept of honor. Honor, to Arabs what "face" is to Orientals, is the central element in the overall culture. In its simplest terms, honor is self-esteem derived through a man's perception of how others see him. Since honor is an externally imposed value, a man's worth in his own eyes depends solely on the opinions of others. Consequently, the key to preserving honor is the assiduous avoidance of shame, defined as anything that might impinge on self-respect. An old Arab proverb that many credit with Lebanese origins perhaps says it best: "Even if I have seen the worm of hunger emerge from my mouth, I shall not debase myself."

The fear of shame is drummed into Lebanese children by mothers, fathers, grandparents, aunts, uncles, and society as a whole. From a very young age a child is constantly subjected to brutal critiques and searing comparisons with other children, all for the purpose of instilling in that child the need to always appear superior. Burdened with such clear familial and societal messages during childhood, the adult is driven to extremes to preserve the image by which others judge him or her. Thus, it follows that most Lebanese are plagued by a paranoid sensitivity to either the approval or the real or imagined slights of others.

Certain normative actions of the Lebanese are in reality exercises in preserving honor. First, there are their statements of status: "I went only to the best schools"; "I live in Ashrafieh. That is the best part of Beirut, of course"; "This is my new car. I bought the most expensive model." Then there are shows of assurance intended to demonstrate authority. Ask ten Lebanese to describe the same event, and with absolute certitude, each will unreel his own interpretation as indisputable fact. In the end, the listener will have no idea of what actually happened or, for that matter, if the event even occurred. The only certainty is that every informant will have looked the listener straight in the eye and unequivocally stated, "Don't listen to the others. I know what really happened."

Finally, there are the Lebanese' pronouncements of self-declared authority: "Don't worry, my friend, I can fix it for you!" A long-time resident of Lebanon once said that "50 percent [of the Lebanese] consider themselves natural leaders, 25 percent think they are prophets, and 10 percent imagine they are gods."

While honor is the greatest imperative in a Lebanese's life, its determination most often hangs on what many would consider superficial criteria: How much money does the man make? Does he entertain lavishly? Are his sons financially successful and his daughters established in suitable marriages? How big is his apartment? Is it in the "best" part of town? Again, while these certainly are measures of success in the Western world, the intensity with which the Lebanese pursue success and the delight they experience in its trappings set them apart to a degree not only from Westerners but also from other Arabs.

Since the Lebanese are hard-working, multilingual fixers and doers to whom commerce and money-changing are second nature, what prewar Lebanese society cared most about was making money. It was an endeavor at which the Lebanese were gifted. "He can make a wine cellar out of one grape" was virtually a national motto. In the years before the civil war, the well-to-do flaunted their money in pursuit of self-esteem. In everything they did, they haughtily mocked the simpler lifestyles of the intellectuals and the middle class and the poverty of everyone else. And in their desperate quest for honor, the rich imposed on society a certain vulgarity. Between 1950 and 1975, Beirut sported more nightclubs, luxury cars, grand swimming pools, and flashy apartments per square mile than almost any other place in the world. With sheer exuberance and outlandish pleasure in themselves, the merchant class, festooned in jewelry, paraded through the streets in their majestic American cars and alighted for elegant lunches resplendent in their Pierre Cardin suits and Christian Dior dresses. As a measure of societal values, the biggest single item in Lebanon's import bill in 1970—nearly 30 percent of all imports—was jewelry and precious metals.

Somehow, whether a man was honest, was employed in a worthy profession, or contributed to the overall good of his community exerted little or no influence on his personal honor as measured by the overall society. This attitude contributed to the brashness of prewar Beirut. Because people were valued almost solely for their wealth, the merchant class reigned as the true princes of the republic. Consequently, professors, lawyers, and doctors who failed to make fortunes never achieved the lofty status accorded the successful businessmen.

Lebanon might have survived the consumerism and egomania of the merchant classes had individual honor been all that was involved. But groups fell prey to the same psychological needs as individuals. It was on the level of societal unity and political compromise among religious groups that the dictate of honor most forcefully thrust its destructiveness on the Lebanese body politic.

The Lebanese divided into various types of communal groups. And it was the communal group that held the collective honor of its members. Within the republic of Lebanon, one group moved against the other to secure power, money or position or to grandly direct Lebanon toward alignment with the West or accord with the Arabs. The competitiveness among these collections of individuals was not just economic or political; it was an exercise in honor, a contest of superiority. As 1975 approached and each side hardened its position regarding the distribution of power and spoils in the political system, it became increasingly difficult to strike the compromises necessary to save the country from war. For a communal group to back down once its stance was struck, to publicly appear weakened, triggered all of the mechanisms involved in preserving personal honor.

As honor confirms a Lebanese's self-esteem, his family establishes his identity. Lebanese society, like all Arab societies, is anchored in the family. And it is the family that is the genesis of all communal identifications.

It is Monday night in a small house in Sidon. The family happens to be Muslim, but the same atmosphere would prevail in any comparable lower-middle-class Christian home. Ahmed, his wife Fadia, their two daughters and son, plus Ahmed's widowed mother are the residents of the house. Yet tonight the women bustle around the kitchen preparing dinner for twelve people—the immediate family; an uncle from the family's village of Machgharah; the son of Ahmed's deceased father's cousin, who lost his job in Kuwait five weeks ago; and his wife, due to deliver their first child in a few days. The remainder of the food on the stove is for other family members likely to drop by during the evening.

Fadia, her faced flushed with the heat of the kitchen and her wooden-soled sandals noisily flapping, hurries into the living room to tend to her guests. Just as Uncle Magid draws his last puff from the narghile, Fadia refills the small brass cup on the top. Lighting the tobacco, she draws a few puffs from the wooden mouthpiece to make sure the tobacco is burning before handing it back to him. Although one child clings to her skirt and another is propped on her hip, no one moves to help her. This is her home and these are her guests, all members of her husband's family.

Just then the bell on the outside gate buzzes. Ahmed rises and goes to answer, joyfully greeting his two brothers. They will eat and stay until bedtime, expecting Ahmed to come to the house of one of them the next night and to the other brother's perhaps the following night. It is in this constant moving of brother to brother, son to father, cousin to cousin that the bonds of family are nurtured. For it is only within the family that a Lebanese truly senses himself.

In Arab culture, the concept of *ahl* (kin) extends beyond the lineal concept typical of most Western cultures. A first cousin is like a brother, and a distant cousin is an integral part of the total family unit. Bonds of family cut across gaps in wealth, education, and social status to unite all those connected through common blood. As in all Arab societies, the extended family claims a Lebanese's first allegiance and provides his first defense against the forces of the outside world. It also demands his total commitment, subverting all other aspects of his life.

The typical Lebanese grows up enmeshed in a multitude of relatives. As an adult, he spends most of his leisure time within his extended family. He often works in the family business or holds a job secured for him by a relative. His earnings help to pay the school fees of younger brothers and sisters or to feed the family of an unemployed cousin. When he marries, the girl most likely will be a relative or someone whose family is closely tied to his. When the couple produce offspring, they will take their place in the total family unit, carrying on the tradition to their children.

These inseverable ties of family span across oceans. The Lebanese are an emigrant people. Like the Jews, they are scattered across the world. But they remain bound to their families in Lebanon. Some leave Lebanon only to earn their fortunes so that they can return to their beloved villages to live out their lives. Others—second and third generations—return to their families periodically or perhaps only once simply to affirm their roots. In the meantime, intricate networks operate between the Lebanese overseas and his family in Lebanon. Even after years of living abroad, a Lebanese often will continue to support various family members in Lebanon. Consequently, there are families all over Lebanon like the one in a tiny village high on Mount Saaneh. Although relatively poor, this large family owns a substantial stone house covered with an expensive tile roof paid for with contributions from various relatives ranging from Los Angeles to Indianapolis, Cape Town to Rio de Janeiro. In fact, remittances have always comprised a large share of Lebanon's total income. In 1961, a sample year, income from emigré remittances equaled 92 million Lebanese pounds, or 40 percent of all of Lebanon's foreign-earned income.

These powerful ties of family have molded Lebanese society into an amalgam of sovereign families bonded together by primordial allegiances governed by the most Arab of all utterances: "My brother and I against my cousin, my cousin and I against the alien."

Kinship is not only the strongest but the only meaningful unit in society.

After the family, the Lebanese's next level of identification is his village or other geographic area. Kinship and village are intimately entwined, especially in Maronite and Druze societies. But this same phenomenon permeates all of Lebanese society. An urbanized Lebanese of prewar Lebanon may have spent his whole life in Beirut. Nevertheless, his identity has remained tied to an ancestral village where he lived, where he retreated on weekends, where he voted, where he expected to find a wife, and where he would be buried. Outside of Ras Beirut, Beirut was a series of neighborhoods where people migrating from the same village clustered together. Despite the cosmopolitan aura that surrounded it after 1950, Beirut never really achieved the integrated status of a city but remained a location in which groups and communities clinging to their villages and their family networks and loyalties happened to live. And in the same way that Beirut failed to integrate families, villages, and religions into an urban environment, Lebanon as a whole was unable to integrate these same entities into a nation.

Lebanon the nation was a facade screening a people fractured into family units rooted in villages scattered over its width and breadth. Although families may have formed extensive economic and political alliances with other families, realistically Lebanon was nothing more than a collection of familial groups, each identified with a specific piece of territory and owing loyalty only to itself. This, in essence, is the cause of the long and terrible conflict in Lebanon. In its simplest terms, war came because "every village, every patch, every bend in the road housed another family, another clan, another way of looking at the world."

The final level of a Lebanese's identification is religion. Historically, confessionals, stripped of their theological trappings, were great clans who competed within the political system of the moment to protect the interests of their corporate members.

After the decline of feudalism in the mid-nineteenth century, religion replaced feudal loyalties as the vehicle for sustaining identity and communal solidarity. It was a process bolstered by the policies of the Ottoman Empire, where religion was the essential element in the social and political structure. All Ottoman citizens defined themselves first according to their religion and second in terms of their sect within that religion. To institutionalize religious identity even further, the Ottoman rulers granted the Sunni Muslims, Christians, and Jews considerable status and gave them formal representation in Istanbul. In return the muftis, patriarchs, and rabbis accepted responsibility for their communities' behavior. In addition to reinforcing the intensity with which people already attached their identity to their religion, the system established the precedent that their political will could be exercised only through a confessional. Rising out of this historical motif, Lebanese politics and religion were melded, a unity that torments the political process to the present day.

Because identity, political power, and economic spoils in independent Lebanon depended on religion, the Muslims, Christians, and other assorted confessionals confronted one another as fervid rivals. Clashes were motivated as much by each group's need to reinforce its innate sense of superiority over all other communities as by theology or politics. During the Golden Age, that mythical time of harmony in Lebanon, Christians and Muslims strove to claim dominance over each other with early morning rituals of loudly ringing church bells on Sunday, the Christian day of worship, or turning up loudspeakers for the early morning prayer call on Friday, the Muslims' religious day. Movie theaters, the scene of Lebanon's most popular form of entertainment, were always potential battle arenas. The occasional cross or crescent that flickered across the screen prompted cheers from one side or the other. Once, during an epic adventure about the Crusades, pandemonium broke out as real-life Christians and Muslims engaged in hand-to-hand combat. With such raw emotion so near the surface, every confessional naturally held its own repository of stories about everyone else. In the Muslim repertoire was a joke about an aged Muslim who on his deathbed called for a Maronite priest, to whom he declared his desire to be converted. His family, gathered around the bedside, gasped in shock and asked him why. He slyly smiled and answered, "Better one of them to die than one of us."

Flashes of humor were superficial to the entrenched prejudices each group sustained through its chronicles of atrocities and injustices inflicted on it by others. These accounts were seldom challenged and their presumptions rarely disproved by experience because communities lived among themselves, largely isolated from one another. Out of a confessional's self-written history devel-

oped clichés passed from one generation to the next that portrayed
affiliates of other confessionals not as members of the same society
but as aliens. More than mere slights of one Lebanese against
another, they were delivered as racial slurs. The Druze were liars;
the Shiites were masochists; the Sunnis were incapable of practicing democracy because of their religion; the Greek Orthodox were
ossified in a dying faith; and the Maronites were, to a man, corrupt. These fierce communal identities based on the assumed
superiority of one's group and inferiority of everyone else were
essential elements of the Lebanese psyche that coalesced around
religious labels.

It is tempting to conclude from the simplicity of the religious
animosities among the Lebanese that theology was the cause of the
civil war. From the beginning, the West naively conceived of the
war in Lebanon as religious, a twentieth-century replay of the
Crusades. But the Lebanese component of the war is mainly tribal,
pitting family against family, region against region, and feudal
loyalty against feudal loyalty. Whether the Almighty is called God
or Allah is not what is at stake; rather it is historical identification,
family rivalries, past grudges, territory, and, on rare occasions,
political philosophy. These same elements were also present in
conflicts among families or regions within every confessional. As a
result, prewar politics operated on two levels. On one, a politician
sought to consolidate his power within his own confessional. To this
end, he crossed confessional lines to strike deals with other politicians maneuvering against their own communal rivals. And so it
was with cavalier disregard of both religion and ideology that the
right-wing Maronite Pierre Gemayel and the left-wing Druze
Kamal Jumblatt periodically allied themselves. But on the other
level, the unity of the confessional was sacrosanct. Lebanon's political system was built on confessionals with the Maronites and the
Sunnis holding the number one and number two spots, respec-
tively. Any challenge to a realignment of power closed Maronite
ranks and caused the Sunnis to circle their wagons in defense
against the Druze and Shiites.

Thus, religious hostilities really were ongoing rivalries among
closed groups protecting their members' multiple interests. Because the Lebanese had never developed class consciousness or
societal organizations strong enough to mount primordial loyalties,
religious identity, more than anything else, defined a Lebanese's

basic interests and constituted the vehicle through which he exercised his political will. And it was along confessional lines that politics ultimately was waged. Consequently, the system left no room for debate on national or class issues. Politics and public policy broke down into squabbles among tribal councils, each representing a highly competitive collection of families and fealties. When war finally came, it "exposed the tribalism of a deeply sectarian country whose civilized forms were only a cover for biases and prejudices, an escape from realities known by its inhabitants."

In assigning honor and kinship its highest priorities, Arab culture builds in a strong propensity toward conflict. All Arab societies are conflict-prone, but in Lebanon conflict reached levels unusual even for Arab culture. It was as if the other side of the Lebanese' celebrated urbanity was ugly enmity. Before the war, the streets were battlefields where passion and short tempers were spent in oral combat. The Lebanese, bred in a highly verbal, gesticulating society, approached minor rush-hour traffic jams like war. They jumped screaming from their cars or yelled out their windows extending four fingers together close to the thumb, the universal Arab sign of *dageegah*, or "Wait a minute!" These streetside shouting matches were inconsequential to the overall stability of Lebanon. They were merely a symptom of other forms of conflict, less open or benign, that permeated the society. It was the communal clashes of family vying against family, region fighting region, religion battling religion, and culture confronting culture that established conflict as a distinguishing characteristic of Lebanese society, making the long periods of cooperation on the national level that much more remarkable. It was not just the rivalries and conflicts themselves but the inability to achieve a resolution that turned Lebanon from a nation into an arena of quarreling cliques. And every lost argument, every dispute that left either party dissatisfied, released the bile of revenge, creating another vendetta.

Every family and group in Lebanon, like every confessional, carries a detailed index of each slight or wrong it has suffered over generations and perhaps even centuries. To deliver revenge, to get even, is crucial to restoring group honor. The West understands these types of conflicts primarily in terms of mountaineer feuds between clans such as the celebrated Hatfields and McCoys or within Mediterranean immigrant groups such as the celebrated Mafia families. It is not the concept but the intensity that distinguishes revenge in Lebanon. In the milieu of Lebanon, revenge is extracted where possible, not necessarily where desired. If the original culprit is out of reach, his allies will suffice for the short term. An old Lebanese saying is "Kiss the hand you cannot bite and pray to God to break it." In the meantime rivals meet, converse, even socialize, but internally the aggrieved party waits to inflict his vengeance.

Because the Lebanese were superficially so polite to one another, conflict was something the West never discerned in the placid image it held of Lebanon before the war. Violence was not alien to Lebanon just as it is not alien to the West; it was alien only to the West's concept of Lebanon.

The many levels of conflict made guns a part of life. The Lebanese stashed weapons in corners, hung them from the walls, or stuck them in armoires. Both Muhammed in his village and Emile on the Rue Hamra had guns. And both would charge that all the Druze cut their teeth on guns. A gun was an emblem of manhood, a phallic symbol. It was also deemed an essential tool for group survival. Bypassing both the police and the courts, individual and communal rivals preferred to settle their own disputes. During the Golden Age, the sketchy murder statistics kept by the languid bureaucracy placed Lebanon's homicide rate well ahead of the United States'. With accurate records, no one knows what the actual rate might have been. Still, the violence that was endemic in Lebanon escaped the eyes of Western tourists and was largely ignored by Western residents. Part of the mystique of prewar Lebanon was its overall low crime rate. Muggings and other stranger-to-stranger street crimes were rare, especially in areas frequented by Westerners. The violence was submerged, waged among the Lebanese themselves. It was communal, it was political. Nabih Berri, leader of the Shiite Amal, once said, "You know, if you take us Lebanese as individuals, we are very civilized people. But if you take us as a group, you'd think we were back in the Middle Ages."

Violence was corporate as well as individual. Historically, communal conflicts were frequent, intense, and often violent. In 1857, British resident David Urquhart, whose tenure in the Levant produced a series of biting comments on the Lebanese, observed, "If the work ceases for a time suddenly it [violence] recurs without apparent cause, as if springing from a periodical necessity giving to the annals of the country a harmonious march of atrocity: no season lacking its expelled prince, its stabbed rival, its ravished district."

From the latter part of the nineteenth century until 1920, communal groups in Lebanon engaged in outright conflict. Then came a stage of relative accommodation that lasted, except for the political eruption in 1958, until 1975. But even within this period of superficial harmony the feuds and vendettas proceeded along their bloody course.

In northern Lebanon, Jaafra and Kobeyat lie nestled in a fold of mountains surrounded by vineyards, orchards, and stony fields. In 1958, when Lebanon fought its first civil war, the eight thousand inhabitants of Kobeyat supported Camille Chamoun, and the two thousand villagers of Jaafra backed the largely Muslim opposition forces. During the fighting Jaafra stormed Kobeyat, killing a woman and wounding five other villagers. Custom dictated that Kobeyat respond. Before the harvest politics, revenge, and a dispute over grazing rights produced an attack on Jaafra that killed its leading citizen. As winter approached, the score was even.

Then, in February, Kobeyat was to celebrate a wedding between one of the village girls and her Syrian cousin. The groom's three brothers, all Maronite priests, traveled along the narrow, twisting road toward Kobeyat. As their car rounded a curve, the night crackled with gunfire. One of the men was killed. The survivors were rousted from a ditch, robbed of their money and watches, and marched off to Jaafra. Entering their village, the gunmen fired their weapons in the air and shouted, "We got blood!" The villagers poured out of their houses, greeting and shaking hands with the surviving clerics. And then they apologized: "We do not shoot men of God, no matter of what religion—not even if they are from Kobeyat." Quickly the two Maronites were fed—for, after all, the preservation of Jaafra's honor demanded hospitality as well as revenge—and sent on to Kobeyat. The letter that accompanied them expressed regret for attacking priests, but it also stated that nothing regarding the feud was changed.

In official Lebanon, such an episode would have been simply another quarrel in a country racked with such incidents. But it came at the same time as a religiously motivated murder in Sidon and a lynching in Tripoli. The issue of vendettas therefore landed on the parliamentary agenda. Consequently, after 1959 a murderer could no longer plead as a mitigating circumstance the defense that Lebanese had honored for centuries—a blood feud.

The artificial serenity of the Golden Age deluded the Lebanese and everyone else into believing that Lebanon held the secrets of communal tranquillity. But it was only adjustment, not cooperation, that allowed communal groups to coexist. The men who kept the peace were the *zuama*, a coterie of political bosses who reflected the purely Lebanese component of Lebanon's culture.

In the feudal society of Mount Lebanon, the social structure rested on the concept of fidelity, or a man's obligation to his overlord. A *zaim* was to Lebanese society what a feudal lord was to medieval Europe. But unlike in Europe, fealty in Lebanon refused to die with feudalism, tenaciously surviving into modern times. Rising out of kinship and other communal ties, fealty was not only an integral part of the society; it characterized Lebanese politics. Hardly a phase of the political process remained untouched by it. And as a potent component of the tribal system it was, in the end, one of the major causes of the civil war.

A *zaim*, with some exceptions, was the unquestioned leader of a tightly knit community rooted in family, religion, or confession. Reflecting the importance of personal relationships in Arab culture, a *zaim*'s link to his followers was personal, not ideological, not programmatic. The authority he commanded was partly traditional and partly charismatic. Rarely was it rational.

A *zaim* originated from one of two sources. He was either the oldest son of one of the powerful families entrenched in Lebanon's feudal past or he rose to power within his communal group through his position as a rich businessman or banker or, on rare occasions, as the spokesperson for a political ideology. All *zuama* were movers and shakers, merchants of influence. The feudal lords, like the Franjiehs and Jumblatts, were a constant in the political arena, gaining or losing a bit of power to their rivals from time to time. The *zuama* who emerged from business or political movements came and went depending on how much they were able to deliver for their clients. For a *zaim*'s follower was a client in every sense of the word. Green or seasoned, the *zaim* worked his district like a ward heeler. Reeking of expensive cologne, he attended births, weddings, and funerals, planting kisses on the cheeks of the men and washing the women in elaborate flattery. When a new shop opened in his district, he and his entourage arrived in a fleet of cars laden with flowers, fruit, and chocolates. From his office, which operated like the members' room of a men's club, he found a job for an unemployed father of four; pulled strings for a belea-

guered businessman in need of a loan; and snared government
contracts for his clients. When one of his clients got into trouble, he
never called a lawyer—he called only his patron. According to one
story in 1968, three men, hardly more than thugs, were arrested
for brawling in a dumpy coffeehouse near Beirut's notorious red-
light district. The door on the cell at the central police station had
barely closed before the minister of the interior called and ordered
his client released. Within minutes, the minister of justice called
and directed that his client be freed. As the jailer stood aside to let
him pass, he looked at the third man, motioned him through the
open cell door, and, shrugging his shoulders, said "Let there be
justice."

In gratitude for past favors and anticipation of future ones,
clients pledged their loyalty to the *zaim*. Once the relationship was
established, the *zaim* sustained it through a combination of charm
and authoritarian displays. No *zaim* exercised authority to the
same degree as the Sunni political boss Rashid Karami. On November 22, 1970, Lebanon's independence day, Karami arrived in
Tripoli to lay a wreath on his father's grave. It had rained that
morning, and pools of water stood in his path. Karami eyed the
mud, looked at his expensive European shoes, then turned and
snapped his fingers. His three bodyguards, members of his entourage, lay face down in the mud while he walked over their backs to
place his floral tribute on his father's grave.

Lacking either ideology or commitment to the common good, a
man stood for public office as an inherent right. In the months
before an election, newspapers routinely announced the intention of
one or another of the reigning *zuama* to hold office once again:

Sabri Hamadeh, the traditional political *zaim* of the Shiite
community in Baalbek, declared his intention to seek his 25th
nomination as Speaker of the Chamber of Deputies—the second ranking position in the formal hierarchy of power in
Lebanon. Like most other veteran politicians . . . Hamadeh is
an absentee landlord, a descendant of a feudal family that can
trace its genealogical descent to the 15th century and the
undisputed head of an extensive clan. Typical of the traditional *zuama*, he has been a prominent figure in the political
life of Lebanon close to half a century, and has succeeded in
representing his constituency in every parliamentary election
held thus far. He served as minister a score of times and has

had a virtual monopoly over the speakership of the Chamber
of Deputies. Of all forty-two regular parliamentary sessions
since independence, Hamadeh was elected twenty-four times.
. . . In declaring his intention to seek the speakership yet
another round, Hamadeh identified no program or platform
other than his purely personal whim to cap his political career
by celebrating a golden jubilee.

The system worked because the Lebanese, largely a product of
Arab culture, possessed no clear sense of institutions. Because of
the primacy of personal relationships, political loyalty belongs to
individuals rather than organizations. As a result, bureaucracies
respond only to men in power. And government most often functions to appease individuals, not necessarily to ensure the public
welfare. In prewar Lebanon, the *zuama* expressed little interest in
ideological commitment or the public interest. At least they were
not hypocrites. Leader and follower alike recognized that a *zaim*'s
political legitimacy depended on his successful cultivation of his
personal ties with his clients. Bashir Gemayel summed it up when
he said, "This is the Levant. You have to answer the telephone
yourself—no secretary—listen to each conversation, and receive
each visitor." Regardless of how the West perceived them, the
zuama made no pretense about being political leaders in the Western sense of the term. As creatures of Arab culture rather than of
Western institutions, they were not expected to grasp and articulate public issues and problems. They existed to deal in personal
favors, not ideology and public policy.

Each confessional sported its own political dynasties. The
Eddes, Franjiehs, Solhs, Salams, Jumblatts, and others formed the
old guard who, except for periodic raids by upstart politicians, ran
Lebanon through private deals among themselves. Young politicians established their political base by inheriting or, less frequently, building up a personal entourage of clients and followers
but seldom by articulating a program or taking a stand on a
specific issue or problem crucial to Lebanon's stability. Never did
more than a third of the members of the Chamber of Deputies even
claim to belong to a party. The few political parties that did exist
were so closely identified with sectarian groups that they collapsed
upon themselves when they failed to deliver on the patronage at the
fingertips of the *zuama*. Periodically political blocs and fronts
emerged, but Lebanon's political structure was so absorbed with

parochial and personal rivalries that it was incapable of mobilizing the population to grapple with the broader aims of society. Behind every public debate were "the personalized pragmatic politics of patronage, transaction relations and changing factional alliances, in which the prize to be won was not victory for one set of values over another, but the achievement of high political office and personal gain." Government was of men, not law. George Naccache, publisher of the French-language newspaper *L'Orient*, once cynically remarked that the Lebanese government was "an arrogant alliance of money and the feudal system."

Since a *zaim*'s power depended on the level of patronage he could deliver, patronage was a potent and permanent phenomenon in the Lebanese political system. Patronage dispensed by the *zuama* was the only game in town, because agencies and institutions with a chance to offer alternate avenues to privilege and opportunity were shot down by the *zuama*'s collective action. As competitive as they were, the *zuama* stood shoulder to shoulder against any entity that threatened to erode their power. Labor unions, benevolent associations, merchant groups, and student organizations were all channeled through confessional organizations under the watchful eyes of the respective *zaim*. With no competition from either governmental or private agencies, only the *zaim* effectively provided services, goods, and favors for his clients. The recipients of these benefits were so beholden to their particular *zaim* that they reciprocated by adopting near filial loyalty to him. At election time, the *zaim* expected and received the votes of his grateful constituents. And when he died or retired, they voted for his son.

Since they arose from confessionals and at the same time competed for clients within them, the *zuama*, except for threats to their mutual interests, were intense rivals. In this context, among the Maronites the Franjiehs battled the Gemayels; the Solhs, Salams, and Karamis vied with one another among the Sunni Muslims; the Jumblatts outmaneuvered the Arslans within the Druze community; and so on through every confessional. Elections frequently degenerated into miniwars as the *zuama* marched out their militias and hired thugs to intimidate the opposition. In the 1951 parliamentary contest between Pierre Gemayel and Raymond Edde for the Metn district, three people were killed and twenty wounded before the Phalange militia ensured that Gemayel won by

149 votes. The *zuama* played their political games for keeps and, when they lost, proved they were masters of revenge. Many of these old rivalries continue to be fought out within the parameters of the civil war. However, few boast the vehemence and audacity of the Franjieh-Gemayel feud.

As major families among the Maronites, the Franjiehs and the Gemayels have vied for years for influence and turf in the northern mountains. In the late spring of 1978, three years after the civil war began, a new and brutal episode of that rivalry opened. The issue was two-pronged. On the national level, both families were positioning themselves for the presidential election scheduled for 1982. Suleiman Franjieh was the reigning president. In seeking to perpetuate the family's hold on the presidency, the elder Franjieh was maneuvering his son, Tony, toward election by the Chamber of Deputies. Tony's main rival was expected to be Bashir Gemayel, the aggressive commander of the Phalange militia and son of the old Phalange political boss, Pierre. But blood feuds run deeper than political contests. On the local level, the Phalange was moving in on Franjieh territory around Zghorta. Phalangists fanned out through the mountains siphoning off the Franjiehs' clients and threatening their rackets and monopolies, including their rights to a cut of the cement and roofing business in the northern coastal town of Chekka. Early in the confrontation, Tony Franjieh warned the Gemayels that if they put one foot north of Jounieh the Franjiehs would break it.

But the Gemayels struck first. At 4:00 A.M. on June 13, 1978, a contingent of Bashir's militiamen crept through the early morning darkness toward the Franjiehs' summer home in the northern hill town of Ehdene. Aroused from sleep by the collision between the attackers and his security guards, Tony Franjieh collected his family and servants around him. But there was no defense. He, his wife Vera, their three-year-old daughter Jehan, a maid, and the chauffeur were gunned down in the courtyard of the house while still dressed in their nightclothes. The family dog lay dead beside them. Before the Phalangists retreated, a total of thirty-four people had died. The cry for revenge was swift. Father Yussef Yamin, a Maronite priest in the Franjieh camp, declared, "All those who profaned Ehdene will be killed, particularly those of the Gemayel clan, those and their descendants for generations until not a single man or woman remains." Thus, the Ehdene massacre took its place in the annals of Lebanese vendettas.

It was a year before the Franjiehs struck back. On the anniversary of Tony's death, Pierre Gemayel was riding along a highway north of Beirut in the back seat of his glistening white Buick. As the car glided past an innocuous-looking Renault parked along the side of the road, a remote control device ignited a jerican of gasoline that fired a 120-millimeter mortar round and 44 pounds of TNT. Scathed and shaken, Pierre Gemayel somehow survived.

The failed attempt simply prompted another try at vengeance. On February 23, 1980 Bashir Gemayel's green Mercedes 450 SEL blew apart in front of Lebanon's foreign ministry. It took sixty-six pounds of explosives stashed in a parked car to kill the chauffeur and Gemayel's two-year-old daughter. Bashir himself was not in the car, but his turn would be next.

In September 1982, twenty-two days after he was elected president of Lebanon, Bashir Gemayel was assassinated by a bomb planted in the ceiling of his headquarters. The Franjiehs immediately became prime suspects in a crime that has never been solved. After all, at the time of the Ehdene massacre it was assumed that Bashir Gemayel had signed his own death warrant. Denying responsibility, the Franjiehs nonetheless expressed subtle satisfaction at the calamity that had befallen the house of Gemayel.

To be a successful *zaim* required energy, hard work, intense public relations, complex and acrimonious negotiations with rivals, and a modicum of larceny. So why did the *zaim*, from generation to generation, thirst for office? Ego was certainly a factor. This was the peerage of Lebanon. People paid homage to the *zuama* as they would have lords of the realm. The press reported their every coming and going. Beirut streets bore their names—Bishara Khoury Street, Sami Solh Avenue, the Pierre Gemayel Corniche. It was heady stuff for a society enslaved to the concept of personal honor. But it was power and money that crowned their success.

Although they skimmed the cream off the economy and paralyzed the development of any alternative to their personal rule, the *zuama*'s government-by-patronage was not entirely bad. It provided some measure of political integration among the widely divided and hostile confessionals. It maintained a modicum of stability and harmony in an otherwise fractured social structure. With the exception of the Shiites, it gave individuals and groups some leverage in securing benefits, services, and a more equitable distribution of resources. But the system was rife with cataclysmic flaws. The *zuama* ran Lebanon like a private club, swapping cabinet offices, government contracts, positions in the bureaucracy, and favor in the private sector as spoils of the privileged. As a result, Lebanon was plagued with endemic corruption, nepotism, and favoritism. The entire political process was reduced to squabbles over political spoils and the boundaries of each *zaim's* territory and influence. In the process, no one came to grips with policy issues of national concern and long-range planning was sacrificed for short-run expediency.

The split went even further. There was always extreme competition among the *zuama*. Only by delivering for his clients could a *zaim* stay in power. This meant he had to protect his own business interests as well as his clients'. In a society in which conflict is a national pastime, the competitiveness of the *zuama*, the men at the top of the political system, only added to Lebanon's already precarious stability.

The *zuama* controlled Lebanon because the nature of the society allowed them to rule. They were a symptom of a society and political system crawling with the same nepotism, bribery, opportunism, and petty rivalries that plagued the *zuama*. Lebanon was corrupt, at least in the Western understanding of the term, from top to bottom. The people themselves did not expect a politician to be honest; they demanded only that he be a fixer and doer in pursuit of his clients' interests. And since the Lebanese held in admiration anyone who could turn a fast dollar, activities of public officials that would have been questionable in the West escaped general condemnation in Lebanon. The *zuama* were tolerated, even held in esteem, because they reigned as the kings of the shady deal. The movement of influence and money was so fast and pervasive during the Golden Age that virtually every politician was on the take from someone—a Lebanese seeking a favor, international business interests, some foreign power, or all of the above. One Gulf oil state openly kept a former Lebanese prime minister as an influence peddler on a private retainer of several thousand dollars a month.

Still, there were voices in the wilderness protesting the licentiousness of Lebanon's political climate. When Bishara Khoury was president (1946–1952), the Maronite Archbishop Mubarak wrote to him, "[I]n Lebanon there is no peace, justice or happiness—only

graft and injustice and murder, robberies and thefts committed by
men in office, and government intervention to prevent free elections
and make easy the victory of a group which has sacrificed every
public interest for its personal profit." But it was the rare politician
who was called to the bar of public censure.

Bishara Khoury was one. Khoury was the first president of
Lebanon. He was fat and friendly and nicknamed "Abu Kirsh"
(Father of Belly) affectionately by his political friends and deri-
sively by his opponents. While Khoury himself was still riding high
on public esteem from his role as an architect of Lebanese independence, those who surrounded him were tarred with blatant corruption. As soon as Khoury became president, his son Khalil's law
practice and business deals began to show enormous profits. So did
his brother Fuad's cement plant. The wife of his brother Caesar
was a notorious influence peddler. Khoury's friend Henri Pharon,
banker, boss of the taxi drivers' union, and owner of a racing
stable, was widely known as the man who could put the fix on any
kind of problem. But the last straw for the Lebanese' excessive
tolerance of such activities was the president's wife. In 1952 Mrs.
Khoury left Lebanon for Paris carrying $100,000 in gold, whose
ownership was distinctly cloudy. When the story surfaced, President Khoury was challenged in the Chamber of Deputies on the
source and use of the money. The president's reply was "Mrs. el-
Khoury has already spent this money in the interests of the Lebanese republic. . . ." It was too much even for the Lebanese, and
Khoury was forced to resign amid charges of corruption and
nepotism.

Much of the Lebanese' passive acceptance of their leaders'
corruption occurred because no one perceived himself as being
cheated. The government of Lebanon, as guarantor of a Lebanese's
security and an entity for which all people shared responsibility,
was beyond the Lebanese experience. Security was the function of
the family or the communal group. Loyalty was to the leaders of
that group rather than to some ephemeral notion of a nation-state.
Before the war, it was estimated that two-thirds of the Lebanese
never paid their taxes. For the rich and powerful, ignoring taxes
was another prerogative. For the poor, taxes represented a form of
theft by some vague central authority to which people owed no
allegiance. When the tax collector approached a village, warnings
of his arrival spread among the inhabitants like an alarm. As he

went from house to house, the best treatment he could expect was veiled contempt. Normally his assessments were greeted with bickering from the men and tears and lamentations from the women. Undeterred by their protests, he collected what he could in cash and impounded a goat or some household item from families with no money. After all, he had to protect his percentage. Trekking back to the main road herding his collected livestock and balancing an assortment of household goods, he was often met by relatives of those who had suffered confiscation offering to pay the taxes of their kin so they would be spared the shame of losing their possessions.

Laws, like taxes, were ignored, or at least skirted. To be put in jail for graft or nonpayment of taxes was a misfortune rather than a disgrace. As a result, almost no one was above a little larceny. In 1968, a prominent banker who was also a professor at AUB was arrested for fraudulent bankruptcy. Before the arrest, it was rumored that Kamal Jumblatt had given him refuge in his palace at Mukhtara, and while he was in jail awaiting trial, the president and the prime minister had casually visited him in his cell. Taxi drivers accumulated so many unpaid traffic tickets in the course of a year that annually the government wearily declared an amnesty.

Laws were brushed aside not because the Lebanese are inherently dishonest; rather, legalities fell outside the purview of the group to which a Lebanese owed his allegiance. Kinship, fealty, and confessional loyalties always superseded loyalties to the nation. A Christian, a Sunni, a Druze, or a Shiite thought of himself first as a member of a given family, tied by heritage to a specific region, and confirmed in a confession. Finally, he might think of himself as a Lebanese if doing so posed no conflict with his other identities. This mindset spilled over into the Lebanese attitude toward the authenticity of Lebanon's government and its ability, or even right, to exercise any control over its citizens. The image of the central government as an extension of the corporate body of citizens simply did not exist in the sphere of Lebanese reason, a fact demonstrated by the 1969 political crisis, when Lebanon lived without a government for seven months. Without the constant handwringing by the press, it is possible the population never would have noticed.

Groups' distrust of one another was so pervasive that for years cynics claimed that the only thing that held three million Lebanese of sixteen officially recognized religions together was their para-

noid fear and loathing of one another. An Anglican priest whose
prewar congregation was largely Lebanese once observed with
deep sadness, "The way different groups betray each other is worse
than animals."

Lebanon was a nation of minorities, each marginal to the
others. It touted a culture that enshrined individualism and indif-
ference to such a degree that the Lebanese seemed to be quasi-
mercenary mercantiles willing to live under any regime provided
they continued to make money. "Such a culture, which begins at the
cradle and is developed on the benches of schools and universities,
must sooner or later end with the disintegration of the city."

Tragically, the seeds of Lebanon's destruction lay in the Lebanese themselves. Lebanon was ruined not only by religious conflict
or the meddling of outsiders but by the very nature of its society. In
1920, less than seventy years ago, France took the Lebanese with
their identity dilemma between East and West, their religious
communalism, their lack of commitment to common goals, and
their endless cycles of conflict and revenge and forged them into a
political entity that never achieved the most basic unity demanded
of any nation.

France Granted Mandate by League of Nations
St. Louis Post Dispatch
September 2, 1920

SIX

THE FRENCH LEGACY

O n September 1, 1920, the diminutive General Henri Gouraud, standing erect on a brilliant red carpet at the top of the steps of the French headquarters in Beirut, grandly declared in the name of France the State of Greater Lebanon. If the French were not already aware of the diversity of the population within their League of Nations mandate, a cursory look at the assembled crowd confirmed it. The Maronite and Melkite patriarchs, adorned in the ornate robes of the Eastern Christian church, flanked Gouraud. On Gouraud's left, the turbaned head of an initiated Druze bobbed left and right as he tried to gain a better view of the proceedings. Behind the Druze, a small, tight knot of Shiites in *kaffiyehs*, the square-checkered head cloths of their desert ancestors, stood, almost defensively. On Gouraud's right, the monotony of the Maronites' ordinary Western business suits was interrupted by a rotund figure wearing an embroidered vest over the wide-sleeved blouse and baggy pants distinctive to the Ottoman court. Obviously, the French had failed to grasp the true Levantine mix of East and West in their new territory. As the French military legation saluted, the dapper Gouraud raised his eyes to the unfurling flag of Lebanon, bold red stripes on a white field emblazoned with a cedar tree—the symbol of the Maronites.

Greater Lebanon was largely the result of the confluence of European interests in the Levant and the Maronites' search for a foreign protector. In the latter part of the nineteenth century, the Christians of Mount Lebanon reveled in their protected status, a position the British and French had imposed on the Ottoman sultan, the nominal colonial lord of the Mountain. But the Ottomans' alliance with Germany freed Sultan Muhammed V from British and French pressures when World War I broke out in 1914. The sultan moved swiftly to reestablish his direct rule and, in the process, delivered the disastrous wartime administration of Jamal Pasha to the Mountain. Between 1914 and 1917, an estimated 100,000 Lebanese, virtually all of them Christian and mostly Maronite, died of disease, starvation, and execution. Thus, with almost 25 percent of the total population of the populous mountain region destroyed, the Christian Maronites emerged from World War I terrified about their future if they fell under Muslim administration. But France, as a result of the secret 1916 Sykes-Picot agreement, eventually won Syria, albeit as a mandate from the League of Nations. With the mandate, French ambitions for territory in the Levant, Maronite hopes for Western security guarantees, and Muslim fears of Western domination were all realized.

With their persons secure, the Maronites sought to further their economic well-being. Immediately they began to press the French to annex the old Phoenician towns of Sidon, Tyre, and Tripoli, the Roman breadbasket of the Bekaa, the southern farmlands settled by the Arabs during the surge of the Islamic Empire, the northern Akkar, which traditionally belonged to Syria, and the city of Beirut to the Mountain. For without them the Mountain was an isolated island completely dependent on surrounding Muslim territory. Without Beirut and much of its agricultural and commercial hinterland, the Mountain as defined by its Ottoman administrative boundaries was a poor and weak version of the Lebanon to which the Maronite nationalists aspired.

The French supported the demands of the Maronite militants, arguing that Lebanon's Catholic population was France's only reliable ally against the rising tide of Arab nationalism in the Middle East. Thus, the interests of the Maronites and those of the West became one. In 1920, responding to the Maronites' rallying cry "Truly France is our benevolent mother," France created Greater Lebanon. Within its borders, the French locked together a

Muslim minority who bristled with suspicion at any threat to its
own culture and a bare Christian majority who slavishly imitated
the West.

Greater Lebanon was so new, yet so very old. With little real
awareness of the new political configuration, the Lebanese continued to move to the rhythms established by the centuries. Caravan drovers still herded their camels through the streets of Sidon
beneath tattered awnings dyed the same purple hue of Phoenician
fame. The farmers of the Bekaa tossed their wheat in great round
reed trays, winnowing the wheat from the chaff, while the peasants
of Jabal Amil lay metal and muscle to yet another boulder to clear
their rocky fields. Armed Druze, heavy ammunition belts slung
across their chests, stood guard, as always, over their sectarian
lands. And in the hills, Maronite priests wearing woolen robes and
high-crowned liturgical hats still hurried toward their churches.
Only Beirut, poised for the metamorphosis from village to nation's
capital, grasped the new reality of a Levantine country almost
equally divided between Christians and Muslims. Optimism was
so high that the Beirutites even cast their illusion of a nonsectarian
Lebanon into statuary set in Martyrs' Square. Memorializing
Lebanese soldiers who had died in World War I, the bronze figures
of two proud women, one veiled and one unveiled, their hands
clasped in unity, turned their faces up to the eternal sun of the
Levant.

The oneness of Greater Lebanon the women represented was a
myth from which other myths flowed. The French embraced the
illusion that they could enter into an alliance with the Maronites to
promote France's national interests in the Levant while successfully placating the other groups who now were incorporated into
the mandate. The Maronites, for their part, grasped France's
mandate over Lebanon as their eternal salvation against the
masses of Middle Eastern Muslims who surrounded them. In their
imaginations, they saw Lebanon as a never-changing utopia of
Christian villages nestled among the mountains, protected by
French ships standing guard off the coast. The Maronites were so
caught up in this illusion that on December 8, 1920, their patriarch
al Huwayyik proclaimed,

And now has the noble French nation given us . . . a new and
brilliant proof of her love for us and our welfare, and her

concern for our affairs. Her righteous policy has triumphed in this land and confirmed the hopes to which we have tenaciously and affectionately adhered, and has offered to our cherished Lebanon her independence, extended her boundaries, and reestablished for her people a living nation which, God willing, will stand with honor among the civilized nations.

The melancholy truth was that the French and the Christians, led by the Maronites, believed their own fantasies. However, annexing new territories to the Mountain was like introducing a Trojan horse into the new Lebanese entity. The population of the annexed territories was overwhelmingly Muslim, largely Sunni in Tripoli, the Akkar, and Sidon, and predominantly Shiite in the Bekaa and south and east of Tyre and Sidon. For these Muslims, the mandate was little more than a new Crusader state.

Stripped of the promise of an Arab nation by the greed of the European powers after World War I, the Muslims bitterly resented their subjugation to yet another foreign power—this time from the West. The French occupation struck at the very core of the Muslim psyche, the sense of impotence induced by the West's technological superiority and military might and fed by the conviction that the West was bent on destroying Islamic culture. The French, unprepared for the depth of communal hostilities, fantasized that under their rule Christians would accept Lebanon as an Arab country with an Arab language while the Muslims would accept Lebanon's continued intellectual ties with the West. Instead, the confrontation between Islam and the West that had been going on for centuries entered a new phase. The new Lebanese entity was split between two fundamental groups, one looking toward the West and the other pulling toward the East.

Once in control of Greater Lebanon, France rejected Lebanon's Arab side and began its civilizing mission. French became the official language. Government, the courts, business, and polite society were all conducted in French. Almost all schools required French, and in many schools teachers, influenced by their own French training, rigidly stood before their classes and taught history, the social sciences, literature, and the humanities as if all their students were French nationals.

The entire fiscal and economic policy of Lebanon was run by

the French. French investors owned and operated the railways, public utilities, and banks. Contracts went to French concerns or Lebanese companies with strong French ties. Consequently, those who could speak the French language were the ones who benefited the most from the mandate's economy.

Christians, particularly Maronites, gained an enormous advantage over Arabic and English speakers through their French education. Command of the French language opened the door to government positions, access to the French colonial officials, and, most important, to a wide range of business opportunities.

But the greatest failing of education under the mandate was that it made no attempt to build any kind of Lebanese nationalism. Although state schools existed, 70 percent of all education was financed by religious organizations that drew on capital resources from abroad. Lebanese youth entered the foreign mission schools and emerged twelve years later ignorant of everything concerning the history, geography, and social life of their own country. Further, children passed through the schools of their own confession, often barely meeting children of another faith.

France has been roundly condemned for its divisive policies in Lebanon. But by the beginning of the French mandate, the dynamics of Lebanese politics were already cast in their fateful mold. Patterns of identity based on blood ties, shared religion, geographic attachments, and various external ties already had produced a political system in which politics and communalism were inextricably linked. The French, in essence, ruled Lebanon in much the same way that the Ottoman Empire had ruled through various religious groups. The *zuama* governed their own communities and guaranteed their acquiescence to French rule. The few efforts the French made to develop conventional political links that crossed communal or regional boundaries were frustrated by indelible communal affinities and the self-interests of the *zuama*. Only by acknowledging the existence and power of communal groups could France hope to turn its mandate into a functioning entity.

The French colonial government was three-pronged. The high commissioner, appointed by the French government, presided over its own bureaucracy in Lebanon. The governor of Lebanon, also a Frenchman, presided over local government. And the *zuama* made it all work by offering services and protection to their clients in return for their allegiance and votes. Under the mandate, the old feudal system of the Mountain simply imposed itself on Greater Lebanon. Lebanon remained more a complex montage than an authentic country.

Perhaps if Greater Lebanon had stagnated economically rather than thrived, opposition to French colonialism and cultural imperialism might have hardened. But under the mandate, the Lebanese undeniably enjoyed the highest standard of living in the Levant. They possessed schools superior to any others in the area. Interconnecting roads and a fledgling transportation system fostered commerce. Modern medical care existed in the towns. And in Beirut, the new capital, an American-style soda fountain whipped up authentic chocolate milk shakes. In short, life in Lebanon was attractive, its allure far exceeding that of neighboring countries. Slowly, the affluent Muslims' enthusiasm for union with Greater Syria cooled.

Yet resistance was far from quiescent. In 1925 the Druze, garbed in ammunition belts and waving rifles, whirled out of their mountain redoubts demanding more rights and greater autonomy. Having allied themselves so closely with the Maronites, the French authorities were all but paralyzed in meeting the crisis. By 1926, the colonial authorities had recovered enough to put forth a new plan for placating the rampaging Druze and addressing Muslim fears of Christian domination. Lebanon was proclaimed a constitutional republic in which all citizens enjoyed equal rights under the law. A formal system of representation in which the people elected representatives to a single-house parliament was inaugurated.

This republic was a feeble attempt to neutralize some of the animosities alive in the communal system, a structure that the French, by both choice and necessity, had used to govern the mandate. Charles Dabbas, who as an Orthodox Christian was more acceptable to the Muslims, Druze, and the other Orthodox than a Maronite could ever be, was appointed president. While this choice was a response to Muslim sensitivities, the French nevertheless established a tacit understanding that the president of Lebanon would always be a Christian. Four years later, when it appeared the Muslims were poised to force the election of a Muslim to the presidency, the constitution was suspended, throwing the mandate into crisis.

The 1932 political crisis produced the all-important 1932 census, the only official census Lebanon has ever had and the one on which the distribution of political power is still based. According to the official poll, Christians accounted for 396,746 people out of a total of 793,226. This gave the Christians a real majority of only 226 over the combined total of all other people. But the results of the census, like everything else in Lebanon, were part truth, part illusion. If the Jews, Alawites, Baha'is, and other groups marginal to either dominant religion were excluded, the Christians actually outnumbered the Muslims by 10,000. Yet the official census established that the Christians outnumbered by 54,000 the Muslims and Druze combined. This difference of 44,000 in the actual number of Christians in Lebanon and the official count was accounted for by Lebanese living abroad who had retained their Lebanese citizenship and registered on the census rolls of their villages. Of these, 50 percent were Maronite.

The Christians' dominance in Lebanon's power structure rested not on overwhelming numerical superiority but on two other factors. First, the French colonial government allowed the large emigré population living outside of Lebanon to vote in Lebanese elections. Second, the Druze and the Shiites, fearful of being engulfed by the Sunni majority of the Arab world, stayed out of Sunni-led Muslim politics. Thus, the combination of an absent block of Christian voters and a quiescent block of Muslim voters led the Christians to know perhaps better than anyone else that their hold on majority status was frail and transient. At the same time, Lebanon's French masters realized that the time would come when the Muslims, with their significantly higher birth rates, would become the majority, threatening French interests as well as Christian interests. As a result, the French "insinuated to Maronite and other Christian leaders in Lebanon that their security against a Muslim tidal wave required full trust in France and cooperation with French rule." On the basis of the census, the French declared that the ratio of Christians over Muslims stood at six to five. Seats in parliament and positions in the bureaucracy were distributed in the same ratio. Tragically for the future of Lebanon, this six-to-five ratio assumed the aura of holy writ, immune from demographic realities.

Ironically, the crisis of 1932 nourished nascent Lebanese nationalism among certain factions within the Christian and Sunni Muslim communities. The Sunnis divided between those who refused to let go of their cherished commitment to reuniting Lebanese territory with the rest of the Arab homeland and those committed to building a new Lebanese identity hand in hand with the Christians. It was the latter group that began to take control of Sunni politics.

Lebanese nationalists such as Riad Solh saw no conflict between Arab nationalism and Lebanon's Western pretensions. Solh, like most Muslim leaders of the 1920s and 1930s, accepted the notion that the Arab world was in need of reform. And it was to the West that they looked for models in science and technology and for the value of free thought with which to wage that reform. The interwar years were a time when Muslims accepted certain Western models and values as universal—practices and philosophies that any people could incorporate without damaging their own culture. It was a viewpoint that would suffer in the frenzied Arab nationalism of the 1950s and 1960s and die with Iran's Islamic revolution.

Even within the Maronite fold, the idea of an independent Lebanon in which the Muslims had a legitimate role gained ground. Led by the *zaim*, Bishara Khoury, the group conceded that Lebanon could survive only if the various confessions shared an independent national identity and solidarity that overrode communalism. Like other nationalists, Khoury recognized that the Maronite community had to choose between its French protectors and an acceptable partnership with the Muslims of Lebanon. They could not have both.

Khoury's vision of a pluralistic Lebanon was anathema to Francophiles like Emile Edde and his ilk. The archetypal Maronite Francophile, Edde studied law in Paris and in the process embraced French culture in its totality. His office functioned as a salon in which he and his peers discoursed at length on French philosophy, cinema, and politics in their adopted tongue. Refusing to think beyond this closed society, Edde disparaged all Muslims as lesser products of the backward East. To Edde the Muslims posed a sinister danger to Lebanon, which he perceived solely in terms of a Christian refuge belonging to the same Mediterranean world as France. Though they differed markedly in their attitudes toward the Muslims, Khoury, Edde, and all Maronites were united on one issue: the insistence on a protected status for the Christians of Lebanon.

As World War II approached, developing Lebanese national-
ism led Christians and Muslims into a tenuous united front against
French colonialism. When France fell to Nazi Germany in 1940,
General Mittelhauser, commander in chief of French forces in
Lebanon, pledged loyalty to Vichy France, thus putting Lebanon in
the feeble grip of the Nazi collaborators.

With French rule in reality suspended by World War II, the
stage was set for the Lebanese to attempt some reconciliation of
their communal differences in preparation for complete independence. The National Pact emerged as the solution to generations of
malevolent confessionalism. It was the most momentous political
decision the Lebanese ever made.

The National Pact, or Mithaq, was an informal agreement
negotiated between the Christian president, Bishara Khoury, and
the Muslim prime minister, Riad Solh, to establish a workable
government to replace the French mandate expected to end with
World War II. From the outset, the pact guaranteed the Christians
a dominant role in government. Using the flawed 1932 census as its
basis, the six-to-five ratio of Christians to Muslims was accepted
for the distribution of parliamentary seats, cabinet offices, and
positions in the bureaucracy. Under the electoral scheme, the
president was to be elected by the parliament and would always be
a Maronite Christian. The president, in turn, would choose the
prime minister, who would always be a Sunni Muslim. The position
of speaker of the parliament was reserved for a Shiite Muslim and
the command of the army for a Maronite. To win the support of the
Druze, Greek Orthodox, and Greek Catholics, each was granted
special preserves of political power and patronage.

Incredibly, the National Pact, the accord over which the Christians and Muslims have shed so much blood, was never committed
to writing. Instead it was accepted as an understanding among
Lebanon's *zuama*. Like the Christian-Muslim ratio established by
the 1932 census, this understanding became the ark of Lebanese
political life until it collapsed in 1975. Still not buried, the National
Pact is like a corpse over which the various factions continue to
snarl.

On one level, the National Pact was absurd. It was based on
assumptions—first, about the relative proportion that each confessional constituted in Lebanon in 1932 and, second, that those
proportions would stay static. The "Christians," including the

Armenians, who could not vote, and the Jews, who were not even Christian, were granted a 52 percent share of the population. The Muslims, comprising the Sunni, Shiite, and Druze communities, none of which had compatible interests about the future of Lebanon, were granted 48 percent. The pact was never affirmed by the people. The Lebanese simply acquiesced to the dictates of a group of tribal chieftains, each jealous of his own prerogatives and protective of his community's turf.

The reason the National Pact became an article of faith for the Lebanese was that it seriously attempted to create a balance between Christian and Muslim anxieties. Its essential element was the declaration of Lebanon as an independent republic, bound by neither its European nor its Arab ties. Christian Lebanese pledged their respect to Lebanon's Arab character and promised to reject any formal alliance of protection with a Western power. Muslims, in return, agreed to accept Lebanese sovereignty and to shun any attempt to integrate Lebanon into a broader Arab or Islamic state. In this commitment to Lebanon's independence, the Lebanese sought to ensure their sovereignty in an Arab world and to reconcile their two basic orientations—to the Christian West and the Muslim East.

Khoury and Solh firmly believed they had laid the foundation for an interconfessional political order whose ultimate goal was to eliminate sectarianism, which Riad Solh described as "an obstacle to national progress, impeding the representation of the national will and poisoning the good relations between diverse elements of the Lebanese population." But regardless of its intention, the National Pact, in practice, formalized and hardened the need for confessional balance, making it virtually impossible to move away from a political system based on confessions.

Rather than eliminating confessionals, the Mithaq established a pragmatic *modus operandi* through which religious groups with basically different overall political orientations and frames of reference could coexist. Like predatory animals, the Sunni and Maronite establishments quickly developed a strong common interest in marking the confessional system as their special preserve, thus retaining for themselves control of a powerless national government. Nabih Berri, in another of his sagacious comments, would say of Lebanon, "[We] behave like tribes instead of like people of one country. The 1943 Pact that we created is a partitionist pact. It helped make us build a farm, not a country. . . ."

Lebanon was granted independence by the Free French government in December 1943. But when France was liberated from
the Nazi occupation in 1944, interest in the empire rekindled in the
DeGaulle government. In 1945, France landed five hundred Sene-
galese troops from its cruiser *Jeanne d'Arc* in Lebanon to reclaim
its former mandate. Suddenly the Maronites found France, though
not French culture, abhorrent. Christian and Muslim anger
erupted against the Christians' once benevolent France. When the
demonstrations ended, fire-blackened ruins stood silhouetted
against signboards from which all but Arabic words were blotted
out.

Yet in the midst of their nationalistic fervor, the Maronites
brooded over their next foreign ally. Zionist moves to create a
Jewish state in Palestine piqued interest among some factions. If
the Zionists succeeded in their dream of creating their own state,
the new entity would offer the Maronites a non-Arab ally in their
confrontation with Arab nationalism in the region. The Edde
faction within the Maronite community went so far as to send an
emissary to Zionist leader Chaim Weizmann to discuss the incorporation of southern Lebanon into a Jewish state in Palestine. Later
the Maronite patriarch dispatched his leading aide to the newly
born United Nations to urge establishment of a national home for
the Christians modeled on U.N. proposals for the Jews. These were
merely auxiliary considerations. After World War II, the Maronites
looked inexorably farther West. The United States had become
their ally of choice.

When a small contingent of the U.S. Army arrived in Lebanon
as part of the Allied forces' mopping operation in the Levant, the
Maronites embraced them as the symbol of their new savior. Troop
trucks rumbled through the mountain villages with the Stars and
Stripes proudly raised while small boys held high their fingers in a
V for "victory" and little girls blew kisses. One American soldier in
the convoy wrote, "It was an advantage to be known as an American." Increasingly the muttered phrase "America must help us"
passed through the Maronite communities on the Mountain.

It was 1946 before the last French soldiers left Lebanese soil.
But the independence that came after their departure produced
neither stability nor security. The incessant question friend and foe
alike asked was whether Lebanon, a small state of marginals, could
survive in the stormy sea of Arab and international politics.

With independence, the *zuama* took charge of Lebanon. Poli-

tics was a family business in which fathers passed on power to their
heirs. Between 1943 and 1975, twenty-six families held 35 percent
of all parliamentary seats. In the 1960 Chamber of Deputies, for
example, almost a quarter of the members had inherited their
parliamentary seats from their fathers. During its term, four
sitting deputies died. As expected, three were succeeded by their
children, one of whom was Myrna el Khazin, the only child of Emile
Bustani and the first Lebanese woman to serve in the parliament.
Although individual seats could be hotly contested, elections to the
Chamber of Deputies usually anointed the leading *zuama*, affirm-
ing their right to their cherished place in the power structure.

Like the established right to serve in parliament, the presidency was a crown bestowed by the recognized leaders of the
Maronite community in consultation with the *zuama* from other
confessionals. The premiership tended to rotate among four Sunni
Muslim families—the Solhs, Karamis, Yafis, and Salams. Like
dukes of the kingdom, members of certain families slid into designated ministerial posts with each change of government. The
Melkite Taqlas family reigned over the Ministry of Foreign Affairs
while the Ministry of Defense was virtually the reserve of the
Druze Majid Arslan. Although unwilling to come to terms with the
system's divisiveness, the Lebanese appreciated its absurdity. One
story that made the rounds of the coffeehouses depicted a senior
army officer—a Maronite, of course—visiting a platoon on the front
line during the 1948 Palestine war. All of the soldiers were lying
under the trees napping, their guns carelessly tossed aside. When
the officer asked the Greek Catholic lieutenant why the platoon was
not in action, the latter replied, "One of our men was just killed. We
have to wait for three Maronites, two Sunnis, two Shiites, two
Greek Orthodox, and one Druze to be killed before we start fighting again."

In truth, Lebanon's much touted democracy was another of the
illusions that the West so readily believed. While the Lebanese
possessed more of a democracy than any people in the Middle East,
the reality beneath the veneer was that Lebanese democracy was
little more than a corrupt consortium of the political establishment
that the electorate was allowed to rubber-stamp at the appropriate
time.

Government worked because the National Pact was created
and sustained by politicians who were masters at the art of flexibil-

ity and compromise in protecting the only two fundamentals on which they agreed—a free economy that served their commercial interests and a political system that abetted the patron-client relationships on which their power rested.

Because there was no sense of the common good, politics was a convolution of Byzantine maneuvers among the political bosses that approached in complexity the maintenance of the international balance of power. In a grudging collective acceptance of each group's existence, alliances formed through manipulation and intrigue shifted from election to election.

The arena of battle was not the floor—or even the closet—of the Chamber of Deputies but the food table of the grand hotels. At lunch, the politicians assembled in the dining room of the Phoenicia or on the terrace of the St. Georges but seldom at less prestigious locations because celebrated surroundings and big tabs were part of the game. Politicians entertained politicians, businessmen courted ministers, organizations hosted their patrons, and patrons dined their clients.

These lengthy meals ended near cocktail time, when the *zaim* crept home through the snarled traffic and collected his stout, lacquered-haired, bejeweled wife to begin the round of evening functions. Through one affair after another, wives kissed one another's cheeks, jangled their heavy bracelets, and exchanged grudging compliments while their husbands, honoring the Levant's penchant for intrigue and oiling their encounters with Mediterranean manners, cut the latest deal.

No social event that might involve potential subtle shifts of power escaped the politicians' attention. Shiites and Christians, for instance, always took intense interest in who was elected president of the Sunni's Islamic Society of Benevolent Intentions in Beirut, for he might emerge as the country's next premier. And because of Lebanon's small size, all local disputes demanded careful tending by all interested parties before they exploded into national issues that would threaten existing coalitions.

Elections were like time bombs. First, they were provocations to family feuds. Any contest, from the election of a member of parliament to the appointment of a village night watchman, provided a chance to even the score in old vendettas. Since election confirmed a *zaim*'s power, the potential for violence exploded as *zaim* jockeyed against *zaim*. With such high spoils, elections were always expensive affairs for those elected to parliament and for the man they in turn would elect president. In the 1960s, it took anywhere from $50,000 to $100,000 to win a Beirut district. The money went into parties for supporters, bribery for newspapers, and salaries for musclemen who kept a *zaim's* supporters in line and intimidated the opposition. A healthy portion of the election budget always went into vote buying, a widespread and fairly open exercise in political behavior. *Paris Figaro* once charged that elections were so corrupt that in many Lebanese districts the registered voters outnumbered the population by ten to one. For those with sufficient capital the cost of getting elected was inconsequential, for these initial outlays were always recoverable for men who were judged to be among the most corrupt in the Middle East.

The other criterion for winning a place in government was religion. Every electoral district was assigned its religious quotas. Aley, a town in the mountains just east of Beirut, was allotted three deputies to the parliament. Of the three one had to be a Maronite, one a Druze, and one a Greek Orthodox, a reflection of the district's communal composition. A voter could vote for whom he chose as long as his selections were one Maronite, one Druze, and one Greek Orthodox. Forcing candidates to run interconfessional slates was one of the few practices that promoted rather than sabotaged intercommunal cooperation. But it was not enough to overcome all the other obstacles in the path of a national, nonsectarian government.

If the system was parochial, corrupt, and unresponsive to a national agenda, where did the fault lie? The answer came across the tea table from a bright, AUB-educated woman in her mid-fifties who has watched the years of civil war in Lebanon. Musing over the tragedy of her country, she said, "The big problem was tribal politics. Elections were corrupt. We were bolstered by violating the rules instead of obeying them. Lebanon was run by the *zuama*—'the big bosses.' It was not a joint venture. We were not good citizens."

Ironically, the National Pact, the covenant of the political system, which was meant to dilute rather than entrench sectarian divisions, played the largest part in preventing Lebanon from developing a strong central government. Not only was the president dependent on the Chamber of Deputies for election; the religious communities and political clans stood together to ensure that the man they elected would never have sufficient power to govern. Further, any president who attempted to take charge was checked by the bureaucracy and the army. The bureaucracy was over-staffed, underpaid, dilatory, corrupt, and incompetent. Unlike in Arab countries in which jobs in the bureaucracy of powerful governments are prestigious, the Lebanese bureaucracy was plagued by the low status government employment was accorded by the the upper and middle classes. Ambitious fathers discouraged their children's interest in government service by telling them that the family had not scrimped to send them to university to be a disgrace. The result was that government jobs were left to those who failed to become doctors, lawyers, and businesspeople.

The impotence of the army was even more debilitating to a central government. The military was structured along confessional lines. The higher-echelon officer corps was Christian, the foot soldiers were Shiites, and the ranks in between were filled by members of the other confessionals. For the Christians, the army was one of the ultimate guarantors of the Lebanese political system and its Christian character. For the Muslims, control of the army was one of those goals key to power in Lebanon. Consequently, no one dared send the army into action in defense of government integrity for fear that the confessionals' carefully balanced accommodation would tumble like a house of cards. A Lebanese president essentially controlled no army to protect the central government against internal or external threats. Defense of the country, like defense of the political system, fell to the *zuama* and their private militias. And the *zuama*, like highly trained attack dogs, always stood ready to thwart a strong presidency. This Disneyesque political system worked well for the first ten years after the National Pact largely because the Christians were so clearly in control. The other components of the partnership were given freedom to maneuver and a share of the spoils as long as they kept their places. But in 1952, the traditional balance of power was challenged head-on by the forces of Arab nationalism.

The problem began in 1948 with the birth of Israel on the soil of Palestine. Although Lebanon, as the Middle East's "Little Switzerland," would in future years be doomed by the human fallout from the first Arab-Israeli war, the Lebanese convinced themselves that they could walk the fine line between acceptance and rejection of Israel, between the view of Israel as a buffer for the

Christians against the Muslims and the condemnation of Israel as a
tool of Western imperialism bent on colonizing Arab land. Lebanon
showed its Arab character by sacrificing ten of its men for Palestine in the 1948 war and later joining the Arab League. But
Lebanon also ended the war with Israel by signing an armistice
with the new Jewish state that recognized Israel and the Lebanon-
Palestine border. And Lebanon never joined its Arab neighbors as
a confrontation state. Instead it tried to follow two courses at once:
to stay within the Arab fold and to pursue commerce with the West.
That policy succeeded until Gamal Abdel Nasser seized the government of Egypt and threw down the gauntlet of pan-Arabism,
the dream of uniting all Arabs under one banner.

With his dashing good looks and passionate oratory, Nasser
overnight became the new Saladin of the Arab world and the terror
of conservative establishments, including Lebanon's. His picture
sprouted everywhere. Enormous posters plastered the walls of
public places, and tiny plastic stickpins highlighting his magnetic
smile decked the visors of taxicabs. Nasser's charisma among
Muslims was so strong that Lebanon's Muslim political leaders
were compelled to travel to Cairo to receive his blessings to pacify
the crowds in the streets of Lebanon's Muslim areas who were
chanting his name. The Sunnis were enthralled with Nasser's
blazing rhetoric. Glued to his broadcasts from Cairo over the
"Voice of the Arabs," the Sunnis' nostalgia for Greater Syria
dimmed in the wake of Nasser's clarion call for the restoration of
Arab dignity. The Arab Renaissance had arrived.

In 1953, Christians were jolted when the Muslims challenged
the status quo in Lebanon through an anonymous English-lan-
guage pamphlet titled "Muslim Lebanon Today." Airing Muslim
grievances, the tract demanded abandonment of the National Pact
and called for a new census, deprivation of citizenship of the largely
Christian emigrés abroad, and citizenship for the Palestinians.
Shaken by this publication, the Christians went on the offensive
and succeeded in forcing judicial proceedings against the suspected publishers.

The following year the Christians, as though to affirm their
central place in Lebanon, staged an elaborate celebration to mark
the centenary of the adoption of the dogma of the Immaculate
Conception by the Roman Catholic Church. The massive celebration culminated in a huge procession from downtown Beirut to the

shrine of the Virgin overlooking the bay at Jounieh. The Muslims responded a month later. Demonstrating their rival strength, they celebrated Muhammed's birthday with a resplendent torchlight procession in downtown Beirut. Fire broke out, and in the ensuing panic twenty-one people were trampled to death, a statistic that Christians observed with grim satisfaction and a conviction of divine intervention. At the time, few appreciated the fact that these Christian-Muslim demonstrations were omens of the shift of politics out of the posh hotels and into the streets.

Nasser derived his power by doing what no other Arab leader had ever done: He molded together socialist economic doctrine with pan-Arabism to create a new ideology labeled "Nasserism." Nasser's mobilization of the Arabs unnerved the West, particularly the United States, which saw in Nasserism a fundamental attack on the existence of Israel and on Western economic philosophy and interests throughout the Middle East. The United States, caught in confrontation with the Soviet Union across the globe, shuddered at Nasser's bold moves toward the Soviets, who responded by pumping copious quantities of arms and advisers into the Middle East's most populous country. While the West worried about the Soviet moves into the Middle East, Lebanon's establishment fretted over Nasser's left-leaning economic policies.

In Lebanon, the ideology of pan-Arabism and social equality had inflamed those embittered by their economic impotence. Even more, by raising high the issue of Arab unity, Nasser seriously threatened the destruction of the critical balance of power in Lebanon achieved by the Maronite, Druze, and Sunni *zuama*. The frustrations of those who failed to achieve their goals of Arab unity when the Ottoman Empire was dismembered, who chafed under the Western rule of the French, and who strained against the Christians' dominance in the National Pact had finally found in Nasser a visionary for Arab aspirations. Why accept a secondary position in a state dominated by Christians with ambivalence toward Arabism when Arabism was on the threshold of its finest hour? Suddenly pan-Arabism was the new force of the day, the catalyst for Lebanon's first crisis with its fragmented political system.

It may be forever argued whether the crisis of 1958 was brought on by Camille Chamoun's clever power plays to control the direction of Lebanon's domestic politics and foreign policy or was simply the result of his own stupidity. In the 1957 parliamentary elections Chamoun, without warning, jettisoned the alliances that guarded the establishment in favor of new alignments more sub-missive to his ambitions. Chamoun backed up his blatant moves with the emerging power of the right-wing Phalange militia, the armed might of the Parti Populaire Syrien (PPS), and briefcases full of Lebanese pounds personally delivered in a gold De Soto attached to the American embassy. With military muscle at his disposal, Chamoun was able to bar the election of politicians cru-cial to the old order, such as Rashid Karami and Kamal Jumblatt. But not without a fight. Three days of violence erupted in which dozens were injured and the home of Sunni leader Sami Solh was reduced to rubble. One contingent of Muslims tried to smuggle bazooka shells into central Beirut in a coffin surrounded by wail-ing women. During the upheaval, Saeb Salam, the former prime minister, was beaten with truncheons by the police and thrown into jail for leading a demonstration. The next day he met the press in his dressing gown, his heavy, melancholy face swathed in bandages and stated, "The Lebanon's function is to be the Mid-East's window on the Western world. But it must remain a window, it must not be converted into a base." In all, over fifty people were killed in disturbances throughout the country. Even more of a sham of the democratic process than usual, the election produced a new Chamber of Deputies that represented only about 10 percent of the electorate. As soon as the election was over, Lebanon exploded with rumors that Chamoun would arrange for the new parliament to elect him to a second term as president, violating all the rules of office swapping that kept the establishment united.

The 1957 election was the first step in an escalating crisis that finally exploded in war in the spring of 1958. The causes of this, Lebanon's first civil war, were as multifaceted as everything else in Lebanon. There was the affront that establishment politicians such as Karami and Jumblatt suffered in the 1957 elections; the Muslims' ongoing demand for more political power in Lebanon; and the question of what role Lebanon should play in pan-Arab causes and particularly in the United Arab Republic.

It was the unification of Syria and Egypt into a federation called the United Arab Republic (UAR) in February 1958 that turned Lebanon's internal squabble into an international conflict. In uniting two Arab countries under one government, Nasser was hailed as having accomplished the first step in his drive to unite all Arabs. When he arrived in Damascus for the formal signing of the unification agreement, thousands of Lebanese sympathizers rushed to the city to see him and Sunni leader Saeb Salam proclaimed him leader of the Arabs. Some Lebanese—largely Sunni Muslims from the urban areas—agitated for Lebanon to join the newly formed UAR. The fiery debate over Lebanon's possible membership in the UAR was more a symptom of stress for the besieged Chamoun government than it was a realistic possibility.

Chamoun had taken office in 1952, the same year Nasser came to power in Egypt. By the middle of his six-year term, Chamoun's extreme pro-Westernism and the burgeoning Arab nationalism espoused by Nasser locked in battle. In 1956 Chamoun, unnerved by the Nasser phenomenon, dashed consensus politics and adopted a one-sided, pro-Western foreign policy. To the consternation of both the Muslims and the Lebanese nationalists, he refused to oppose the Baghdad Pact, a British-sponsored alliance formed to thwart Soviet moves along the USSR's southern flank. He refused to break off diplomatic relations with Britain and France in 1956, after the Europeans attacked Egypt along the Suez Canal to avenge Nasser's nationalization of the waterway. And in 1957, his greatest affront to Muslim sensitivities, Chamoun placed Lebanon under the Eisenhower Doctrine, the American pledge to defend friendly governments against outside threats. The doctrine, aimed specifically at Syria and Egypt, thrust Chamoun in opposition to his own Arab nationalists and also to some Christians, including the Maronite patriarch, who saw the move as dangerous to Lebanon's internal balance. The more Chamoun's Western resolve stiffened, the more the Muslims bitterly accused him of replacing France with the United States as the protector of the Christians.

Chamoun's opposition—including all the major figures defeated in the 1957 election—joined forces under the name of the National Front and called a general strike in May 1958. Having no effective access to constitutional opposition from within the parliament, the adversaries resorted to both innuendo and terrorism. The government retaliated, and nationwide violence ensued. Forged letters were published showing that Charles Malik, the Christian foreign minister, was corresponding with Israel's Abba Eban; pro-Chamoun forces accused the Egyptian ambassador of conspiring against Lebanon; and Syria claimed it had uncovered an American plot to overthrow the government with Turkish troops. In quick succession Najib al Matni, the left-leaning Maronite editor of *al Tiligraf*, was assassinated by men suspected of being government agents, and Tripoli rioted. Symbolic of the ugliness and violence was the attack on the border post of al Masna on the Beirut-Damascus highway by a band of two hundred armed men who crossed into Lebanon from Syria. The small army garrison was composed of five Christians and one Muslim. The commandos castrated and disemboweled the Christians and incorporated the Muslim into their ranks.

As violence escalated, Chamoun pleaded with the army commander, General Fuad Shihab, to intervene. Shihab refused, reasoning that to suppress the insurgents would be to thrust the army into an internal conflict whose aim was to keep a particular government in power. This would destroy the army's impartiality and probably its cohesion as Christians and Muslims within the ranks split to join one side or the other. Shihab's decision to keep the army neutral was probably the wisest choice any Lebanese government official has made since.

Except for Kamal Jumblatt's offensives that seized positions overlooking Beirut, attacked the presidential palace at Dayr al Qamar, and threatened the airport, the war was a process of holding actions and vitriolic radio broadcasts. The "Voice of Free Lebanon," the "Torch," and the "Voice of the Arabs" all furiously attacked Chamoun. His defense was delivered by the Phalange's "Voice of Lebanon" and the government's own national station. At one point, the battle of the airways shifted to ground action. The government radio station was seized by the National Front, which substituted Arabic music for a program of Western classical music. The station was soon recaptured. Immediately the Arabic records were smashed and in their place Beethoven's Fifth Symphony thundered over the airways in celebration.

The Lebanese probably would have been left alone to settle their own quarrels had revolution not struck in Iraq. Suddenly Lebanon, as it would increasingly in the future, was caught in the trap of the politics and national agendas of its larger, more powerful neighbors.

On July 14, 1958, Arab nationalists overthrew King Faisal, the pro-British monarch of Iraq and the key pillar in the Baghdad Pact. In a frenzy of hatred against a ruler whom the nationalists considered a Western lackey, Faisal and his family were killed and the king's body dragged through the streets of Baghdad. The next day two thousand U.S. Marines landed in Beirut, not to save the Chamoun government but as a show of power to convince the pro-Western governments of Pakistan, Turkey, and Iran that the United States would enforce the Eisenhower Doctrine.

Except for the fact that between two thousand and four thousand people were killed, the 1958 civil war in Lebanon, and the American invasion in particular, contained elements of absurd comedy. The U.S. Marines splashed ashore amid bathers and ice cream vendors, who moved off the beach just long enough to allow the leathernecks to pass. The following day, when American troops redeployed into downtown Beirut, they were preceded by three columns of Lebanese policemen on motorcycles and jeeps, followed by boys on streamer-decked bicycles and Lebanese civilians, honking the horns of their big American cars. All the while the premier, Saeb Salam, sat behind his sandbagged command post, which displayed a small, decorous sign "Appointments 9 to 1 and 4 to 7."

The fourteen thousand American troops stayed in Lebanon three-and-a-half months. In the process, they lost three men—one to sniper fire and two to drowning while swimming off Beirut's beaches. The operation had been swift, clean, and successful. But its very success instilled in American policymakers a naïveté concerning intervention in Lebanon's affairs that, in another civil war, would come to haunt them.

While the Americans were still in place as reassurance to the Christians, Camille Chamoun became convinced of the wisdom of resigning. Once he announced his decision, the major bone of contention dissolved and the civil war quickly wound down. Peace was accelerated because the military stalemate was disrupting the economy, a situation more intolerable to the *zuama* than political deadlock. As a result, both sides accepted decisions that restored the equilibrium. The Arab nationalists decided they were unwilling to sacrifice independent Lebanon for union with Egypt or any other Arab state. Chamoun and his supporters decided they did not want to become so tied to the Western alliance as to jeopardize Lebanon's trade links with the rest of the Arab world.

The civil war of 1958 has never been called a "war" by the Lebanese, who simply refer to it as "The Events." The 1958 event was one in which points were scored but nothing was resolved.

Chamoun had gone too far in both his personal ambitions and his pro-Western stance. In striving to be president again, he violated the spirit of the National Pact. In maneuvering the defeat of leaders such as Salam and Jumblatt, he desecrated the spirit of compromise under which Lebanon had survived.

The American intervention is often condemned for maintaining the status quo, for stepping into an internal revolution, and for thwarting the emergence of Muslim politics. A powerful case can be made that the American intervention was ill-advised because it identified the West with reactionary forces in the Middle East and implied that the United States was anti-Arab. But it is probably just as accurate to argue that the U.S. invasion gave the parties involved an excuse to reach accommodation over issues they were not yet ready to attack.

What saved Lebanon from disaster was that the sharp divisions in the body politic were not along sectarian lines. Although the war challenged the status quo, communal lines were fuzzy. It was a war of personalities among the *zuama*. All sides were fragmented, removing from the conflict its most insidious communal aspects and its clear challenge against Christian dominance. Internal divisions within the various confessionals prompted by competing *zuama* taking opposite sides kept violence at a minimum and hyperbole at a maximum.

Although the war was the most serious challenge to Lebanon's independent existence since its founding, it was more a squabble between grasping politicians and their disappointed rivals than it was a confrontation over great ideological causes or demands for revolutionary change. Its major result was that it made clear the parameters beyond which Lebanese leaders could not go without jeopardizing the country's independence. It revealed the extent to which real power rested in the hands of forces other than the government. And, to the consternation of the Maronites, it showed their vulnerability and how little they could depend on the support of the Western nations the Christians had chosen to protect them. As much as anything else, the war served to reveal lines of power and of loyalty usually buried beneath the benign hypocrisy of normal times. In the end, "The weak and hydra-headed party system, consisting of a dozen or more groupings of one or another religious group centered around a single strong leader, continued to operate according to a kind of political logic indigenous to Lebanon alone."

Fatefully, the events of 1958 mistakenly confirmed the illusion that the easygoing Lebanese were incapable of waging a serious civil war. Camille Chamoun's words seemed to speak of Lebanon as much in 1958 as they had when he uttered them three years earlier. "The great creeds and philosophies have lived together for 5,000 years without seeking to destroy each other—Phoenician and Greek philosophies, Persian and Assyrian divinities, Roman and Byzantine cultures, and finally the divine religions of Christianity and Islam."

By late fall, the levelheaded—and, in the opinion of all parties, neutral—General Fuad Shihab was installed as president. Christian hegemony was in place, and *la dolce vita* was once again in full swing. On the last warm afternoon before winter, a corpulent, hedonistic Christian, his hairy barrel chest protruding above low-slung swimming trunks, waddled down a chic beach strewn with shapely, bikini-clad women and made the final pronouncement on the events of 1958: "This is the Lebanon they want to destroy!"

But Lebanon was not yet ready for destruction. One remaining group had yet to take its place within the jumbled mosaic—the Palestinians.

SEVEN

OUTSIDERS, INSIDERS— THE PALESTINIANS

T he luminous yellows and pale purples of the spring wildflowers dotted the hills of Galilee, clustering between folds of sand-colored rock that bisected the hillocks like furrows in a field. The arching sky was cloudless, allowing the sun to cast its warmth into the very bottom of the smallest ravine. Yet the tranquillity of nature was counterposed against the turmoil of man in the spring of 1948.

On the dusty roads out of Galilean villages with names like Khirbet Jiddin, Deir al Qasi, Az Zib, and al Bassa, a steady stream of refugees trekked north toward Lebanon to escape the uncertainty and fear generated by the war for Palestine. Stout women in black dresses embroidered in traditional Palestinian designs balanced large bundles on their heads, supporting them with aching, outstretched arms. Behind, the fortunate among the men herded overburdened donkeys, but more often it was the men themselves who were bent over toting the weight of their families' possessions. The heavy quiet surrounding the scattered columns was broken only by the sound of gravel kicked up by an occasional car carrying the affluent onward, out of Palestine. Most of the rich already had gone by steamer from the port of Haifa to Beirut. But the poor

128

walked, driven from their villages and farms by the collapse of
their society and by the panic caused by the real and imagined
threats from the army of the new state of Israel.

The exodus continued through the parched summer of 1948.
By the end of that year, 130,000 Palestinians had flowed into
Lebanon. Those with capital and skills quickly made their way into
Lebanon's mercantile world or established themselves in the pro-
fessions. Armed with money and skills compatible with Lebanon's
expanding economy, they slid into the upper strata of society. But
the vast majority of the Palestinians—roughly 104,000—were uneducated products of the land. Generation after generation their
families had worked the fields and orchards of Palestine. They
knew nothing but farming. But now their land was gone, and with
their land went not only their livelihood but their identity.

Clinging to the hope that they could return home once peace
was restored, the farming class huddled in the south of Lebanon
near the Israeli border. Lebanese authorities, alarmed by the
concentration of refugees in the south, dispersed them to camps
around the country. In all, seventeen camps administered by the
United Nations Relief and Works Agency (UNRWA) were established across Lebanon from Tyre to Tripoli to Baalbek. The largest
was Ein al Hilweh, just outside Sidon.

Except for size, Ein al Hilweh was depressingly like the other
camps. People lived in anything that put a roof over their heads—
tents, Quonset huts abandoned by the military at the end of World
War II, packing cases, or simply corrugated tin supported by
scavenged cement building blocks. Often sick and almost always
poorly nourished, the refugees survived on basic rations handed
out by the United Nations, which they supplemented with comb-
ings from an adjacent garbage dump. Lebanese authorities ra-
tionalized the deplorable conditions as no worse than those in
refugee camps in Jordan, Syria, and Egypt. After all, they were
temporary. Soon the refugees would return home to Palestine. But
as time moved on, the Palestinians in the camps ceased being
temporary refugees and became permanent residents of Lebanon.

The Palestinians posed both a philosophical and a practical
problem for the Lebanese. From the beginning, the Palestinian
issue trapped Lebanon between its Western and Arab identities.
Although sympathetic to the plight of the Palestinians, the Chris-

tian Lebanese, largely the Maronites, felt less animosity toward the State of Israel than the Lebanese Muslims. In fact, Christian Lebanese saw Israel, a non-Muslim state in the heart of the Middle East, as a potential ally to a Christian-dominated Lebanon. But when the Lebanese Muslims looked at the State of Israel, they dredged up all the timeworn images of the Crusades.

Rational or not, much of the Arab enmity toward Israel arose from the fact that most of the early Jewish settlers and those who fought in the 1948 war were Westerners—Jews from eastern and western Europe. For the Muslims, the Western orientation of the Zionists and the considerable support they drew from Western nations cast the new state of Israel into an instrument of Western imperialism. Consequently, in the eyes of Lebanon's Muslims, Israel represented little more than a stalking horse for Western designs against the Arab world, yet another threat to Islamic and Arabic cultures. Just as the Crusaders came to conquer Islam, just as the Europeans imposed on the Ottomans a special status for the Christians of the Mountain, just as Western imperialism ravaged Arab nationalism after World War I, so did Israel, with Western help, establish itself on Arab soil. Israel was the new Crusader state.

With Israel challenging the duality of Lebanese identity, the Palestinian presence ripened into another deep, divisive issue between the Christians and Muslims. Since 90 percent of the Palestinians were Sunni Muslims, they offered Lebanon's Sunnis a potential ally in their struggle for political parity with the Christians. But all the Maronites saw in the Palestinians was the threat they posed to the confessional balance in Lebanon and the Maronites' tenuous hold on political supremacy.

Nevertheless, on the economic level the Christians and Muslims of the establishment, as they so often did when their common interests were at stake, united against the threat both saw the Palestinian refugees posing to Lebanon. The Palestinian influx of the late 1940s increased by one-twelfth a population long plagued by its own demographics. From the mid-nineteenth century onward, serious unemployment in Lebanon was held in check only by heavy emigration. For an economy already burdened with chronic unemployment, the addition of 120,000 Palestinians let loose from the camps to seek their way in the Lebanese economy smacked of disaster. Therefore, the *zuama* huddled and decided to impose stern limitations on the Palestinians. Unlike Jordan, which granted the Palestinians citizenship, or even Syria, which allowed them to serve in the army and hold government jobs, Lebanon classified the Palestinians as "nonnationals," a designation of banality guaranteed to isolate them in their refugee status. Most Palestinians held neither Lebanese citizenship nor a Lebanese passport. Instead, they were issued permits to reside in Lebanon, a right that could be canceled upon any type of exit from the country.

As "nonnationals," the Palestinians were barred from government employment, both civilian and military. Their children generally were blocked from entering the state school system, so that they were thrown back on the schools run by UNRWA or on scholarship assistance to the private schools. Palestinians were disqualified from state benefits, although many contributed to the system through deductions from their salary checks. Therefore, the fate of most Palestinians in Lebanon was that of unskilled and cheap labor, confined in refugee camps with no political voice.

Acutely aware of their hosts' sensitivity, the Palestinians outside the elite in Lebanese society shrank into their camps and neighborhoods, becoming a passive and desperate people living off international assistance. As humbled refugees, they provided ready targets for the Lebanese' cruel derision. A favorite epithet for the Palestinians was "monkeys," a brutal allusion to refugees reaching through the bars of the camps to pick up their food rations. Ein al Hilweh was even called "the zoo." Over time a Palestinian refugee learned his place. On the streets of Beirut, he instinctively pressed himself to the building walls of narrow side streets when the Cadillacs of Lebanese entrepreneurs and Arab oil sheikhs passed him by like so much rubbish. After they were gone he walked on disconsolately, head lowered and eyes averted from the allure of the shop windows catering to affluent Lebanese and Western tourists. With little income and few rights, the Palestinians were simply another minority living within the Lebanese mosaic, a people taught by hard experience to heel.

Gradually the Palestinians, who were as motivated and ambitious as the Lebanese, built their own society in the camps. Temporary shelters gave way to a jumble of dwellings crowded along narrow pathways. The one-room cinder-block houses financed by relief agencies were expanded with whatever materials their inhabitants could afford. Although unsightly, cramped, and bare, they did provide a semblance of permanence. Small shops selling vegetables, fruits, eggs, and live chickens sprang up along the pathways. Merchants operating in the front rooms of families' quarters offered a pitiful assortment of goods for sale. Butchers hung newly slain sheep carcasses outside their shops and piled the severed heads in wooden crates on the sidewalk. Metal crafters wielded their hammers before jury-rigged forges, relieving the camp of another of its dependencies on the outside economy. Schools opened to provide the legions of Palestinian children thronging the streets with a coveted education. Clinics, staffed by starched Palestinian nurses, checked the weight of babies and dispensed medicine. In the grayness, overcrowding, and deprivation, the camps were inordinately clean, a statement of the inhabitants' pride in being Palestinian.

By 1958, the Palestinians constituted one-tenth of the population of Lebanon. However, because they were politically quiescent, they played no part in the "events" of 1958. The 1958 war was a political upheaval among the Lebanese themselves over the nature of the Lebanese state. When Camille Chamoun stepped aside as president to end the crisis, the *zuama* elected as his successor Fuad Shihab, the commander of the Lebanese army. Shihab was perhaps the only choice, for it was his refusal to inject the army into the conflict that had prevented the disintegration of Lebanon. Shihab understood, as perhaps no man since has, the delicate nature of Lebanon's position between East and West. Only by addressing both Lebanon's Western exterior and its Arab soul could the country survive. With this philosophy, Shihab steered Lebanon out of the crisis and into the greatest stability the republic of Lebanon ever knew.

Fuad Shihab was born in the town of Jounieh in 1903, a beneficiary of some of the most important bloodlines in family-conscious Lebanon. His ancestors reached back to the most prestigious of all Arab tribes, the Quarayshi tribe of the prophet Muhammed. Shihab himself was a direct descendant of Bashir Shihab II, who during the early 1800s extended his rule over the whole of Mount Lebanon, the Bekaa Valley, the northern Akkar, southern Lebanon, and a sizable portion of Palestine. A Maronite by confession, Fuad Shihab nonetheless was influenced by the secularism that defined the rule of the great Bashir Shihab. He was one of the few true "neutrals" in Lebanon. At the time of his election, he possessed the aura of a savior-hero. To this he added his other assets—an authoritative personality and a base of power in the army. The result was a political figure who joined Riad Solh and Bishara Khoury in that exclusive triad of statesmen that Lebanon produced between 1943 and 1975.

Shihab based his administration on three principles unique to the Maronite presidency. First, he sought to strike a balance between Lebanon's Christian face and the Arab nationalism that at the time was burning its way across the Middle East. Second, he attempted to address the great disparities in wealth in Lebanon, understanding that only by pulling the lower-class Sunnis and the alienated Shiites into Lebanon's prosperity would the country avoid the destructiveness of wide economic divisions. Last, Fuad Shihab was committed to building the power of the president at the expense of the *zuama*. He recognized that Lebanon could endure only by becoming an authentic nation rather than continuing as a disjointed piece of territory that greedy tribal chieftains divided and redivided among themselves. Shihab had greater success with his first two goals than with his last.

Under Shihab, Lebanon managed to walk the fine line between the West and the Arab world. In this he was helped immeasurably by the relative lull in hostilities between Israel and its Arab neighbors and by the fact that the Arab governments were speaking for the Palestinians rather than the Palestinians speaking for themselves. Shihab conducted a slightly pro-Nasserite foreign policy but at the same time managed to convince anti-Nasser forces—the Western bloc, Israel, and the conservative Arab regimes of the Persian Gulf—that their interests in Lebanon were secure. Thus, Lebanon was able to trade with both the West and the East, handle money for both, and act as host for businesspeople and pleasure seekers from California to Kuwait.

With Lebanon temporarily removed from the Arab-Israeli struggle, Shihab turned to domestic problems. Despite the superficial prosperity of the 1950s, large areas of Lebanon remained poor. Much of the Akkar, the northern Bekaa, and the neglected south lacked modern roads, irrigation systems, electricity, educational facilities, and decent housing. These areas were victims of Lebanon's shallow and unbalanced economy.

Lebanon's free-market economy, low taxes, and apparent social progress obscured an economy with no real roots. Much of

Lebanon's productive capacity was destroyed in the late nineteenth century by the introduction of European-manufactured goods into the Levant. Its labor-intensive industries that produced textiles, rugs, and copperware were decimated when the cheap imported goods began to arrive from Europe. Soon the gossamer silks meticulously woven by Lebanese craftspeople were supplanted by machine-made cotton from the mills of Birmingham. Within a painfully short time, the Lebanese became subservient to Western economic might. Their economy survived by trading the goods of others rather than creating their own. It was a position from which they never recovered.

The economic expansion of the 1950s did little to stimulate manufacturing. In 1960 only 12 percent of Lebanon's gross national product (GNP) was produced by industry—all of it small. For a country reputed to have the Middle East's most capitalistic, aggressive economy, the output of the industrial sector was meager. A company that turned out $8 million of copper cable a year represented Lebanon's industrial strength. Only the two oil refineries at Sidon and Tripoli, which produced 14.5 million tons of fuel a year, could be considered major industries. From the standpoint of productive capacity, Lebanon's economy compared poorly even with Syria's.

With meager natural resources and almost no industry, Lebanon sustained itself on "invisible income." This revenue was derived from banking, transit trade, various forms of brokerage, remittances from the Lebanese emigrés scattered from Europe to the United States to Latin America, and a healthy slice of smuggling and drug dealing.

Despite the various identifiable sources of income, Lebanon's prosperity remained somewhat of an enigma. One Western economist called in by the Lebanese government to study the country's fiscal structure reported back to officials, "I can't understand it. But my advice to you, since things are going so well, is don't ask too many questions. . . ."

If too many questions had been asked, Lebanon would have been exposed as "a nation whose vaunted economy was in reality a 'jungle,' a case of 'Robber Baron capitalism.' " In a society with few social concerns and a laissez-faire economy operating with essentially no government controls, the rich got richer and the poor got poorer. By the time Shihab assumed office, the bidonvilles of

Beirut were proving fertile breeding grounds for various ideologies of the Nasserites, Baathists, and other left-wing groups in the Middle East. Although the rhetoric of these groups was their commitment to Arab nationalism, the other side of Arab nationalism was the leftist challenge to the existing economic order. And nowhere was that economic order more discriminatory than in Lebanon. To Lebanese leftists, Lebanon ranked slightly below Babylon in decadence. The leftists attacked the existing system because it served the interest of the elite and further widened the gap between the power of the Christians and the impotence of the Muslims. This is the issue Shihab sought to address in his economic reforms. Unfortunately, he lacked the temperament and the political power to defeat the *zuama*.

The tall, ramrod-straight Shihab was intelligent, methodical, circumspect, introverted, and possessed of integrity—all qualities that divided him from the flamboyance and power grabbing of the *zuama*. Shihab stayed largely to himself, running the country through a group of close advisers tagged "the *awlad*" (Arabic for "children") by political pundits. The *zuama*, who had run Lebanon since the arrival of the French, were quarantined, separated from the levers of power they could manipulate so destructively. Shihab made no secret of his intention to build the power of the presidency, to squeeze "*les fromagistes*" ("cheese eaters," as he scornfully called the *zuama*). *Al Nahj*, the way of Shihab, mobilized Shihab's control of the army, his social and economic reforms, his reputation of neutrality among confessionals, and his independent set of advisers to build the power of the presidency. His eyes, ears, and muscle, his opponents charged, was the Deuxième Bureau, the intelligence section of the Lebanese army that behaved like a cross between Scotland Yard and the CIA. But Shihab's failing was that the very qualities that separated him from the *zuama* also prevented him from building a grass-roots movement capable of sustaining his reforms. He had no charisma, no burning ideology, and he shunned the heavy use of patronage to buy supporters. In order to rule he was forced to fall back on a number of key leaders, such as Pierre Gemayel, Kamal Jumblatt, and Rashid Karami, to act as liaison between the president and the traditional power structure.

At the end of Shihab's term, the presidency as an institution was still subservient to Lebanon's tribal leaders. Although Shihab failed to topple the *zuama*, he had made the system strong enough to irritate them. Given another six-year term, perhaps he could have reformed it. But to run for president again required repealing Lebanon's one-term rule, a move that threatened a replay of 1958. Consequently, as the 1964 presidential election approached, the *zuama* clustered like vultures to pick the bones of "Shihabism." The *zuama*, some of whom so despised each other that they hardly spoke, gathered to defeat either Shihab or his chosen successor, Elias Sarkis. Camille Chamoun, Saeb Salam, and Raymond Edde were the spearheads of the anti-Shihab movement. Suleiman Franjieh was with them. Even the Maronite patriarch Meochi had turned against Shihab because the president consistently chose to ignore his temporal advice. Of the most powerful *zuama*, only Kamal Jumblatt, Pierre Gemayel, and Rashid Karami stood with Shihab. But because Jumblatt and Gemayel were so alienated from each other that they could not even discuss strategy, their bloc disintegrated.

The failure of Shihab's ambitious economic and political reforms was less important in the long run to the survival of Lebanon than was his failure to solve the Lebanese' fundamental dilemma over their identity. Shihab labored in vain to redirect the conservatives among the Maronites and other Christians who continued to view Lebanon as a Christian nation closely linked to the West. The best he could do was coax moderate Christians to the point where they could accept Lebanon's Christian character as implicit rather than explicit. But on the basis of Lebanon's identity with the West, they stood with the conservatives.

And so Fuad Shihab left office, and with him went the aloof but enlightened rule of Lebanon.

In 1964 Charles Helou, publisher, diplomat, cabinet minister, and retired politician, became president of Lebanon. Helou was the perfect compromise candidate for the *zuama*. He had neither supported nor opposed Camille Chamoun in 1958, choosing instead to join the neutral "Third Force." He shared Shihab's concern for socioeconomic reforms and enjoyed a close rapport with the former president. But best of all for the predatory *zuama*, he had retired from politics in 1960.

Helou in Arabic means "sweet." Thus, Helou's election was hailed as the dawning of the "sweet era." And sweet it was. The period from 1964 to 1967 was perhaps the pinnacle of the Golden Age, the time when all the illusions about Lebanon were still intact.

When Helou took office, Beirut was reaping $3 billion a year in revenues from the Persian Gulf's oil sheikhs. From Kuwait, Bahrain, Qatar, and Saudi Arabia, the royal and merchant princes flocked to Beirut to deposit their ever growing wealth with the banks and real estate developers and to play among a people who both spoke their language and understood their needs. Escaping the conservatism of their own societies, they drank at the fountain of libertine Beirut.

And Beirut gushed forth as only Beirut could. For tastes dulled by mutton and rice, the restaurants airfreighted in French oysters, Scotch salmon, Danish ham, and English beef. For men whose behavior had been arrested at adolescence by the rigidity of their society, hotels and shops stocked their shelves with the world's most expensive liquors. The Casino du Liban provided delectable show girls, and the Bourg Central Square supplied prostitutes. And merchants dangled before their eyes a dazzling array of tacky merchandise, all instantly available for a price. The Gulf Arabs just released from poverty and cultural confinement had no idea of what was "good" and what was "bad"—it was the Lebanese' job to make sure they never discovered the difference.

Beirut possessed a titillating element of ribald wickedness. It was a brash, flashy embodiment of commercial success pulled off by a Levantine assortment of Christian, Palestinian, Armenian, and Druze entrepreneurs. High-rise buildings financed with oil money sprang up everywhere. The streets were so congested with traffic that a proposal was made to ban cars with odd-numbered license plates from the streets on odd-numbered days and cars with even-numbered license plates on even-numbered days. Even Lebanon's sectarian problems were treated with panache. Ziad Rahbani's gifted sketches and musical comedies portrayed the deepening pathologies of Lebanon's pluralism to audiences more interested in pleasure than anxiety.

But the panache served to mask Lebanon's weak infrastructure and divert attention from its mounting social and economic inequities. Public services were appalling for a country sporting the pretensions of Lebanon. Even moderate rainstorms routinely knocked out power and telephone lines. Roads outside of the major routes leading to Beirut were narrow and broken. Public education was hopelessly inferior, forcing parents either to endure deprivation in order to scrape up school fees or to condemn their children to a poor public education in a highly literate and competitive society.

The inequities Shihab had sought to address escalated. Rapid but uneven economic growth challenged the already precarious republic. The level of Sunni participation in the political and economic life of Lebanon belied their numbers. The small farmer grew increasingly impoverished as Lebanon's economy shifted more and more toward trade and services. The move away from agriculture hit the Shiite population of the south the hardest. By the late 1960s, 56 percent of the farmers in southern Lebanon were forced into second jobs, usually as laborers. Those unable to find employment in Jabal Amil left the land and migrated to Beirut. There they settled in squalor and misery alongside the Palestinians and Lebanon's other immigrant communities.

Economic issues followed religious lines. Christian predominance over Muslims in commerce, trade, industry, and services was approaching a margin of five to one. Except for the leading *zuama*, the Sunnis sought a redress of their grievances in pan-Arabism and reform of the political equation created by the National Pact. In the name of the Druze, Kamal Jumblatt fought for a realignment of Lebanon's political system and an upending of its laissez-faire economy. And the Shiites sank further into ignominy. Those who defended the Lebanese myth called to mind what Thomas Paine said of Edmund Burke: "He pities the plumage, but forgets the dying bird."

Just as Lebanon's superficial prosperity masked deep-seated inequities in the economic system, the artificial harmony of the religious communities disguised profound communal divisions. The pretensions of the Lebanese, who thought of themselves as Occidentals and regarded their country as another Switzerland, were fast approaching the point at which both of these myths would collapse. Cultural identity and economic disparities among the Lebanese were splitting the country apart at the very time the West was celebrating Lebanon's glory as the prototype of intellectual freedom and economic well-being, the fruition of communal harmony. But at the peak of the Golden Age, Lebanon's culture was as Levantine as ever and its political system more riddled by tribalism than ever before. It was a tribute to the negotiating skills of the *zuama* who kept it all together.

Left alone, Lebanon might or might not have survived. There are two diametrically opposed views on why Lebanon destroyed itself. One school of thought argues that Lebanon's problems were internal, that Lebanon caved in on itself. According to sociologist

Halim Barakat, "[T]he current civil war in Lebanon is a culmination of a confrontation that has been building up between the forces of change and the forces of maintaining the established order against all odds and quite often in opposition to the professed principles of society and government."

Still, Lebanon, as part of the Levant, did not live in isolation as either succeeding or failing in charting its own destiny. The other side of the debate about the cause of the civil war is that Lebanon was the victim of outside forces. According to this argument, Lebanon would have survived one way or another had it not been trapped in the violence of the region.

Halfway through that apparently idyllic presidency of Charles Helou the most momentous event in the Levant since 1948 occurred—the Six Day War.

At 7:30 A.M. on June 5, 1967, Israeli Mystère and Mirage jets streaked westward out to sea, then wheeled back eastward to skim below radar range. In wave after wave, they bombed airfields in Egypt, Syria, and Jordan, wiping out the air forces of their enemies on the ground. Without air cover, the Arab armies fell before the Israeli ground advance toward the Jordan River, into Syria, and the desert of the Sinai. By 4:30 P.M. on June 10, the 100,000 Egyptian, Jordanian, and Syrian troops had surrendered and Israel held the Sinai Peninsula, the west bank of the Jordan River, the Golan Heights, and the city of Jerusalem. When bulldozers cleared the jumble of homes and shops surrounding the Wailing Wall, the remaining wall of Solomon's temple and the point to which Jews of the Diaspora had prayed for nearly two thousand years, the victory was complete. Gamal Abdel Nasser's blockade of Sharm al Sheikh, Israel's gateway to the Red Sea, and his vow to destroy Israel utterly had both failed. In the euphoria of the moment, the Israelis believed they had destroyed Nasser, pan-Arabism, and the Palestinian issue in six glorious days of combat. Nasser never recovered from the defeat, but for the Palestinians it was only the beginning. The Six Day War ignited the fire of Palestinian nationalism and let loose the passions of 150,000 Palestinians crammed into the camps of Lebanon.

Rashid Karami was prime minister of Lebanon at the time of the Six Day War. He ordered Lebanon's army into battle against Israel, but the army, under the command of the Christians, refused. This confrontation between the Sunni prime minister and the Christian-led army was short because the war was so short. A spate of anti-Western demonstrations was the sum of the war's immediate repercussions in Lebanon. Installations of Shell Oil and Mobil near the port of Beirut were destroyed. Scattered Western embassies were attacked, prompting evacuation of AUB's Western faculty. Random mobs torched some of the Lebanese' much loved American cars and ripped down billboards advertising Coca-Cola, Kodak, and Austin Motors. But it ended quickly, which lulled Lebanon into believing it could continue to walk the fine line between Israel and the Arabs.

In the aftermath of the Six Day War, the Lebanese steadfastly held to the illusion that no matter what unfolded on their borders they would not only survive but prosper by trading on both their Western and Arab sides. All Lebanon needed to do was stay aloof. As one shopkeeper said, "Since 1943, we have followed a policy of letting the big powers protect us. Why not in the future as well?"

Between 1948 and 1967, the Palestinians scattered around the borders of Israel had been represented by a combination of the old leadership establishment from Palestine and the countries of the Arab League. Neither truly spoke for the bulk of the Palestinians. The old *mukhtars*, or elders, were not from the refugee camps. They lived in the towns and cities, where they ran their businesses or worked at their white-collar jobs. They came to the camps only to cultivate their followers. Although they were important in the early years following 1948, the longer exile continued and the more permanent the camps became as fixtures of Palestinian life, the less influence they wielded. The same was true for the Arab states that laid claim to the Palestinian cause. In the early years the Palestinians, disorganized and disoriented, looked to the Arab countries to uphold their rights and redress the injustice of their exile. In the glory days of Gamal Abdel Nasser, the airways of the Middle East resounded with Nasser's call for the destruction of Israel and the return of the Palestinians. On their cheap radios in the camps and on the shortwaves of the Palestinians working in the Gulf, they listened in rapture to Nasser railing against Israel. But in the end, Nasser failed to deliver anything to the Palestinians. After 1967, the Palestinians took charge of their own affairs.

It was late afternoon. The buildings along Corniche Mazraa absorbed, then radiated the setting sun, painting the drab stucco shades of rose and orange. Inside one of the buildings, a five-foot, four-inch-tall, pear-shaped man dressed in baggy military fatigues, a black and white *kaffiyeh* with its corners turned up to expose the stubble on his cheeks, and unpolished boots trudged up yet another flight of stairs. At the top, he turned and moved down the hall. Identifying the office of one of Beirut's newspapers, he entered and handed an editor a press release from the Palestine Liberation Organization (PLO) titled "Military Communique No. 1." The year was 1965, and the man was Abdul Rahman Arafat al Qudwa, or Yassir Arafat.

At its summit conference in Cairo in 1964, the Arab League gave birth to the Palestine Liberation Organization. Because League members were tormented by the fear of a large Palestinian presence in their own countries, the organization was by design a sterile symbol of Arab support for the Palestinian cause. Discouraged by its ineffectiveness, various activists within the Palestinian movement drifted even before the 1967 war. They coalesced around a leader or an ideology, or both. The two most important of these renegade groups were Yassir Arafat's Fatah and George Habash's Popular Front for the Liberation of Palestine (PFLP).

Fatah was organized on an isolated beach in Kuwait in 1957 by a cadre of Palestinians, including Arafat, who were employed in the Gulf at the time. From the beginning, Fatah claimed no ideology other than the return of the Palestinian people to their ancestral land of Palestine. The PFLP, on the other hand, began as a nationalist organization but by the 1967 war had incorporated Marxist ideology as an essential element in its platform. This ideology allowed the PFLP to establish ties with some of Lebanon's more extreme leftist groups.

When the 1967 war destroyed Gamal Abdel Nasser and every other Arab leader purporting to speak for the Palestinians, Fatah, the PFLP, and other splinter groups were there to fill the vacuum. What these groups did was establish an identity and a strong nationalistic sentiment for the Palestinians that was distinct from the pan-Arabism of the Nasser era. Yassir Arafat spoke to the Palestinians' new philosophy when he said,

We waited and waited for the justice of the U.N., for the justice of the world and the governments of the world gathering in the U.N. while our people were suffering in tents and caves. But nothing of this was realized. None of our hopes. But our dispersion was aggravated. We believe that the only way to return to our homes and land is the armed struggle.

Even before the 1967 war, arms made their way into the Palestinian camps in Lebanon, allowing nascent guerrilla groups to stage pinprick raids across the border into Israel. After 1967 the guerrilla movement burgeoned, fed by thousands of young Palestinians in the camps with neither jobs nor hope. The commando with his gun and his zeal now symbolized the Palestinians of Lebanon.

While no more than half the Palestinians in Lebanon lived in camps, after 1967 their strength and leadership came from Ein al Hilweh, Nabatieh, Shatila, and the other camps. The fedayeen, or commandos, were from a major segment of the Palestinian population rather than from the population as a whole. The road across the Lebanese-Israeli border beckoned to the Palestinian guerrilla army. From their camps and enclaves in Lebanon, they struck against Israel. And Israel responded tit for tat, carrying every commando raid back into Lebanon.

On December 28, 1968, Israeli commandos landed at the Beirut airport and systematically blew up thirteen planes belonging to Middle East Airlines (MEA). Israel had delivered its ultimatum: If Palestinian incursions into Israel continued, Lebanon would pay. Israel was holding the country with the least cohesion and the least ability to deal with the Palestinians responsible for their behavior. Suddenly Lebanon was thrust beyond the Lebanese' own squabbles into the throes of the Palestinian-Israeli death struggle. The sweet era of Charles Helou had ended.

The flaw in Israel's policy of retaliation was Lebanon's inability to control the Palestinians. Lebanon was a country in that it possessed defined borders, but it was not a state capable of exercising a national will or controlling either police or military power. The Palestinians had succeeded in grabbing power in Lebanon precisely because the Lebanese state was so weak and fragmented. The Palestinians had built a separate world within Lebanon's own domestic anarchy. Despite repeated Israeli reprisals against Lebanon, armed commandos continued to roam southern Lebanon's roads at will. The camps still functioned as autonomous territories that government authorities dared not penetrate. All the Israeli reprisals against Lebanon did was to drive yet another wedge between the Maronites and those Lebanese possessing an Arab identity.

The Maronites reacted against the Palestinians with increasing consternation and anger, blaming them for recklessly drawing Israel's bloody reprisals into Lebanon. Behind the immediacy of the military situation was the fear that the Palestinians were undermining the political balance of the National Pact and Lebanon's Western facade. The Sunnis openly embraced the Palestinians, most of whom were themselves Sunnis, to strengthen their stance against the Christians.

But there was yet another point of view about the Palestinians, held mainly by their "fellow deprived," the poorer Sunni and Shiite Muslims, and by the Druze and some Christian intellectuals who shared the revolutionary aspirations of the Palestinian movement. Out of these groups rose some hope that the Palestinians, radicalized by their dispossession from both Palestine and Lebanese society, would stoke the process of change in Lebanon to eradicate the massive social inequalities and corrupt practices of the political elite.

And so emerged a symbiosis between the Palestinians and segments of the Lebanese political spectrum, particularly nonestablishment Sunnis. To attack one was to attack the other. Following the Lebanese practice of seeing things only as they wish them to be, the Sunnis failed to recognize that the Palestinians had an agenda of their own. Neither the redistribution of political power in Lebanon nor the ideologies of the leftists could compete with the Palestinians' passion to return to Palestine.

The Palestinians were both victims and villains in Lebanon. Cast out of the society and deprived of a political voice and of economic opportunity, the Palestinians, particularly those of the camps and lower socioeconomic groups, epitomized the downtrodden. But the Palestinians could be as arrogant and contemptuous of Lebanon and the Lebanese as the Lebanese were of them.

By 1969, Palestinian commandos swaggered through the streets, brandishing guns and defying the authorities to stop them. Palestinian neighborhoods often refused to pay for electricity, telephone service, garbage pickup, and other public services. Street toughs accosted university students receiving U.S. AID funds on the day their stipends arrived and forced them to donate twenty-five Lebanese pounds to the Palestinian cause. In southern Lebanon, where their numbers were greatest, the Palestinians collected protection money from the poverty-ridden Shiites and defied village elders who opposed their presence around their

villages. Although many Palestinians who felt they owed Lebanon
a debt of gratitude for the refuge it had provided them led lives as
model citizens, others were willing to sacrifice Lebanon in the
interests of an elusive Palestine. To these, Lebanon was a corrupt
society incapable of acting like a nation even in its own defense.

The excruciating dilemma the Palestinians presented for the
Lebanese government continued to mount. To send in the army to
quell the Palestinians would risk splitting the nation along its
communal and economic divides. Yet to do nothing challenged
Lebanon's very sovereignty. In 1960, Fuad Shihab had prophetically said of Lebanon and the Palestinian problem, "How tragic it
is, either we crush them and we will be the oppressors or we
remain inactive and we will be the oppressed."

April always seems a harbinger of violence in Lebanon. In
April 1969, Lebanese authorities finally agreed to act to establish
some control over the Palestinians. But all the army's actions
accomplished was to trigger a wave of procommando sentiment
across Lebanon. Left-wing political parties joined students and
Palestinians from the camps in violent demonstrations against an
already enfeebled Lebanese government. In the Burj al Barajneh
camp alone, fifteen people were killed and one hundred injured in
the rioting. Amid the melee, an aged Palestinian leaned against his
heavy, homemade bomb and wearily declared, "I have the will to
use it but not the strength."

The Palestinian issue was striking all of the chords in the
Lebanese' own disunity. The Maronites wanted to crush the resistance movement but were fragmented into various camps headed
by jealous *zuama*. The Sunni establishment was torn between its
Arab and Lebanese nationalism. Of the major *zuama*, only Kamal
Jumblatt was decisive. For Jumblatt, the Palestinian resistance
represented a rising force from the left, and for that reason he gave
it his full support.

Not only were Lebanon's political leaders burdened with the
country's own endemic disunity; they had to face the reality that
the Palestinians were drawing the ominous shadow of Lebanon's
neighbors into the arena. The Israelis were already there. Now
Syria stepped up its presence. The Syrians, long covetous of a
commanding role in Lebanon, funneled supplies to the Palestinians
along the "Arafat trail" running between Syria and southern
Lebanon. In addition, they financed and supported Saiqa, a faction
of the PLO subservient to Syria. Lebanon was under attack.

In October 1969 General Emile Bustani, commander of the Lebanese army, launched an operation aimed at cutting Syria's supply line to the PLO and establishing some semblance of control over the south. Within days Lebanon was on the threshold of war with Syria, factions of the PLO, and elements of its own population. A frightened and powerless Lebanese government ran for the only escape hatch—the Cairo Agreement of November 1969. Brokered by Gamal Abdel Nasser, this pact set the terms for the PLO's coexistence with the Lebanese government and, in so doing, marked the point of no return for Lebanese sovereignty. Under the agreement's provisions, the PLO was consecrated as a state within a state in Lebanon. It won the right to govern its own camps, establish training bases in the south adjacent to the Israel-Syria borders, and command free access to Syrian supply lines. The agreement in effect ceded Lebanese sovereignty over a twenty-seven-square-mile area in southern Lebanon to the PLO, an area that became known as "Fatahland."

Lebanese politicians on both sides of the communal divide acquiesced to the Cairo Agreement first because there was no other choice. But second, the Maronites understood that any further challenge to the Palestinians threatened to destroy the climate of accommodation established by the National Pact. The Palestinians, as the Lebanese Muslims' most visible symbol of Arabism, had succeeded in symbolically throwing down the gauntlet to Israel and by inference to the West. The Maronites were still flexible enough to recognize the risk of challenging that symbolism, especially at a time when all of the Arabic-language newspapers were carrying the famous photograph of president Richard Nixon bowing to Israeli Prime Minister Golda Meir. And so within the ramparts of the Crusaders' castle of Beaufort, the PLO installed its rocket launchers aimed at Israel.

Although at Cairo the PLO had pledged to respect Lebanese dominion over areas outside Palestinian jurisdiction, the promise was short-lived. Commandos flaunted their presence from Fatahland to Beirut and from Tripoli to the Bekaa. Manning illegal roadblocks, they arrogantly stopped Lebanese to inspect their identity cards. They searched homes suspected of harboring their special enemies. At gunpoint, they collected money for the Palestinian cause. The Lebanese were fast becoming captives in their own country.

While other Lebanese complained, the Phalange, the paramilitary political organization founded by Pierre Gemayel in 1936, began to prepare for the defense of Lebanon. The Phalange was as denigrated by the Maronite establishment in the late 1960s as it had been before Lebanese independence. Its membership was still largely lower middle class, with roots sunk in the Maronite orthodoxy of the Mountain. To the establishment, Gemayel and his militia were Lebanese "rednecks."

The Phalange ignored the sneers and moved ahead with its strategy of recruitment and armament. Rapidly the Mountain underwent a transformation. With arms flowing in through the port of Beirut and by way of the Jounieh Yacht Club, military training camps sprouted up on the peaks and in the valleys of the Mountain. Under the shadow of mountain pines, uniformed men smartly stepped in unison and military jeeps sped up and down the twisting roads through Maronite villages, where graffiti smeared across the rock and stucco of buildings declared, "Each Lebanese must kill a Palestinian."

> While some [Phalange] party ideologues continued to plan the reforms deemed vital for the preservation of the Lebanese political system, others were planning in great detail the defense of fortress Lebanon—that part of Mount Lebanon and the coastal plain in which the Lebanese Christian entity could be upheld.

The tumult of 1969 merged into the tumult of 1970, one of the watershed years for Lebanon. Continuing Israeli reprisals joined by Syrian responses further challenged the sovereignty of the Lebanese government; King Hussein's war against the PLO in Jordan reverberated into Lebanon; and the Lebanese faced another presidential election.

The year began with the kidnapping of the night watchman for the Israeli border town of Metullah by the PLO. Israeli forces retaliated by crossing the border into southern Lebanon. They stayed for thirty-four hours. During that time, demolition squads leveled a number of houses in the village of Hebbariyih as punishment for allowing Palestinians to operate from the area. When the Israelis withdrew, young Israeli soldiers proudly posed atop their tank, jeering at an elaborately framed picture of Lebanese president Charles Helou adorned in full state dress.

Helou's office trappings belied his authority. As the Israelis pulled back across the border, 650 members of Saiqa, the Syrian-sponsored faction of the PLO, encamped on Mount Hermon. Helou could do little but appeal to Syria to refrain from involving Lebanon in a war it was unable to wage. Pressed to do something to demonstrate Lebanon's waning power, the parliament upped the authorized strength of the army from fifteen thousand to twenty-five thousand. It was all symbolic. The entire Lebanese army numbered only eleven thousand men, four-thousand below its existing authorized strength. Without a draft, something no Lebanese government could either adopt or enforce, there was no hope of raising the mandated level to twenty-five thousand men. Interior Minister Kamal Jumblatt dolefully admitted, "There simply are no volunteers these days."

The only leverage the Lebanese government had against the internal and external dynamics of the Palestinian situation was the fact that the Palestinians' main political seat was in Jordan. But in the fall of 1970, the Palestinians lost their Jordanian base.

The Palestinians, nearly one-half of the population, were a more potent force in Jordan at the time than they were in Lebanon. They had long ruled their camps, forbidding Jordanian government officials to step beyond the heavy wire gates. Between commando raids against Israel, the PLO plotted the overthrow of the Hashemite king, Hussein. Powerless to rein in the PLO without committing his country to civil war, Hussein struggled to preserve his throne. Finally, on September 16, 1970, he attacked.

For nine days, the world watched as the descendants of the Bedouin army who followed Hussein's grandfather from Saudi Arabia to Jordan leveled Palestinian camps and whole sections of Amman controlled by PLO guerrillas. Dust rose from the hills as tanks ferreted out and destroyed nests of commandos. In the end, Hussein won. The PLO was dislodged, and another wave of Palestinian refugees trekked to Lebanon.

Lebanese Sunnis mobilized their political power to allow the Palestinians retreating from Jordan to settle in Lebanon. Just as the Maronites reached out to the West to strengthen their power vis-à-vis the Muslims, so did the Sunnis grasp the Palestinians to add to Muslim ranks in the old game of political demography. And so the Palestinian presence swelled and with it Lebanon's fragility. By the end of 1970, Lebanon had replaced Jordan as the base from which the Palestinians pursued their political and military agendas.

The civil war in Jordan had barely subsided when Lebanon

elected a new president. On the day of the election Suleiman Franjieh, the godfather of Zghorta, arrived at the Chamber of Deputies accompanied by four thousand Zghortan militiamen. They stood outside while Franjieh battled the Shihabist candidate, Elias Sarkis, to a third ballot, which Franjieh won by one vote. But when Sabri Hamadeh, the speaker, announced that Franjieh's fifty votes out of a possible ninety-nine did not constitute a majority, mayhem broke out. Franjieh charged down the aisle, crying foul. Fistfights erupted, broken up by deputies who had whipped their ever-ready guns from their desk drawers. Outside, the Zghorta militia as well as private militiamen hired by several political chieftains nervously waited for orders to wade in. At last, Hamadeh backed down and reversed himself. Suleiman Franjieh was the new president of Lebanon. His celebrating supporters careened through the streets, wildly firing rifles and pistols into the air with reckless abandon.

The day after the election, the new president received the press. His demeanor reflected none of the disorder his ascension to the presidency had caused or the problems that he faced now that he was in office. Wearing a slightly askew ascot, he reclined aristocratically in a comfortable chair, moving an extraordinarily large string of worry beads one at a time through his thumb and forefinger. The assembled press—and much of Lebanon—knew that Franjieh had won only because of a standoff between two former presidents, Camille Chamoun and Fuad Shihab. Of the three, Franjieh was the least equipped intellectually and temperamentally to be president. Sadly, he would not succeed, for during his term the war broke out.

Franjieh's major problem was the same as Helou's in the last year of his presidency—the growing power of the Palestinians and the moves of both the Maronites and the Israelis to contain that power. The Israel-Lebanon border was fifty miles long. By 1970, when Suleiman Franjieh took office, shelling of one or the other side of the border was part of the normal flow of life. Fear that Israel would annex Lebanon south from the Litani River in retaliation for the Palestinian commando raids grew. The Christian-led Lebanese army began to crack down on Palestinian activity despite Muslim resistance. But with the army divided along communal lines, it accomplished little.

The Phalange, equipped and trained in its mountain strongholds, entered the void. In March 1970 Bashir Gemayel, son of Pierre and a rising star in the Phalange, attacked a group of Palestinian commandos leading a funeral procession past the mountain village of Khale. Ten commandos were killed, setting off violent clashes between the reluctant army and Palestinian guerrillas near the Beirut airport.

On March 25, the PLO retaliated by kidnapping Bashir Gemayel. Hundreds of Phalange militiamen rushed from their headquarters and laid siege to Palestinian refugee camps. Eight hours later Kamal Jumblatt, through the intercession of Yassir Arafat, secured Gemayel's release. Calm returned.

In 1972, the cruise ships still stopped at Beirut and the passengers still poured into the *souqs* and boutiques, still drank at the great fountain of pleasure. But Beirut, like the rest of Lebanon, increasingly was heading toward anarchy. Lebanon's endemic political, economic, and social problems whirled around the concurrent issues of Arab nationalism and the Palestinian movement. Lebanese Muslims who sought reform within the Lebanese state and Lebanese leftists demanding radical reform and trumpeting Arab nationalism linked up with the Palestinians, beneficiaries of subsidies and arms sent to them from countries such as Iraq, Libya, and Syria.

From this spectrum of opposition groups emerged a broad coalition that rattled the cage of Lebanon's old, established order and laissez-faire capitalism. As a result, in 1972 Lebanon was racked by another cycle of chaos. The period was marked by an endless succession of student strikes involving approximately two-thirds of the university students in Lebanon.

AUB, as the most Western symbol in Beirut, was a focal point of much of this unrest. In January a bomb exploded in Nicely Hall, a protest against the university's policy of granting more holidays for Christmas than for the Muslim Eid al Fitr at the end of Ramadan. On the eve of the third anniversary of the 1967 war, a stone bench outside the home of AUB's president was destroyed by another bomb. An American student, a young woman who had imprudently discussed a trip to Israel, was seized one evening and then released after the word "Jew" was carved into her body with a knife.

But disorder was not limited to AUB. Throughout 1972, random violence punctuated life in Beirut. The Gemayel family pharmacy was blown up. The Strand Apartments off Rue Hamra, where Fatah leaders kept rooms, was dynamited. Several horses from a stable near the Bir Hasan settlement were killed by stray bullets when they were freed so that their stalls could be used for protection in a fire fight between the Phalange and the commandos. Fearing its aircraft would become the target of reprisals by one group or another, Middle East Airlines flew its planes to Cyprus for safekeeping. The disorder once again highlighted the government's impotence.

During March, as the almond blossoms released their scent across the landscape, Israel again invaded southern Lebanon. The incursion sent waves of Lebanese, mostly Shiites, fleeing toward Beirut. Once again the army and the government appeared a mockery. Ignoring their dispossession, the state offered the refugees neither protection from the Israelis nor food and shelter as they crushed into the slums of south Beirut. All the refugees got was a pledge from Suleiman Franjieh that he would be tough on the Palestinians. But on the same day the president spoke, a photograph appeared in *L'Orient–Le Jour* showing two uniformed commandos with machine guns slung over their shoulders, lounging against a fence at a football game, idly watching the Lebanese police try to stop the audience's assault on members of a rival soccer team. Amid the chaos, all Suleiman Franjieh could do was hold worried meetings in his Baabda palace residence and issue statements to the public. "Instead of wasting our energies in shouting and unproductive chanting, why don't we give blood generously to the Red Cross so we may care for our casualties?"

That blood would be needed. On May 29, the Popular Front for the Liberation of Palestine and a Japanese terrorist group, the Red Brigade, struck the crowded customs hall at Tel Aviv's Lydda airport. Prime Minister Golda Meir immediately blamed Lebanon for the twenty-six people killed, citing Palestinian training camps in Lebanon. Israel retaliated with a devastating four-day air, land, and sea operation against southern Lebanon. The Israelis succeeded in killing an estimated fifty Palestinian commandos, but they also killed one hundred Lebanese civilians.

In September, when nine Israeli Olympic athletes and a trainer were massacred in Munich by the Palestinian group Black September, Lebanon again paid the price. The death toll in that round of Israeli retaliation was over four hundred.

In the face of brutal attacks against Lebanon's citizenry, the *zuama* played out their petty rivalries and old vendettas. By the end of 1972, the State of Lebanon was in reality only an effete image of a nation, quibbling within itself as Lebanese and foreigners sucked out its very life.

The Maronites still believed that even though they were threatened by the rising Muslim population, their security would be protected by their long-time ties with the West. That illusion was about to receive its final jolt. In October 1973, the Arabs unleashed their ultimate weapon against the West—the oil embargo.

In the two wars the Arabs fought against Israel after 1948, the confrontation states of Egypt, Jordan, and Syria pleaded with the Arab states of the Persian Gulf to declare economic war on Israel's Western supporters by withholding the oil that fueled their industries and powered their cars. Conservative in religion and in politics, the rulers of the oil sheikhdoms, who abhorred Nasserism with its pan-Arabism, socialism, and strong ties to the Soviet bloc, refused. But now Nasser was dead. In his place was the pragmatic Anwar Sadat, who in 1973 envisioned war as a tool for restoring Arab honor, paving the way for accommodation between Egypt and Israel. Before moving his troops into the Sinai, Sadat met with the acerbic, hawk-faced Faisal al Saud, king of Saudi Arabia. Once again he pleaded for an oil embargo. With the world facing an oil shortage and the Arab oil producers bent on obtaining higher crude prices, economics and politics merged. Faisal agreed, and the blockade was on. Overnight the conservative Arab regimes surrounding the Persian Gulf brought the Western world crawling on its knees. In 1973, the last year to reflect the old price levels, the combined income from petroleum sales for Saudi Arabia, Iraq, Kuwait, and the Gulf sheikhdoms was $13.7 billion. In 1974, it was $50.15 billion and escalating wildly.

With the oil boom, the bikini-clad bathers at the St. Georges and Phoenicia hotel swimming pools were joined by rotund Arab women from the Gulf countries, cloaked in black, who sat in the shade and peered out from behind heavy, dark veils. The Muslim Lebanese who waited the poolside tables, picked up towels, and cleaned the dressing rooms silently beheld the shift in wealth from the West to the Arabs. For them, the oil boom had done more than bestow outrageous wealth on their Arab brothers. Money translated into prestige, and prestige into power. In this sense, the oil boom affirmed the worth of Islamic society. To many of Lebanon's Muslims, it signaled the beginning of the Arab renaissance. A quarter-century after the loss of Palestine, the Arabs had regained their pride.

The Lebanese, for centuries brokers and middlemen, shuttled Arab money to the West and Western technology to the Gulf. Capital poured into Beirut's banks, and the Lebanese streamed into the Gulf as entrepreneurs, managers, and workers. Their high salaries returned to Lebanon to support their families and to seek investment in Lebanon's freakish economy. For once it was the Muslims, not the Christians, who were the major benefactors of the economic bonanza. Muslim rather than Christian businessmen won the bulk of the Lebanese contracts that would catapult the Gulf states from the eighteenth to the twentieth century. Lebanese emigration that for generations had gone west now went east.

The oil boom brought with it a period of supreme confidence that spread throughout the Arab world. In the relatively homogeneous societies of much of the Arab world, the oil boom was a period in which to celebrate the nobility of Arab culture. But in Lebanon, with its fragmented society, the oil boom stimulated two movements, each of which would prove disastrous to the fragile coexistence created by the National Pact: The Maronites lost the West's protective shield, and the Palestinian movement exploded on the world scene as a legitimate political movement.

The oil boom struck at the very foundations of Maronite security—the assumed Western commitment to Lebanon's Christians. With motorists lined up at gas stations and consumers fearful of their dwindling supplies of heating oil, the Western nations were in no position to buttress the Maronites' vision of "petite Liban." "In the world that existed prior to the advent of Arab oil wealth, the fantasy of Lebanon as superior to the rest of the Arab world, the fantasy of being of Europe but not in it, of belonging to a distant world across the Mediterranean could be indulged." But now it seemed that one barrel of oil outweighed all the Christians of the Orient.

Fear of extinction fueled the passions of the Maronites. In their apocalyptic mindset, they were the last bastion of a civilization in retreat. Frustration further fed emotion when the Maronites realized that the need to preserve Christian Lebanon was something the West refused to understand, at least in the same terms as the Maronites. For the Maronites, their struggle was not only for Lebanon but for the West as a whole. To them Lebanon was the last passageway between West and East, one that would be closed unless Lebanon, or at least the Maronites' version of it, were saved. But instead of rushing to their defense, the West, blackmailed by Arab oil, chose to relinquish what the Maronites saw as its moral duty to Lebanon's Christians. Envisioning themselves with their backs to the wall, the Maronites decided to fight for their version of order and civilization in Lebanon. Unlike in 1860, the Maronites would save themselves.

The Maronites targeted the Palestinians as the vanguard of the radicalism that was leading to Muslim control of Lebanon. Ever since the Cairo Agreement of 1969, the PLO had developed its political and territorial base in Lebanon at the expense of Lebanese sovereignty. After the 1970 civil war in Jordan, Lebanon became the Palestinians' base of operations. This put Lebanon in the vortex of Palestinian activities. Consequently, when the Arab League acknowledged the PLO as the true representative of the Palestinian people, the Palestinians' capitol was Beirut. And when Yassir Arafat stood in his *kaffiyeh* and army fatigues before the General Assembly to receive the United Nations' affirmation of his cause, it was Lebanon that suffered the aftershocks.

In 1974, the year Arafat was crowned by the Arab League and the U.N., the Palestinians in Lebanon were a formidable force. One person in ten in Lebanon was a Palestinian. The PLO bristled with weaponry and governed its own territories. It was obvious to everyone that the Palestinians would never bow to Lebanese authority of their own volition. Yet somehow the Lebanese still believed that Lebanon had the power to defend its own sovereignty.

That belief was shattered on April 9, 1973, when an Israeli terror squad beached its boat and quietly stole into Beirut. There it murdered three Palestinian leaders, including the poet Kamal Nasser, and claimed control of a section of Beirut for several hours. During the operation the Lebanese army, which had been ordered into action by premier Saeb Salam, cradled its guns and stood watching while the Israelis directed traffic through a busy intersection. Lebanese of all persuasions were outraged. Mass demonstrations erupted forcing the army to attempt to crush the Palestinians three weeks later.

Fighting between the Palestinians and the Lebanese army

lasted for almost two weeks. The Lebanese government, commanding some communal unity, flexed its muscles enough to impose a
curfew on Beirut and close down the pinball parlors, the rage of the
day. It even made a feeble attempt to divert public attention from
the fighting by expanding the broadcasting hours of the state-
owned television station. Omitting the news, the government fed
the public a steady stream of cartoons, reruns of soccer matches,
and the American comedy series "Hogan's Heroes." As if casting
the conflict in terms of the Maronites versus the Muslims, government radio dropped its regular program of Arabic music and
substituted Western classics such as Gounod's *Ave Maria* and
Brahms's *Lullaby* to quell public anxiety.

That confrontation with the Palestinians cost 350 lives and
ended in a negotiated settlement that once again confirmed the
impotence of the Lebanese state. The Palestinians were left in
control of the camps and their southern bases. Both sides agreed to
release their prisoners and kidnapping victims. And the country
spun into another political crisis. A weary Lebanese summed it up:
"The nation is without a premier, the army is angry, the Arab
world is annoyed, the Israelis are poised and the fedayeen, their
backs against the wall, are desperate."

In a sense, the Lebanese civil war began in 1973. The Christians, who at one time thought they would always be the demographic majority, faced a coalition of Lebanese Muslims linked to the
Palestinians and energized by the new wave of Arab consciousness
ignited by the oil boom. Population estimates for 1973 set the
Lebanese Christian population at 1,350,000. Inclusion of the Armenians added another 175,000. Of this number, the Maronites
constituted 900,000. The Sunnis and Druze, together with the
Palestinians, equaled 950,000. (They also drew some support from
the 100,000 Syrians, Kurds, and other Muslim minorities scattered
throughout Lebanon.) Outnumbering any other single group were
the Shiite Muslims, totaling 1,100,000, who stayed outside the
Sunnis' political alliance. The Maronites' claim to power no longer
could rest on a demographic majority rule. The right to dominate
the political system could now be justified only on the basis of the
supposed superiority of a minority civilization, supported by its
own army.

Although the antiestablishment Sunnis and the leftists in
alliance with the Palestinians possessed more power than they had

ever commanded, it was not enough to force the changes that the mainstream Muslims wanted. What the broad left represented was less radicalism than political reform, something the Maronite and Sunni establishments had resisted for decades. Muslim politicians talked of reform but did nothing meaningful other than play to their constituents by making it more difficult for the Maronite president to win Muslim cooperation in forming cabinets and controlling a parliamentary majority.

In 1973, the *zuama* still held the political power in Lebanon. Their incessant bickering with one another was no different, only more symptomatic of Lebanon's grave underlying problems. Preoccupied with protecting their influence, they failed to grasp the changes in Lebanon's political configuration. The *zuama*, particularly those among the Muslim communities, were losing control of their clientele to more radical leadership. Ideology had at last become more important than the politics of patronage. The old art of consensus conducted by the elite broke down. "Older politicians were incapable of coping with threats to the political system but in the tradition of ancient regimes they were powerful enough to block the access to others."

All the cancers were there—confessionalism, provincialism, maldistribution of political power, economic inequities, the presence of the Palestinians as the third largest of Lebanon's minorities, the incursions and chaos caused by Israel, the lengthening shadow of Syria, and, as always, the deep cultural division between East and West. A country that had juggled different worlds was up against the wall, growing more incoherent, frightened, and irrational. Private armies of militiamen erected roadblocks, creating in Lebanon physical fortresses closed, as the emotional fortresses always had been, to members of differing religions or political persuasions.

Even so, the persistent illusions about Lebanon somehow survived. President Franjieh, addressing the United Nations General Assembly on November 14, 1974, declared with ringing voice that Lebanon was a "land of tolerance, of human synthesis, fraternal and peaceful." And sociologists David and Audrey Smock, in work done the same year, concluded, "It is our conviction that the Lebanese approach, while not totally adequate and not exportable in toto, has much to offer other states confronting serious problems of ethnic and racial conflict." Malcolm Kerr, sitting in his office at

AUB, was less sure. Kerr believed Lebanon was reaping the harvest of its endemic schizophrenia produced by its Western and Arab identities. The nation perhaps would not survive.

Kerr's pessimism was justified. The fears and conflicting interests that pitted different factions against one another stoked a deep and dangerous anger that permeated the society. At last the hostility among groups triggered a series of tragic events that led to civil war.

It is perhaps symbolic of the long war in Lebanon that no one definitive event ignited it. It was as if the country slid into war at some indefinable point when anarchy could be sustained no longer.

True to character, every Lebanese identifies a particular event as the start of the war. A professor at Beirut University College insists that the war started when four Palestinian commandos were apprehended by Lebanese security forces outside the American embassy. A young doctor, then a medical student, describes how he was sitting at his desk studying for final exams when he heard shots. Hurrying down the stairs to the street, he found five people standing in front of his building holding what looked like hunting guns. When he asked them what was happening, they said Palestinians from the Tel Zaatar camp five hundred meters across the street had shot at them. A Shiite blames an incident at a Palestinian roadblock in the south. A Sunni tells the same story except for substituting Maronites north of Beirut.

Two events are generally accepted as marking the passage of Lebanon from a kind of chaotic peace to war. One bore all the marks of the Lebanese communal/economic struggles. The other clearly pitted the Maronites against the Palestinians.

Camille Chamoun, the malefactor of 1958, was once again the catalyst of events in February 1975. As part of a plan to modernize the fishing industry, which was dominated by Muslim fishermen, the government had granted extensive fishing rights off Sidon to Chamoun's company that produced protein supplements. This action led to a classic dispute among Lebanese, a conflict of economic interests between rich and poor, a battle between Christian entrepreneurs intent on profit and Muslim fishermen bent on preserving their traditional mode of life. The fishermen, joined by Muslim political factions, marched through the streets of Sidon in a demonstration against the government. Suddenly Marouf Saad, Sidon's mayor, dropped to the pavement, shot without warning by an unknown assailant. Protests turned into riots and extended over several days. Chamoun resisted all entreaties to surrender his concession in order to restore peace. Ignoring the lessons of 1958, when Fuad Shihab refused to inject the army into a dispute with Christian-Muslim overtones, General Iskander Ghanem brought in the army to break up Muslim protests. When Saad died, the Sidon fishing dispute escalated into a showdown between all the forces of the right and the left, between Christian and Muslim, that had simmered in Lebanon for decades.

On March 5, an estimated thirty-five thousand members of the Phalange and Chamoun's National Liberal Party marched from East Beirut to the tomb of the unknown soldier in the city's center to express their full approval of the army's presence in Sidon. And Kamal Jumblatt, accompanied by a heavily fortified contingent of Druze, rushed to Sidon to whip up the left. The lines were drawn. The Maronites stood on one side, and the Sunnis, Druze, a representation of Shiites, and the leftists stood on the other. Gone was the luxury of 1958, when the *zuama* could patch up alliances across confessional lines. Everyone was armed and ready.

On April 13, an incident involving the other level of the Lebanese conflict—the Palestinians and the Phalange—finally threw Lebanon into war. On a peaceful Sunday morning in the predominantly Christian Beirut suburb of Ain al Rummaneh, a Peugeot sedan, its license plates wrapped in dingy cloth, raced toward a Maronite church where Pierre Gemayel was attending mass. As the car pulled even with the entrance, the occupants opened fire. Four people, including one of Gemayel's bodyguards and two members of the Phalange, sprawled dead on the sidewalk.

Convinced that the assassins were Palestinian commandos, Phalange militiamen gathered to deliver retribution. Within an hour, a busload of Palestinians going between the camps of Sabra and Tel Zaatar wound through the narrow streets of Ain al Rummaneh singing Palestinian songs and chanting PLO slogans. The Phalange opened fire. The fusillade lasted twenty minutes, during which time twenty-seven passengers aboard the crowded bus were killed and nineteen others wounded.

As news of the Ain al Rummaneh incident spread, Lebanon erupted. Palestinians joined by Lebanese Muslims battled the Phalange, reinforced by Chamoun's Tigers, for four days in the streets of Beirut, Tripoli, and Sidon. The Maronites laid Palestinian camps under a barrage of fire. The Palestinians and their Lebanese allies blew up shops, factories, and offices belonging to the Phalangists. Pierre Gemayel's pharmacy was destroyed yet again. Near the Tel Zaatar camp, mortars and salvos of rockets launched from both sides smashed into populated areas. The war was on, and there was no one to stop it. President Suleiman Franjieh lay in a hospital bed recovering from gall bladder surgery. But Franjieh's presence would have changed nothing. The Lebanese government was enfeebled by its own history of placing sectarian interests above national ones. The army reflected the deep-rooted confessionalism that plagued the country. And the leadership was a clique of ambitious, quarreling tribal chieftains incapable of rising to a crisis. Not even the imperfect Fuad Shihab was there. The hero of 1958 had died in April 1973.

With no government and no army to stand for Lebanon, each Lebanese group fought its own war. The Druze and some Lebanese leftists fought for power within the Lebanese system. Other Lebanese Muslims fought for a Lebanon that would be part of the Arab world. The Palestinians fought for their own nationalism. And the Maronite militias fought for their vision of Christian Lebanon.

Among the Maronites, only the Phalange was strong enough to bear the brunt of the fighting. After years of quiet preparation, the Phalange's self-assumed role as the armed protector of Christian Lebanon at last was openly proclaimed. For the Phalange, it was a new Christian crusade. A monk from the University of Kaslik, the Maronite spiritual center, was among those who sent the Phalange into battle. Reflecting on the coming action, he said, "They have been good men but they have to kill to defend their homes, families, and land. We are doing nothing but protecting our Christian values, our own church, our own theology, and our own Christ."

The war would pit Christian against Muslim, left against right, Lebanese against Palestinian, Israel against the PLO, and Syria against Lebanon. Yet at its core lay the centuries-old struggle over whether Lebanon was of the West or of the East.

Syrian Troops Occupy Beirut
Wall Street Journal
November 16, 1976

Pax Hebraica in Lebanon?
World Press Review
August 1982

U.S. Marines Digging in for a Long Stay?
U.S. News and World Report
October 11, 1982

EIGHT

THE FOREIGN POWERS

The warm sun of April 1977 once more radiates the blue of the Mediterranean and casts its brilliance on the pine-studded bluff of Ras Beirut. Water-skiers again skim across one another's wakes in the placid waters off St. Georges Bay. All is seductively quiet as Lebanon approaches the second anniversary of the bloody Sunday in 1975 at Ain al Rummaneh. Along the Rue Hamra, the ever-effervescent Nabil stands in the doorway of his coffee bean and nut shop shouting to the passersby, "Come, my friend, I give you a good price!" Money changers are back on street corners turning dollars, francs, riyals, and dinars into Lebanese pounds with rapid-fire motion. The only clue to Lebanon's recent past is the small "No Parking" sign riddled with the perfect circles created when automatic-rifle fire pierces thin metal. Just as Ras Beirut was once a facade of illusion masking Lebanon's fractured society, so is it now a facade of normalcy that hides a scarred and violated Beirut.

The traffic jams are gone and there is little activity on the streets beyond an occasional proprietor picking glass shards from a broken office window. The durable old Normandy Hotel is but a ruin. Up the hill from the waterfront, an abandoned tank lists on a pile of rubble under the canopy of the drive-in registration facility at the Holiday Inn. And the bare salutatory flagpoles stand silhouetted against the charred walls of a hotel caught in war.

Across the street a dirty, faded poster of the late Gamal Abdel Nasser, waving to a massive crowd and smiling his magnetic smile, clings to a crumbling wall. Around every corner is some stark symbol of Lebanon's destructive will. None is more telling than the shell of the Gothic-style Anglican church. Two walls gone, its roof open to the sky, the ruin emits a pathos that extends beyond damage or destruction—it speaks of desertion.

Yet daily life moves on. Throughout Lebanon the singular sign of the compulsion to survive is freshly washed laundry drying in the Levantine sun. In Damour, a family's wash hangs in the open on what two years earlier was the second story of their house, now reduced to a mound of cement and twisted reinforcing rods. In Sidon, four multicolored garments wave through the broken door frame of a roofless house smeared with political slogans. Near Beirut Airport, outside the hovel of a Shiite refugee from the south, a gaunt woman beats the dust from a thin mattress hung over a makeshift fence. The Lebanese have survived the first phase of the war, but at a terrible cost. Out of a population of three million, ten thousand people are dead and another half-million are homeless. The massive physical destruction amounts to an estimated $1 billion. Other damage cannot be quantified. The conditions of war have left Lebanon stripped of its cultural life, and the violence has defiled its humanity. In the jewel of the Levant, the Lebanese are no longer seen as a hospitable and genteel people capable of little more rancor than the comic opera of 1958. The illusions about "little Switzerland" have crumbled. The reality of the profound and intense hostilities the Lebanese harbor against one another at last has emerged. And it is only the beginning.

In 1975, during its early stages, the war jumped from locale to locale. It was a war of opposing militias defending their own self-defined turfs.

After the first skirmishes, the Palestinians retreated to their own territories and stayed removed from the fighting unless their boundaries were challenged. There was no front line, no confrontation of organized armies. Instead, citizen-soldiers fought behind barricades erected on street corners and wore sneakers as often as combat boots. Although casualties were high, no one in the spring of 1975 thought the war would last long. It was still a time when a pet cat killed by a sniper was a calamity shared among friends. As late as June, a malevolent humor overlaid that which was devoid of humor. One avant-garde press published a fictional guide to Beirut's current boutique items—Christian Dior combat boots, a pearl-inlaid automatic rifle by Kalashnikov, an Alexander Calder barricade. Another publishing house distributed the *Bullet Dodger's Guide to Beirut,* which offered instructions on what to say at the barricades of various militias. However, the Lebanese were not the only ones who refused to face reality. In August, the American magazine *Travel* was still reporting that "Lebanon, the Biblical land of milk and honey on the shores of the Mediterranean, just might pack within its tiny borders more good things per square mile than any other place on the globe."

At this stage, the Western press was reporting the outbreaks of fighting as civil war between the Christians and Muslims. But in reality, "neither camp was constituted on a truly communal or religious basis . . . nor could their aims be reduced to communal or sectarian ones."

In its ideological framework, the war in its early stages pitted a status quo coalition against a revolutionary alliance. The status quo coalition, which became known as the Lebanese Front, pulled together the Phalange; the Tigers, the militia of Camille Chamoun's National Liberation Party; and Suleiman Franjieh's Zghorta Liberation Army. The Lebanese Front was right wing and almost entirely Maronite, obsessed with protecting Maronite privileges. The opposition coalition was leftist and largely Muslim, determined to establish a new economic and political order in Lebanon. Known as the National Movement, it was a loose association of Kamal Jumblatt's Progressive Socialist Party (Druze), the Syrian National Party (Greek Orthodox and Muslim), the Independent Nasserites (Sunni), the Amal (Shiite), the Baath Socialist Party allied with Syria, the Baath Socialist Party allied with Iraq, and the Lebanese Communist Party.

At the outbreak of the hostilities, the National Movement set out to destroy the dominant order to make way for a complete economic restructuring of Lebanon. Yet its goal went beyond economics. The National Movement encompassed the deep desire of those Lebanese whose identity lay with the Arab East to turn Lebanon from a country possessing merely an "Arab face" into one whose culture and political system bespoke its Arabness. The National Movement was a challenge not only to the economic and political provisions of the 1943 National Pact but to the vagueness of the Mithaq's definition of the character of Lebanon. After the eruption at Ain al Rummaneh, Kamal Jumblatt whipped up the National Movement by calling for a firm stand against the "hatred being directed at Palestinians and all in Lebanon that is Arab."

Through the summer of 1975, the *zuama* negotiated to strike one last compromise to save Lebanon. It was too late. Confronting the ultimate crisis of the old politics, they possessed no tools with which to turn back the flood. For even before the Palestinian challenge to the authority of the Lebanese state, the crisis in Lebanon was first one of lame political leadership and national institutions. In the tradition of those who governed, the president, Suleiman Franjieh, retreated to the mountains for the summer without ever speaking to the Lebanese people about the war. When Pierre Gemayel and Camille Chamoun pleaded for mobilization of the army as the only salvation for Lebanon, one of their colleagues muttered, "Let's not speak about the army."

Burdened with their old conflicts and weakened by the flow of power to more radical leaders, the *zuama* failed. And as Lebanon polarized, the moderates found themselves with nowhere to go since neither of the battling coalitions encompassed the middle of the political spectrum. With the Lebanese' deep-seated communalism asserting itself, wealthy Muslims reluctantly threw in their lot with the radicals, and moderate Christians grudgingly moved into the arms of the Maronite militias. Both groups contained the core of the politico-economic establishment of Lebanon, which shared neither the alienation of the urban poor nor the "retreat to the mountain" mentality of the Maronite militants. Even the Maronite patriarch was superseded by militant monks.

By September 1975, the fury of civil war had mounted. Ideology began to vanish in a maelstrom of base and petty interests. The Maronite militias killed one another for control of the port of Beirut and the big profits it engendered. They fought for a percentage of the hashish trade and for the right to rob some particular bank. A British national employed by the United Nations became one of the first Western fatalities of the war when he defended his girlfriend from rape at the hands of a militiaman attached to the National Movement. Hanging over everything was the potential for trifling disputes to explode into violence with incredibly disproportionate results. In Tripoli, an argument between two taxi drivers over right-of-way erupted into a battle between the Sunnis and Tripoli's Maronite Christian community that killed two hundred people and gutted Tripoli's economy.

In November, the war took a new turn when the Phalange decided to move out of its strongholds in eastern Beirut into Muslim and neutral areas in western Beirut. The hotel district, as the most recognizable neutral area in Beirut, was a prime target. Consequently, armed Phalange militiamen occupied the Phoenicia, St. Georges, and Excelsior hotels, the pride of cosmopolitan Beirut. When they seized the newly completed Holiday Inn, forces of the National Movement raced to the nearby forty-story Mour Tower, the tallest building in Beirut. Once they secured it, they hoisted Soviet-made Duskas, 20-millimeter cannons, Katyusha rocket launchers, and .50-caliber machine guns up through the skeletal structure still under construction. From the top floors, Muslim forces rained fire down on the grand hotels, those bastions of the moneyed elite whose roots ran back to the creation of Greater Lebanon.

In the West's vaunted playground, 150 tourists who had no part in the war except for their unfortunate choice of hotel were trapped in the basement of the Holiday Inn, fighting fires with anything they could find. Throughout the week of the "battle of the hotels," hundreds of Westerners still left in Beirut gathered daily in front of the Riviera Hotel to make the run to the airport. Carting ski poles, Oriental rugs, and overflowing suitcases, they traveled in convoys by circuitous routes around Palestinian refugee camps. This was also the week that the U.S. State Department declared Beirut—the "Paris of the East"—a hardship post.

The Phalange lost the war of the hotels. The Holiday Inn was the last to fall to the Muslims. Before his final retreat, a Phalange militiaman, as though saying farewell to a bygone era, laid his automatic weapon on top of the bar's grand piano, sat down at the keyboard, and played in a haunting tempo the refrain "Yesterday, all our troubles seemed so far away."

In December, the real savagery of the Lebanese war began as both sides moved to eliminate hostile areas within their own enclaves. Who is to say which of Lebanon's warring militias was the most brutal? The most arrogant was the coalition of the Phalange and the National Liberal Party. On December 6, the Phalange discovered the murdered bodies of four of its members in the village of Fanar. On what is now called "Black Saturday," the Phalange struck, killing fifty-three people—mostly innocent Muslims—and kidnapping at random another three hundred. Before the retribution ended, over two hundred had died.

In January, the Phalange and the NLP laid siege to the Karantina section of Beirut, brutally slaughtering a thousand people. They moved on to Maslakh, where they murdered five hundred Palestinians, Shiites, Syrians, and Kurds. In response to the slaughter at Maslakh, the Palestinians ended their quasi-isolation and joined the National Movement in laying siege to the Christian village of Damour, home of Camille Chamoun. Matching the brutality of the Christians, the Muslims forced thousands of people to evacuate. To avenge Karantina and Maslakh, they massacred the three hundred to four hundred villagers who had stayed behind.

Old vendettas and sectarian strife fueled the flames of war. The Druze of the Mountain battled the Maronites; Christian villages in the lowlands defended themselves against the Sunnis; the Shiites shielded their Beirut shantytowns. But most of all the Palestinians, in defense of their territorial base in Lebanon, brought their power and weapons into the war on the side of the National Movement. The Palestinian arsenal added another element to the nature and course of the war. Urban warfare became a duel of heavy artillery. All sides fired blindly into densely populated neighborhoods, producing 90 percent of the casualties among noncombatants.

By the time the Palestinians joined, the National Movement was splitting into its sectarian elements. As it unfolded, the fight in Lebanon turned out to be less loaded with socioeconomic meaning than the radicals originally had assumed. Religious hatred and fanaticism manifested itself in "identity card killings," in which individuals were kidnapped or arrested at roadblocks and executed if the religion designated on their identification cards did not match that of their captors.

Muslim groups broke into houses and massacred whole families on the knowledge—or sometimes mere assumption—that they were the enemy. Phalangists burned crosses on their victims' bodies and stuck severed testicles into the mouths of the dead. Terrified people shifted from west to east or from north to south seeking safety among those of their own confessionals. Beirut divided along the "Green Line," with the no-man's-land around the National Museum the only crossing point between the two.

The last vestiges of law and order dissolved, and kidnap, rape, and massacre became the common currency of war. Unchallenged by any governmental authority, looters roamed at will. Squatters carrying submachine guns dispossessed residents from their houses and apartments. In Lebanon, the meek inherited nothing.

In the Levant, nothing happens in isolation. With the entry of the Palestinians into the war in December 1975, Syrian interest in Lebanon peaked and with it began a succession of foreign powers into the quagmire.

Lebanon has never been outside of Syria's national interests. Lebanon is Syria's front yard. It is the conduit through which trade and information flow into the Arab hinterland from the Mediterranean. Most important, it was and always will remain in Syrian eyes a part of Greater Syria. The concept of Greater Syria extends to Palestine and the Palestinians. While no Syrian regime after 1948 seriously believed it could destroy the State of Israel, none were willing to allow an unbridled Palestinian presence on the soil of Lebanon to dictate Arab action against the Jewish state.

Syria's failure to exert strong influence in Lebanon between 1946, the year it became independent, and 1975 resulted from Syria's internal weaknesses. Beset by its own religious and political conflicts, Syria was incapable of flexing muscle in Lebanon until Hafiz Assad seized the reins of power as head of the Baath party in 1970. (The Baath Party is pan-Arab, secular, and socialist. The two branches, one in Syria and the other in Iraq, are intense rivals.)

In Hafiz Assad's overall scheme for establishing Syria as a major force in Middle Eastern politics, Lebanon had to remain in the Syrian sphere of influence. At the same time, Assad always had to be aware that a victory by Lebanese radicals would destabilize Lebanon and prompt Israeli intervention. The Israelis, already sitting on the southern border of Lebanon, were within striking distance of the Bekaa, Syria's soft underbelly, only eighteen miles from Damascus. In the event that Israel moved into Lebanon to squelch the Palestinians, "Syria would have to choose between two equally unappealing alternatives—to fight Israel or to suffer the humiliation of failing to do so."

With the Palestinian-Lebanese Muslim forces gaining ascendancy over the Christian forces, Syria faced the possibility of an uncontrolled Palestinian presence in Lebanon. Suddenly the Lebanese war confronted the Assad regime with the prospect of a regional conflict of immense proportions.

Initially Syrian involvement in Lebanon was cautious. In early 1976, Hafiz Assad advanced a peace plan to both sides that balanced power between Christians and Muslims slightly more equitably and hinted at a somewhat improved status for the Palestinians in Lebanon. The Muslims rejected the plan as inadequate, and the war continued. The Maronites, facing defeat, reverted to past behavior and frantically cast around for a foreign protector. The United States, burned by the fall of Vietnam, and Europe, tied to Arab oil, were no longer viable possibilities. The imperfect president, Suleiman Franjieh, with his long ties to Syria, provided the conduit through which the Maronites found Syria. Muslim Syria, the Syrian behemoth, would save the Christians. Thus, in October 1976, Hafiz Assad, in a last-ditch attempt to control events in Lebanon, sent thirteen thousand troops reinforced by T-55 and T-62 tanks into Lebanon to block a Muslim victory. Syria had entered the Lebanese war on the side of the Christians.

The scale and candor of Syria's move into Lebanon altered profoundly the balance of internal and external circumstances that impacted on the Lebanese political system: Syria's position vis-à-vis Israel and the Arab world; its relationship to the leftist Muslim National Movement; and finally the mutual disillusionment of the Syrians and their Maronite wards.

Syria's military intervention ended the Lebanese civil war but not the Lebanese crisis. In the uneasy peace that Syria imposed, the Lebanese tried to recapture their old optimism. The broken Lebanese government attempted to revive mass tourism by buying an advertising supplement to the *New York Times* that included an article by Lutfi Diab of AUB arguing that Christian-Muslim hostility in Lebanon was largely a myth. Developers, following the government's lead, poured money into beach resorts and exclusive swimming clubs aimed at the tourist trade. With rebuilding moving at a fast clip, land speculation returned to its revered niche as the best get-rich-quick game in town. Despite the bravado, Beirut lived in a half-light between security and insecurity, war and truce. There was only enough security to allow people to go about each day feeling vaguely confident that it would not be their last.

The crisis persisted because nothing had changed in the political equation among the Lebanese themselves. The vacuous Lebanese state that had existed before the war was exhausted, not destroyed. The 1972 parliament dominated by the *zuama* survived as the only elected government in existence. The president was so weakened that he could exercise no authority beyond east Beirut. And the hope of turning the Lebanese army into a cohesive force that could establish control over Lebanon in the name of a national government was as illusory as ever. All of the elements that could reconstruct Lebanon were trapped in a vicious circle. The army could not be restored without a political consensus; consensus required political normalization; normalization demanded the framework for a credible state system; and a state system mandated the backing of an apolitical, militarily effective army. In the aftermath of the Syrian invasion, the Lebanese state could be neither transformed nor restored. As a result, power shifted from traditional politicians and factions to new groups fielding their own militias. After 1975, a political leader devoid of military power was irrelevant.

For Hafiz Assad, Syria's invasion was the last defense of his ability to control Lebanon. It was a move blessed by the Arab world's political leaders and tacitly accepted by the United States and Israel as the only feasible way to establish order in Lebanon short of their own intervention. With the backing of the United States, Syria and Israel agreed to observe the "Red Line," an imaginary boundary running from the Bekaa across southern Lebanon.

In effect, it established Syria's implicit recognition of an Israeli security zone in the south as the quid pro quo for Israel's conditional acceptance of Syria's intervention in Lebanon. International recognition bestowed on Hafiz Assad his coveted role as an Arab power broker.

But the Syrian presence in Lebanon also created enormous problems for the Syrian leader within Arab circles. Assad sat at the head of the Baath (Renaissance) Party. Founded during World War II by Michel Aflaq, a French-educated Arab from a Christian family, and Salah Bitar, a Sunni from Damascus, the Baath Party stressed nationalism, unity, and socialism as the three forces that Arab society needed to rejuvenate itself and to restore its once famed brilliance and affluence in commerce, industry, and culture.

After 1970, when Hafiz Assad took charge in Syria, the Syrian Baathist Party stood as the champion of pan-Arabism. But when Hafiz Assad sent his troops into Lebanon, "The Ba'thi regime encountered great political difficulties in explaining to Syrian and Arab public opinion how an Arab ideological party, successor to one of the great legacies in the history of the Arab left, could fight on the side of conservative pro-Western militias against the Lebanese left and the PLO."

The Syrian intervention challenged Lebanon's sovereignty as it had never been challenged before. Although the Christians and the Muslims battled each other over political and economic power, the Phalangists and the Druze were totally committed to an independent Lebanon, a country in which both could claim protection of their minority status in the Arab world.

At first, Kamal Jumblatt saw the Syrian-Maronite alliance as a historic opportunity "to re-orient the Maronites towards Syria, to win their trust, [and] to make them realize that their source of protection is no longer France or the West." But after the fact Kamal Jumblatt, choosing his Druze identity over his socialist identity, refused to accept Syrian hegemony in Lebanon. Jumblatt became as much an aggravation to Syrian president Hafiz Assad as he was to his old political rivals in Lebanon. As the leader of the Muslim-leftist bloc, Jumblatt threatened to complicate Syria's goal of establishing its own devised order in Lebanon. But Jumblatt's struggle against Syria was one he could not win. In Hafiz Assad's mode of operation, all that remained was to remove Jumblatt from the scene.

In March 1977, Kamal Jumblatt and two bodyguards wound through the twisting roads southeast of Beirut into a blazing ambush. The enigmatic Kamal died instantly. The next day, fifty thousand mourners marched at his funeral chanting, "Revenge, revenge, revenge." In delivering that revenge, Jumblatt's followers shot or slit the throats of 170 Christians in the Shuf despite the fact that few doubted the duplicitous hand of Hafiz Assad.

Jumblatt's personality and leadership were indispensable to the survival of the leftist coalition of Lebanese parties and to the separate issue of preserving a united anti-Syrian front. His death resulted in both the collapse of the National Movement coalition and the weakening of the challenge to Syrian power in the name of Lebanese sovereignty.

The semblance of stability that Syrian troops imposed on Lebanon allowed Assad to begin to distance Syria from its uneasy alliance with the Maronites and to move toward some accommodation with the Lebanese Muslims and the PLO. It was a move that ultimately led to the intervention of another foreign power and the most brutal phase of the war.

No longer fearing annihilation as a community, the Maronites looked with increasing disdain at Syrian moves toward the Muslims. A new savior had to be found for Christian Lebanon. But for once, the Maronites would not turn to a foreign protector. Instead Bashir Gemayel, the twenty-eight-year-old son of Pierre Gemayel, rose to become for the Phalange a Lebanese Mussolini. Determined, ruthless, and aflame with ambition, Bashir Gemayel usurped the positions of his father, still the formal head of the Phalange party, and his older brother, Amin, to sound the battle cry of "Marounistan." Bashir Gemayel's formal position was not in the Phalange party hierarchy. He was commander of the Lebanese Forces, a militia formed in 1976 by combining the Phalange with other militant Maronite militias, groups such as the Numur, the Guardians of the Cedar, and the Tanzim.

The motivation of the Lebanese Forces came out of a state of mind that started fourteen hundred years ago with the "problem of the east," the overwhelming Muslim population of the Middle East. That issue was as current as the reigning political crisis—the preservation of the Maronites. Yet the militants' philosophy differed from that of the old-line politicians. The Lebanese Forces manifested a political ethos that rejected old-style establishment politics. It in fact launched a frontal assault on the feudal system that had dominated Lebanese politics since the days of the mandate. Its appeal was antiestablishment, lower middle class. The Phalange was the "revenge of the 'small' Maronite, the hick, the red-neck over the typical figure of the entrepreneur." In saving Christian Lebanon, the Phalange also promised to level Maronite society.

Bashir Gemayel was the leading proponent of military might as a basis of political power. The fragmentations and divisions characteristic of Maronite politics throughout the first phase of the war was a luxury that a beleaguered community, fighting for its future against numerical and political odds, could no longer afford. On that premise the Phalange, the largest and best organized militia within the Lebanese Forces, set out to consolidate Maronite power.

One by one the Phalange eliminated its Maronite rivals. Phalangist gunmen ambushed and wounded Raymond Edde, the symbolic leader of the Maronite moderates, driving him into exile. Similarly, it was Bashir's move into northern Lebanon, challenging Suleiman Franjieh's traditional power base, that touched off the vengeful round of attack and retaliation between the Gemayels and the Franjiehs. In July 1980, Gemayel's militia destroyed the military infrastructure of the Tigers, Camille Chamoun's militia. Chamoun accepted the Phalangist victory, effectively anointing Bashir Gemayel as his own political successor, and Chamoun's own son, Dany, went into political exile in Paris.

Bashir Gemayel had the ability to dazzle and amaze. In the West, he played to a public almost totally ignorant of the dynamics of Lebanon. In April 1981, Geraldo Rivera of ABC's "20/20" depicted Gemayel as a latter-day Crusader doing battle against the Soviet's client, the PLO, in the name of shared Western values. Those who knew Gemayel better argued that he was erratic, restless, and willing to do anything to further his ambitions. But for the Maronites of the Mountain, Gemayel took them back to their roots. For other Christians, he represented integrity and idealism, a refreshing change from the "10 percent" practices of most Lebanese politicians. In this, Gemayel touched a deep longing for a clear, unequivocal leader to cut through the encrusted hatreds of Lebanese society and bring order out of nearly a decade of chaos. Declaring the Christians "a small population . . . fighting alone for liberty, democracy, for the dignity of man against peoples and groups that deny these values," he won over many of the non-Maronite Christians. Succumbing to his rhetoric of the injustices they had suffered over the centuries, the Christians fell behind their confession's most militant leader. Amazingly young in a society that revered age and hierarchy, Gemayel was spoken of reverently as "the boy." Some Protestant Lebanese hailed him as the kind of leader who appears only a few times in history. Burying their socioeconomic contempt for the Phalangists, most Christians were ready to join them at the barricades.

In December 1980, Gemayel published his manifesto: "The Lebanon We Want to Build." In it he argued that the formula of the National Pact no longer applied. He demanded on behalf of all Christians that since the Christians played a special role in Lebanon, they should have a special position regardless of the population figures. This posed the cardinal question of Lebanese politics: How were the Christians to reconcile their desire for a Christian entity in the face of the demographic realities of Lebanon? The answer was that if the Christian ethos and power structure could be preserved, Lebanon would stay unified. If not, the Maronites would opt for a smaller Lebanon created by partition or cantonization. As the last resort, East Beirut, the northern part of Mount Lebanon, and the coastal areas north of Beirut would become Christian Lebanon. The extremist Maronites of 1980 were ready to jettison Greater Lebanon sixty years after their fathers had structured it.

Through the Phalange, Bashir Gemayel developed an infrastructure for an embryonic Christian state. Its future rested on three presumptions: recruits for an army raised by tapping the mentality of Christianity under siege; financial resources garnered from the Christians of the Lebanese diaspora; and a foreign sponsor—this time Israel—acting as an arms supplier and military adviser. Forced to forgo their usual Western support, the Maronites embraced Israel in a new alliance of survival. "Israel was always second best, an ersatz Western power and only an alternative when the Christians' traditional Western friends refused to follow the Phalange down its path of death and destruction."

Since 1948, Lebanon's Christians had seen Israel as both a threat and a blessing. The Lebanese business community feared that Israel would outstrip it economically and would more successfully appeal to the West. But at the same time, the hard-core Maronites identified with Israel as an enclave society that, like itself, was surrounded by the Muslim world. While the Christians' Arab side expressed sympathy for the Palestinians, their Western side demanded that Israel be considered among the Christians' scant instruments of survival. Throughout the Arab-Israeli wars of 1948, 1956, and 1967, the Christians refused to fight Israel over the Palestinians. Yet they did seek to awaken the West to the Palestinians' plight. This strategy successfully maintained the Christians' careful balancing act between the Arabs and the West until the Christians found themselves with their backs to the wall. Then the glib, superficial Arabism of the Maronites met its test—a test it was destined to fail.

The leaders in the Christian community who had known the Arab system and made their peace with it lost to those to whom Arabism and Islam were synonymous and who believed in their own cultural supremacy and in the backwardness of the Arabs. The Maronites, convinced that they were being abandoned by the West . . . , resentful of the post–October 1973 wealth of the Muslim Arab states, losing control over a country that had become too Palestinized and radicalized for their taste and aware that the demographic facts were shattering the myth of Christian majority, did what was previously unthinkable . . . they opted for a full break with the Arab system.

Bashir Gemayel's plans for "Fortress Lebanon" created a natural ally for Israel in its struggle against the Palestinians. The relationship between Israel and the Maronites was not new, only more open. Even before the Lebanese civil war began, Israel was a major arms supplier to the Phalange. Clandestine operations delivered weapons to a variety of places including a cove at Tabarja nicknamed "the Israeli embassy" because of the frequency of its after-hours operation. As important as Israeli arms were to the Phalangist cause, the establishment of militias tied to Israel was crucial to Israeli security concerns. The most open alliance between any Lebanese group and Israel was the South Lebanon Army (SLA).

Determined to build a security zone on its northern border, Israel had enlisted a renegade major from the Lebanese army, supplied him with arms, and put him in charge of his own militia. Saad Haddad, a small, erect man with the reddish hair color of the Syrians, was a Greek Orthodox Christian who marshaled a contingent of Christian military men living in the south into a command structure for his minuscule army. His troops, on the other hand, were largely poor Shiites coaxed out of their villages by the allure of the mercenary salaries paid by the Israeli government. The Christian commanders and the Shiite foot soldiers set out to create a buffer zone between the Israeli border and the Palestinian concentrations in Tyre and Sidon. But Haddad's forces were no match for the Palestinians in southern Lebanon. With access to money and weapons from Syria, Libya, and other friendly Arab governments, the PLO over the years had transformed its fighters from a guerrilla force into a conventional army possessing long-range artillery, tanks, and mobile launchers that could pepper northern Israel with salvos of deadly rockets.

In March 1978, under the guise of a retaliatory raid for a PLO killing of thirty-two Israelis on the Mediterranean coast, Israel unleashed the "Litani Operation," meant to clear the Palestinians once again out of southern Lebanon. Before American president Jimmy Carter forced an Israeli withdrawal by vowing to cut off American arms and aid, 2,000 Lebanese and Palestinians were killed and 250,000 displaced. To establish a semblance of order before Syria felt compelled to act and to salvage Israel's security interests, the United Nations sent its seven-thousand-man United Nations Interim Force in Lebanon (UNIFIL) to patrol the border area. The U.N. forces were another armed element in Lebanon. Already present were the militias of the various Lebanese antagonists; twenty thousand Israelis; thirty thousand members of the Arab Peace Force, including Syria's troops; the Palestinians; the militia of Saad Haddad; remnants of the Lebanese army; and agents of Iran's SAVAK, sent to Lebanon to bolster the Shiites.

The Lebanese army, barely heard from since 1975, was also sent into southern Lebanon to attempt to gain control of Lebanese territory and Major Haddad. Haddad, backed by his Israeli patrons, declared his zone the ministate of "Free Lebanon." Running mosquitolike attacks against the Palestinians, Haddad was as much a PR man as a soldier. The Israeli government bused a steady stream of visiting journalists north for full-dress audiences with the lackluster Haddad, whom the Israelis billed as the West's stalwart defender of Lebanon against the Muslim hordes and godless communism.

Between 1977 and 1982, a sullen three-way stalemate existed among the Christians, grouped behind the Lebanese Forces and armed by Israel; the alliance of the left, the remnants of the National Movement reinforced by the PLO; and Syria. In this situation, Syria held a stronger hand than Israel. Major Haddad could do no more than annoy the Palestinians in southern Lebanon, and the Lebanese Forces, Israel's other ally, were locked in east Beirut and in the mountains north of the capitol. As events built toward the summer of 1982, Israel's settlements in Galilee suffered frequent shellings from Palestinian positions in southern Lebanon. At one time the guns drove out most of the inhabitants of the Israeli border town of Kiryat Shmona. For those who remained, an acrid smell hung over the blackened hillsides and the dreaded boom of distant artillery filled the air. Within a stifling shelter, women and children spent their seventh successive day underground. Everyone knew it was only a matter of time before Israel would once more cross the border into Lebanon.

The grand design meant to turn the swamp of Lebanon into a domain of Israeli security was the brainchild of Ariel Sharon, Israel's minister of agriculture. Sharon, a short man with an expansive stomach hanging over low-slung trousers, moved with the will and determination of one obsessed with destroying the PLO. Possessing a volatile personality, a driving ambition, and an intense hostility toward everything Arab, Sharon had been carefully isolated from the Ministry of Defense by Menachem Begin's Likud party. But in Begin's second administration, Sharon won the coveted post of defense minister, from which he laid the plans to grind the PLO in Lebanon to dust. While other Israeli defense ministers had acted to move the PLO out of artillery and rocket range of the border, Sharon schemed to destroy the PLO by changing the political structure in Lebanon. Sharon meant to do no less than put in place a Lebanese government that he smugly believed could stabilize the military situation on the ground, expel the Palestinians and the Syrians, and enter into a treaty that would formally recognize the State of Israel.

In unveiling his bold plan to the army, Sharon stated,

> I am talking about an action that will mean destroying the terrorist organization in Lebanon in such a way that they will not be able to rebuild their military and political base. . . . The question [then becomes] . . . how to preserve [the advantage of] such a new situation. . . . It is possible to achieve [a long-standing change] on condition that a legitimate regime emerges in Lebanon, not a puppet government; that it signs a peace treaty with Israel; and that it becomes part of the free world. . . . All this demands extreme caution and waiting for just the right moment. . . .

Since the essential element in the impending move into Lebanon was political, the Israelis' alliance with the Maronites was as crucial as the military conflict with the Palestinians. The Israelis had watched Bashir Gemayel develop from the charming, volatile younger son of a veteran political leader into what they believed was the mature head of the single most powerful political and military force in Lebanon. Bashir Gemayel appeared to be the Lebanese ally Israel had sought since the Palestinians had entrenched themselves in Lebanon, a man with the capacity to change the paradigms of the Lebanese polity. Thus, the sides joined, the Israelis believing Bashir Gemayel could be molded into a wedge against the Arabs and the Maronites convinced they had found yet another foreign rescuer eager to protect the Maronites' special position in Lebanon. And so the Phalange did the unthinkable: It overthrew the careful balancing of Lebanon's Western and Eastern sides for an alliance with Israel, the Arabs' most hated enemy. The Israelis were about to be seduced as the French, the Americans, and the Syrians had been seduced into believing they could solve the problem of Lebanon.

All the pieces were in place for Israel's entry into Lebanon. All that was needed was a spark to light the fuse. On June 3, 1982, word reached Jerusalem that Israel's ambassador to Britain, Shlomo Argov, had been shot and critically wounded in London. The PLO, operating from Lebanon, was immediately held responsible by Israel. Two days later, the first Israeli tank rumbled over the barbed-wire fence dividing Israel and Lebanon. Behind it three columns of armored personnel carriers, halftracks carrying antiaircraft guns—giant, self-propelled 175-millimeter artillery pieces that could destroy a target twenty-three miles ahead—communications vans, and supply trucks all rolled north. Lumbering along narrow dirt roads the procession, bedecked with red bunting to make it easy for Israeli warplanes to identify, possessed a cinematic quality that was captured on countless reels of Israeli defense ministry film. When they saw the columns approaching, UNIFIL soldiers, sent to Lebanon to buffer incursions from either side across the border, fled their posts, realizing they were hopelessly outmanned and outgunned. One valiant Nepalese Gurka intent on defending the Khardala bridge over the Litani River finally dove into the water to escape an advancing tank that had no intention of stopping.

On the second day of the invasion, Israeli prime minister Menachem Begin stood before the Knesset and declared that the invasion would clear the Palestinians from a strip forty kilometers (twenty-five miles) deep along the Israel-Lebanon border and then stop. The prime minister assured his nervous nation that the invasion of Lebanon was a modest operation with limited goals. But what Begin blatantly kept from his own people was that Israel's goals went beyond a security zone. What lay behind Operation Big Pines was no less than the destruction of the Palestinian presence in Lebanon.

From the beginning, the strategy of Ariel Sharon and the Israeli hawks was to push the Palestinians as far north as the environs of Beirut. In a second phase, Israeli forces would confront Syria with such overwhelming superiority that Damascus would be forced to withdraw, thereby eliminating the Palestinians' Syrian umbrella. Finally, the all-important political goal of the Israeli invasion would ensure the election of Bashir Gemayel as president of Lebanon. Under a pro-Israeli head of state, Lebanon's political system with its Christian dominance would then be reinstituted. Israel, in effect, would become the "protector of Western and Christian interests [in Lebanon] more enthusiastic and committed than the Christian and Western powers themselves."

The overlooked element in the Israeli plan was that the Israeli-Maronite alliance sparked all the burning hostilities of those Lebanese who identified with the Arab world. It was impossible for Israel to wage a war against the Palestinians without igniting Arab resentment against the West and its surrogates that had smoldered in Lebanon for centuries. The failure to assess the potent emotional symbolism of the West warring against the Muslims was the great flaw in Israel's operation. The brutality of the operation completed its damnation.

Lebanese Christians of the south and even some Shiites welcomed the Israelis. Recognizing that Lebanon itself lacked the might to expel foreign forces, they thought the Israelis had succeeded in doing what the Lebanese were incapable of doing for themselves—namely returning Lebanon to the Lebanese. With the Palestinians in retreat toward Beirut, they deluded themselves into believing that the war was over. Others were less sure. A gnarled farmer, watching the last of the invasion force pass his village, said, "There is great fear of the Israelis. They have gained a reputation for being merciless."

And merciless they were. The first stages of the invasion killed ninety-five hundred civilians and wounded sixteen thousand others, most of them civilians. Hospitals were overrun with victims such as the frail fifteen-year-old girl and her wan seven-year-old brother who lay side by side, their legs blown off by Israeli shells. So many people died that there were not enough coffins; the dead were rolled in sheets, blankets, and tablecloths before hastily shunted into shallow graves. Terrified refugees fleeing before the advancing Israeli military columns swelled the already dense population of Muslim West Beirut to 1.2 million. The Palestinians were equipped to deal with their displaced. Gathering them into the camps, the PLO sheltered, fed, and clothed them from their well-stocked coffers. That left the Shiites, desperately short of food, water, blankets, and medicine, to fend for themselves.

On that fateful second day of the war, Menachem Begin flew by helicopter into Beaufort Castle, that massive relic of Saladin's great victory over the imperialist Crusaders, to declare it, at last, free of Palestinian gunners. At the same time, tanks and personnel carriers reached Damour in one more violation of a town reduced to little more than rubble since 1975. And then the columns paused. The Israeli Defense Force (IDF) was already beyond the stated forty-kilometer limit of the invasion. Beirut, with thousands of PLO guerrillas holed up in camps and apartments, lay just ahead. With the order to advance, the whole of Sharon's plan unfolded before the Israelis and their Western allies.

From a distance Beirut still looked beautiful, its scarred buildings masked by a thin blue haze. The city was quiet, lying in wait for the next assault on its waning civility. And then the stillness broke. Israeli planes, streaking low over the city, dropped leaflets warning the PLO and the Syrians to withdraw or subject Beirut to its impending fate. The Syrians hastily evacuated their checkpoints, leaving them vacant for the first time in six years. But the PLO stood firm. As Israeli forces closed their pincers on Beirut, trapping the Palestinians inside, Yassir Arafat vowed to turn Beirut into "the graveyard of the invader and the Stalingrad of the Arabs." But despite the rhetoric, they had no other choice. A PLO major manning a gun behind a sandbagged emplacement said the obvious: "We will fight here to the last man. We have nowhere else to go."

Having come this far, Israel had two choices: to empty Beirut of the Palestinians through negotiations or to clean them out by force. To soften the city for either option, the Israeli army blockaded Beirut, cutting water and electricity to Muslim West Beirut and barring fresh fruits, vegetables, and bread from entering the city. Like hardened war addicts, people hunkered down in basements for the siege.

In a letter to President Ronald Reagan regarding the impending Israeli assault on Beirut, Begin defended Israel's actions by putting the PLO on the same plane as the Nazis: "In a war whose purpose is to annihilate the leader of the terrorists in West Beirut, I feel as though I have sent an army to Berlin to wipe out Hitler in the bunker."

But Israel had no intention of subjecting its army to a guerrilla war in the streets and alleys of Beirut. Casualties would have been intolerable for the Israelis, who knew the name of every lost soldier. It was the Lebanese Forces that Israel expected to take West Beirut. But for Bashir Gemayel, as leader of a small force representing a community haunted by a sense of steady demographic entrenchment, casualties were every bit as important as they were to the Israelis. From Gemayel's point of view, if Israel wanted to act as a regional power forcing political change through a military campaign, it ought to pay the price that the capture of West Beirut was bound to extract. And so the dilemma. Israel had to expel the PLO from Beirut. Having already defined its purpose in terms far more ambitious than those originally announced, failure to evict the PLO would constitute a distinct victory for the Palestinians. Unwilling to commit its troops, Israel decided to force out the PLO from the air.

For seventy days, the Israelis pounded Beirut with bombs and mortar rounds. Shelling came from the south, from the hills, and from the sea. Night after night, the skyline exploded in flashes of orange and yellow accented by ascending spirals of white smoke from exploding munitions. Israeli gunners, known for their precision, landed rounds on hospitals marked with red crosses and crescents as well as on the headquarters of the International Committee of the Red Cross. Hysterical people piled into basements they knew could become tombs if the building above were hit. Guests nervously huddled in the Commodore lobby quavered at the uncanny imitations of incoming artillery rounds squawked out by Coco, the hotel's parrot. Nowhere was there shelter from the Israeli-imposed horror.

Israel nearly succeeded in killing Yassir Arafat in an aerial manhunt. Informers supplied with radios by the IDF reported his whereabouts to the command center, which called in Israeli jets for the strike. Eight buildings were destroyed on information that Arafat was there. At one point, the PLO commander operated from his car, moving constantly.

Civilian casualties were high in an operation that drew no distinction between the enemy and the innocent. Surgeons worked around the clock performing what they dubbed the "Begin amputation" of limbs shattered by the cluster bombs provided to Israel by the United States. Others were wounded by shells whose exploded casings buried in apartment walls carried the message "Made in the USA." To everyone except the Phalangists and some of their Christian supporters, this hell was being delivered as much by the United States as by Israel. To the Lebanese Muslims, Israel's silent partner in the carnage was the United States. It was American shells, American money, and American political support that had created the Israeli monster.

The pummeling of Beirut went on and on. To speed up the city's surrender, Israel ordered saturation bombing on the scale of the World War II attack on Dresden. Known as "Black Thursday," it began at dawn on August 12 and continued uninterrupted for eleven hours. The city burned and there was no water to quench the flames, for the Israelis had shut off the flow. In West Beirut, where only about one in eighty people was a Palestinian guerrilla, five hundred civilians died.

When the shelling finally stopped, the Israelis were back at their roadblocks, stopping food supplies from entering the western section of the city. Thousands of people, their homes destroyed by the intense bombing, were living in the streets or in the lobbies of damaged office and apartment buildings, while UNICEF fretted over the potential for plague from rats, typhoid, and cholera.

By the end of July, Yassir Arafat realized that the PLO must leave Beirut. After standing pat throughout the siege, Arafat made clear his belief that prolonging the city's punishment would serve no useful purpose. The PLO had withstood the onslaught long enough to save face and salvage its honor from the ruins of military defeat.

All sides looked for a way out, and ironically it was to the United States that they turned for a negotiated settlement. Much of the irony arose from the fact that U.S. Secretary of State Alexander Haig had silently assented to the Israeli invasion. Haig represented those in the Reagan administration who believed Israel was the anchor of U.S. strategic interests in the Middle East. To Haig, Israel was the counterweight to the Palestinians, Syria, and, by projection, Soviet power in the area. Therefore, U.S. interests were compatible with those of Israel's, a view not shared by others in the administration, including some of Haig's own State Department aides.

Accepting the U.S.-Israeli connection, Yassir Arafat pressed

for an American security screen to cover an "honorable" evacuation
from Beirut for his guerrillas. Israeli prime minister Menachem
Begin angled for a U.S. operation to clean up his PLO problem and
save his army from the trauma of a final assault on West Beirut.
Caught in the middle of the Israeli-PLO showdown, most Lebanese
welcomed any intervention that might stop the bloodshed. The man
chosen to effect a solution was U.S. special envoy Philip Habib.
Time was Habib's worst enemy. No one doubted Ariel Sharon's
warning, "If the PLO is playing for time you should know that our
army is ready for the worst scenario. I want to see the PLO on
buses, on ships or boarding planes at the airport. I want them to
leave."

But to get the Palestinians out of Beirut and end the siege,
some place had to be found for them to go. Habib succeeded in
convincing seven Arab countries to agree, albeit reluctantly, to
accept the Palestinians, with Tunisia designated as the new headquarters of the PLO. The scene was set for the evacuation of Beirut.
The rationale behind the Reagan administration's intervention in
Lebanon was the determination to tie a solution of the Lebanese
crisis to the next phase of the Arab-Israeli peace process. Consequently, on September 1, 1982, President Reagan announced his
Middle East Peace Plan. Under the proposal, the Palestinians on
the Israeli-occupied West Bank and on the Gaza strip would be
given autonomy under the supervision of King Hussein of Jordan.
Israel immediately rejected the proposal. After having thrown a
symbolic gesture to the Arabs, the Reagan plan lay dormant and
finally died when King Hussein renounced all claim to the West
Bank in the summer of 1988.

From the beginning of August to the end of September 1982,
events in Lebanon tumbled one on top of the other to suck yet
another foreign force into the imbroglio—the Multi-National Force
and its American contingent.

On August 8, Habib assured all sides that the United States, as
part of the Multi-National Force (MNF), would provide up to one
thousand U.S. Marines to help maintain order and to escort and
protect PLO guerrillas boarding ships, planes, or vehicles for the
exodus from Lebanon. Like all plans devised in haste and desperation, this scheme was full of traps. First, there were the physical
risks to the Marines. One Reagan administration aide conceded,
"You're putting kids in combat and asking them to be policemen.
They don't know what the hell to do. Can you imagine them figur-

ing out the differences between Druze, Muslims, Maronites and Israelis?" Second, there were the further political risks to the United States' already problematic Middle East policy. A State Department official worried, "Anything that would provoke some of the Marines to fire on the PLO would just confirm the worst fears of being seen in league with the Israelis from the start." Nevertheless at precisely 5 A.M. on a clear morning, a landing craft pulled into the port of Beirut and Lance Corporal James Dunaway of Hattiesburg, Mississippi, flag bearer for the 32d Marine Amphibious Unit, stepped ashore. For the second time in twenty-four years, U.S. Marines had landed in Lebanon.

Over the course of twelve days, 8,144 Palestinian guerrillas gathered at the port of Beirut to go into yet another exile. Before he left, every Palestinian under arms in Beirut received orders to report to his headquarters where he was given a haircut, shaved, and issued a new uniform for his exit from Beirut. Meanwhile, Yassir Arafat paid all of his organization's outstanding debts to Beirut's merchants and landlords. The PLO would leave Lebanon with pride.

The Palestinian fighters arrived at the dock with bravado, waving their fists in victory and firing their weapons into the air before turning them over to the MNF. Then came time for the good-byes. Only 664 women and children accompanied their men into exile. The rest stayed in Lebanon as part of the evacuation deal, assured of protection by the Western forces now in place. Most of the good-byes were said back in the camps but one eleven-year-old boy, tears streaming down his face, stood on the dock clinging to his father, prolonging that last moment together.

Although the United States had sealed the deal to extricate the PLO from Beirut, America was no hero to the Palestinians. Handing his gun to a Marine, a bearded pharmacist-turned-guerrilla spat out vehemently, "I'll tell you what this war taught us. It taught us that the real enemy is the United States. It is against you that we must fight. Not just because your bombs killed our people, but because you have closed your eyes to what is moral and just."

The leadership of Fatah, their political organization intact, stood proudly before their men until the last one left Beirut. The sixty thousand shells and countless bombs that Israel had poured down on Beirut had not buried the PLO.

Before the evacuation plan could be completed, the tattered and depleted 1972 Lebanese parliament had to gather once again to elect a new president. The Phalange intended to anoint Bashir Gemayel, but he faced opposition from the old Sunni *zuama*, from the Gemayels' archrivals, the Franjiehs, and from Camille Chamoun. However, the political phase of Israel's war in Lebanon demanded Gemayel as president, and so the Israelis set about guaranteeing his election. Parliamentary delegates in Israeli-controlled areas were produced for the election with instructions on how to vote. For the remainder, the Gemayel forces themselves reverted to the time-honored practices of Lebanese politics. Chamoun was bought off with political promises and cash. The rest of the deputies Bashir needed were just bought off, at a cost of about two million Lebanese pounds apiece. Thus, on August 23, two days after the Palestinian evacuation had begun, Bashir Gemayel was elected president of Lebanon in an East Beirut military barracks surrounded by armed Phalangists. When his election was announced, Phalangists uncorked champagne bottles and filled the sky with so much celebratory gunfire that they killed five people. With the PLO steadily moving out of Beirut and Bashir Gemayel in place as president, the Phalange-Israeli axis seemed a reality.

The last goal of Israel's Operation Big Pines was a formal peace treaty between Lebanon and the State of Israel. But here Israel ran into the Lebanese' dual identity. While Gemayel was willing to use his Western identity to pull in outside support for his own political ambitions and to rid Lebanon of the Palestinians, he was unwilling to sever all of Lebanon's ties with the Arab world by formalizing his relationship with the Zionist state. Bashir Gemayel echoed old Pierre: "We must remain on good terms with the Arab world. We are a part of it." To the consternation of Israel, the treaty was shelved.

For forty-five days, Bashir Gemayel prepared Lebanon for his assumption of the presidency. The United States and other members of the MNF, accepting him as the best hope for a stable Lebanon, threw their support to the Christian president. Believing that Lebanese affairs were at last on track, the American government and its European allies withdrew their forces on September 10.

Through his control of the information services, Gemayel created an image of stability. He appeared to reconstitute the bureaucracy and create in Lebanon what a former Chamoun supporter called "a proper country." Radiating the aura of power, the handsome, dashing Bashir convinced most Christians that the defense of Christianity in the Middle East lay securely in his hands.

Then, on September 14, Gemayel drove to the Ashrafieh branch of the Phalange party to address a seminar of young women activists. At 4:10 P.M., while vowing to his audience that the Muslims would learn to accept the new order in Lebanon, Habib Tanious Shartouni, a Christian member of the PPS, detonated a two-hundred-pound bomb planted in the ceiling above Gemayel's head. The entire building collapsed with a mighty roar.

The first reports said the president-elect escaped with minor injuries to his leg and hand and was being treated at a nearby hospital. The Voice of Free Lebanon, the radio station of the Lebanese Forces, even quoted the president-elect as thanking God for his miraculous escape. But as the hours ticked by with no one actually seeing Gemayel, fears mounted. Finally at 9:45 P.M., his body, head all but blown away, was identified at the Hotel-Dieu Hospital. Distraught Phalangists gathered at the scene of the explosion, sat on the curb, and wept when the news of Gemayel's death reached them. At the funeral the next day, thousands of Phalangist militiamen carrying giant portraits of their fallen leader marched through the streets chanting, "Bashir lives! Bashir lives!" as though their chants would bring him back.

While the Phalangists buried Bashir Gemayel, the Israeli Defense Force (IDF) moved into the Palestinian and Shiite neighborhood of Sabra and the camp of Shatila to flush out any remaining Palestinian guerrillas and to secure West Beirut. Originally intending to use the revived Lebanese army, the Israelis instead allowed the Phalange to enter an area in which eighty thousand Palestinians were encircled. The inhabitants of Shatila were mostly the young and old and the wives, mothers, and sisters the *fedayeen* had left behind under Western assurances of their safety.

At sundown on September 16, squads of Phalangists crawled over the earthen embankments and disappeared into Shatila's narrow alleyways. A hardened Phalangist militiaman whose relatives were killed by the Palestinians at that first bloodletting at Damour said as he crept into Sabra, "I've been waiting years to get in here." The Phalange intended to carry out the dead Bashir Gemayel's vision of the final act of the war for Lebanon.

For two nights and a day, while the IDF stood outside the gates and periodically sent flares over the area for illumination, the

Phalangists gutted their victims with bayonets, trampled infants
to death, and slaughtered whole families in a frenzy of revenge for
Bashir, for Lebanon, and for Christendom.

Israeli soldiers suspected what their commanders refused to
acknowledge. One young soldier from atop his tank, peering down
into the carnage, demanded of a Phalangist why his people were
killing women and children. The militiaman shouted back,
"Women give birth to children, and children grow up into terrorists." Finally, the Israeli military hierarchy was forced to acknowledge the magnitude of the *dabah,* or slaughter, and ordered the
Phalangists out. Before leaving at 7 A.M. on September 18, the
Phalangists summoned bulldozers to conceal as much of the blood-
bath as possible.

Journalists, alerted by rumors over the preceding days, broke
into the camp at mid-morning. The bulldozers had left enough
evidence uncovered to haul both the Phalange and the Israeli
government before the bar of world opinion.

In a one-hundred-square-yard space inside Sabra, seventy
corpses overlapped one another. Ninety-year-old Adnan Noury, a
gaping bullet hole in his left temple, sprawled next to his seventy-
year-old neighbor, Muhammad Diab. A few steps to the right,
blood-splattered bodies were draped over rubble left from the
siege of Beirut. In the doorway of a meager house, a three-year-old
child cuddled as if asleep next to her dead mother. Phalangist
revenge had rained down on the poorest of the poor among the
Palestinians. All that was left was to bury them in a mass grave
marked with a simple inscription: "Long Live Our Deaths."

No one may ever know how many were killed in that act of
infamy. Israeli intelligence set the number at seven hundred to
eight hundred, while the Palestinian Red Crescent claimed two
thousand. Whatever the number, it was too high. The West's guarantee of safety to the Palestinians had failed. Within forty-eight
hours of the final act of killing at Sabra and Shatila, President
Reagan ordered the U.S. Marines back to Beirut.

Israel's failure to establish some political control in order to
extricate itself from its own flawed policy thrust upon the United
States the burden of acting as peacemaker in Lebanon. After
refusing to become involved at the beginning of the civil war, the
United States was at last the captive of the Maronites.

In some ways, Lebanon was another victim of the Vietnam

war. The American effort in Indochina had collapsed in April 1975, the same month Lebanon was plunged into civil war. Thus, the blood feuds of the Levant became lost in the Washington shuffle. Whether the United States could or should have acted in 1975 was by now moot. In 1982, the United States faced the reality that Lebanon represented the West's last open door to the Middle East.

The election of Amin Gemayel, Bashir's older brother, as president provided the cornerstone of U.S. policy. Looking debonair even in a flak jacket, Amin Gemayel on the surface is a repository of Western manners and mores. He prefers Western classical music, especially Beethoven and Wagner. He plays tennis in designer whites. And he claims the Maronites are "fighting for values, values we have in common with the West." But Amin Gemayel is more attuned to the Levantine character of Lebanon than his brother ever was. Therefore, at the time of his election, he was at least reasonably acceptable to the old-line politicians, if not to the radicals. "To Muslims, Amin Gemayel represented a compromise. It was like the class of 1943 rising from the grave. Innocent of ties with Israel, convinced of the need to get along with the Muslims, and involved in business like any self-respecting Lebanese, Amin represented a return to the past."

Amin Gemayel sought U.S. support to shore up his shaky regime and to get the Israelis and Syrians out of Lebanon, giving the National Pact one more chance. But the National Pact was by now light-years away from reality. The political and economic changes that should have come before 1975 were unavoidable after the summer of 1982, when the Maronites constituted only about 30 percent of the population.

Unfortunately, the Reagan administration knew even less about the realities of Lebanon than the Israelis did. Like Israel, the United States painted a grand design for Lebanon. On paper, it was impressive:

The American formula for success in Lebanon was relatively straightforward. First, the US would use its undeniably close relations with Israel and President Gemayel to help work out an agreement on withdrawing Israeli forces. Once this was achieved, the Lebanese, with Arab and American help, would work on the Syrians to get them to withdraw. Then Gemayel, with these two victories behind him, could work to broaden his political base by drawing into his government some of the leaders of the Muslim communities. While the diplomatic initiatives proceeded, the US would help to strengthen the Lebanese army, so that Gemayel would be able to go into political reconciliation talks with a force of his own with which to confront the various militia leaders, including those of the Lebanese Forces.

With their own country stabilized, the Lebanese could move into the Middle East peace process by making peace with Israel.

However, the Muslims perceived the United States' whole operation as nothing short of collusion with Israel and a grand scheme to ensure continued Maronite control of Lebanon. In important aspects, they were right. Israel, unable to finish the job it had started without an intolerable loss of life, fell back on the United States to pull its chestnuts out of the fire. In rescuing Israel, the United States clutched at a government put in place by Phalangist deal making and Israeli military might. Even accepting the argument that Lebanon could emerge from war only under a strong central government, that government was worthless if it guaranteed Maronite hegemony and failed to represent the majority of the Lebanese people. In protecting the Christians, the West again was, in the eyes of the Muslims, denigrating the Muslims and Islam.

If the use of Amin Gemayel to build a new order in Lebanon was not enough to doom U.S. efforts to stabilize Lebanon, the war itself had made another ninety-degree turn. With the death of Kamal Jumblatt in 1977, the leftist front that originally had entered the war against the Maronites faded. From the Syrian intervention in 1976 to the Israeli invasion in 1982, the foreign elements of the war—Syria, Israel, and the Palestinians—dominated the action, carrying along a changing array of Lebanese allies. But with the Israeli invasion, the sectarian aspects of the war finally overshadowed any unity the left enjoyed. The Druze, the linchpin of the leftist alliance, shunned the leftists' socialist ideology for their communal survival.

The four-thousand-strong Druze militia had been developing in quasi-underground conditions since 1976. After Kamal Jumblatt's death, Druze leadership fell to Jumblatt's only son, Walid. No one expected much of the owl-eyed Walid. Rumored to have a "weak character," a mercurial personality, and an alcohol addiction, he further shocked the establishment by dressing in faded blue jeans and a worn leather jacket and riding a motorcycle. But Walid, displaying surprising political savvy and aided by the strength of the Druze militia, succeeded in keeping all—the Syrians, the Phalangists, and the Palestinians—out of the Druze' historic lands in the Shuf. On the eve of the Israeli invasion, Walid reigned over a united flock that shouted its loyalty to its leader: "With blood and spirit, we will sacrifice to you, O Walid."

As part of its invasion strategy, Israel had entered the Shuf in the summer of 1982. The IDF met little resistance, because the Druze assumed they could cut a deal with Israel: In return for keeping the Palestinians out of the Shuf, Israel would recognize Druze autonomy. Instead, Israel allowed the Lebanese Forces to move into the Shuf, igniting all the old enmities between the Maronites and the Druze of the Mountain.

The Lebanese Forces set about establishing their control over the Shuf with the same tough tactics they had used elsewhere. But the Druze struck back. They were armed with a huge arsenal of Syrian- and Soviet-supplied arms and reinforced by emigrant Druze who had returned from jobs abroad to make the stand for their ancestral lands. War councils of Druze military commanders met around the swimming pool of the Sunnyland Hotel and planned the defense of the Shuf. When they moved, the Druze pushed the Lebanese Forces out of most of the southern mountains and trapped the remaining pockets of Maronite resistance in the hills. The only thing that stood between the Maronites and a rout at the hands of the Druze was the Israeli army.

When the IDF abruptly pulled out of the Shuf in August 1983, the Druze embarked on a rampage of slaughter in Maronite villages, writing another chapter in a 140-year vendetta. On the first anniversary of the massacre in Sabra and Shatila, the Maronites lost sixty villages to the Druze, suffering one thousand dead and fifty thousand homeless. A bitter Maronite, hunched over in a refugee center on the edge of Jounieh, blurted out his anger: "The world wept over Sabra and Shatila and shed not a tear for Dayr al Qamar." Among the villages looted and burned was Beit al Din, which lay just across a narrow ravine from the Christian town of Dayr al Qamar, scene of the notorious massacre of 1860. The hard-pressed Maronites sent out their call to the Western forces of the MNF.

The nations of the Multi-National Force, seemingly naive as to the labyrinthine nature of Lebanon, walked into the chaos in 1982 sincerely believing that the West could serve as an honest broker between the warring sides. But it was the United States that embraced the grand strategy of stabilizing war-torn Lebanon in order to lead it into peace with Israel. The "May 17 Agreement" was the pinnacle of American diplomatic ineptitude in the Levant. The agreement centered on a series of clandestine understandings between Israel and the State of Lebanon as represented by Amin Gemayel. Its key provision was a secret letter from Israel to the United States that pledged a phased Israeli withdrawal from all of Lebanon upon a simultaneous withdrawal of Syria and the remaining Palestinian forces. Free of foreign intervention, the reconstituted Lebanese government could pursue peace with Israel. The agreement's fatal flaw was that the United States, the Gemayel government, and Israel had entered into a pact on Lebanon's future without consulting two of the major players in Lebanon—the Druze and Syria. Hafiz Assad, in concert with Walid Jumblatt, whirled into action to destroy it.

Syria mobilized groups in Lebanon opposed to the Gemayel government into a coalition called the National Salvation Front. Suddenly, the United States stood face to face with the incredible complexity of Lebanon, where "the ingrained fragmentation and volatile partnerships of Lebanon were no more responsive to position papers than they had been to bombs and shells."

In the months following the birth of what Assad termed "the stillborn agreement," the tangled skein of alliances and rivalries in Lebanon demonstrated the true complexity of the political-military mix. Some of Syria's allies in the anti-Gemayel coalition hunted for new backers to protect them from this new assertion of Hafiz Assad's power. Walid Jumblatt decided he was willing to forgive Israel the "perfidy" of its invasion if it would support a Druze canton in the Shuf and provide the Druze with a modicum of independence from Syria. Arafat, pushed into a corner by a rebellion of pro-Syrian factions among the Palestinians, suddenly discovered the possibilities in an alliance with the Phalange, who were only too happy to supply weapons and Israeli ammunition to his last stronghold in Tripoli. In the midst of this shifting of alignments, the Americans, like latter-day "innocents abroad," maneuvered through the maze of the Levant.

Washington belatedly realized that Amin Gemayel sorely

lacked the political leverage and personal stature required to play the role envisioned for him. With the Israeli withdrawal from Beirut and its environs, the leading force in Lebanon was now the Syrian-backed Druze and the Shiite front ensconced in the Shuf. To prove the impotence of the Gemayel government, shells rained out of the hills onto Beirut and the president's Baabda palace. Caught in the middle were members of the Multi-National Force.

Like the first heady days of any foreign intervention in Lebanon, the return of the MNF after the massacre at Sabra and Shatila was greeted with the joy accorded liberators. Across the confessionals, the Lebanese believed—or wanted to believe—that the presence of Western forces would end Lebanon's long nightmare. The two thousand men of the French Foreign Legion manned Beirut proper. Twenty-one hundred men from the Italian contingent were entrenched in the southern suburbs. And twelve hundred U.S. Marines burrowed down behind sandbags at the Beirut airport. When unarmed patrols were sent out into the Muslim quarter, children waved, and older boys who casually carried machine guns instead of schoolbooks let them pass checkpoints with a nod.

But eventually everyone who comes to save Lebanon ends up being destroyed by Lebanon. When the shooting from the mountains began, the U.S. Marines, sitting in an exposed position at the airport with instructions not to fire, were the biggest sitting ducks of the MNF. All the old arguments about putting the Marines into Lebanon in the first place resurfaced. George Ball's words came back: "We would imprudently hazard the lives of our Marines to commit them to an area where anti-Americanism is a dominating sentiment."

With the Druze, joined by others within the National Salvation Front, rampaging through the Shuf during September 1983, Amin Gemayel desperately grabbed at the remnants of American and MNF support for his government. When a unit of the Lebanese army, commanded by Christians, was besieged by Druze militiamen in Souq al Gharb in the mountains above the airport, Ronald Reagan declared the tiny village of strategic importance to the United States. From their positions off the coast, the cruiser *Virginia*, the destroyer *John Rogers*, and the battleship *New Jersey* sent six hundred rounds of seventy-pound shells zooming over Beirut and crashing into Muslim villages in the Shuf. French aircraft streaked in after the shells in an aerial mop-up operation. Incredibly, U.S. and Allied policymakers still clung to the MNF's original premise that it was supporting the legitimate government of Lebanon. Yet for antigovernment Lebanese, American warships shelling villages inhabited not only by Druze but by Shiites and some Sunnis presented the spectacle of a superpower battering a small, determined community. Throughout the Arab world, television screens flickered with the awesome display of Western military power and scenes of anguished Arab mothers clutching their dead or dying children. The West did save the Lebanese army from defeat, but at the price of convincing the Muslims that the United States was in Lebanon only as the guardians of Israeli interests and the protector of Lebanon's Christians. With the battle of Souq al Gharb, intense anti-Westernism exploded in Lebanon.

The mountain war ended as all the major eruptions of fighting had ended. In its aftermath, the battles for turf among rival militias continued. Lebanon had been at war for eight years. Life, particularly in Beirut, was reduced to coping—to staying sane.

By the fall of 1983, Lebanon had sustained at least $12 billion to $15 billion in physical damages. Yet the Lebanese continued their cycle of build and destroy. A resident of a seafront apartment replaced all his windows three times in 1983, and businessmen rebuilt their shops and offices as many as six times. Somehow humanity and barbarism lived side by side. After the big battles, rescue workers buried bodies and cared for the wounded while others stole water from ambulances and robbed the dead of their gold. Yet Beirut's dimmed sparkle still struggled up through the destruction.

The population did not become animals: if anything, family relationships grew stronger during the war because there was no one else to depend on. Curiously, most people became obsessively orderly, organizing every aspect of their lives down to the smallest detail. At the height of the siege of Beirut, one man gathered up the neighborhood children and put them to work scrubbing the street with detergent.

War also unleashed the Lebanese' insatiable appetite for material goods. Holiday seasons in Lebanon always invited moods of compulsive, almost manic shopping and extravagant spending. But in the aftermath of the Israeli invasion, department stores, shops, makeshift stalls, and street vendors unfurled a dazzling assortment of goods exceeding anything before the war. "The compulsion to buy became a national pastime, an outlet for traumatized individuals in their futile attempt to restore their damaged self-regard and personal worth." Yet while the shops glittered with gadgetry and gaudy luxuries, the fetid streets and sidewalks were littered with rancid garbage and the effluents of gushing sewers. With introspection the Lebanese criticized their own adaptability, citing it as one reason for the war's long duration. A favorite saying was "If you keep a frog in a frying pan and warm it up slowly, the frog stays. If the pan is heated fast, it jumps out."

In the absence of any plausible explanation for the many acts of violence that terrorized their lives, the Lebanese indulged in the simplistic, often incredible rationalization that the blame for their travail rested solely on the Syrians, the Israelis, or some grand superpower conspiracy—anyone but themselves. Perhaps the Lebanese knew the outsiders could not have done it alone. Perhaps they knew they had proven incapable of settling their own political differences. While mournfully portraying themselves as impotent victims of international rivalry, they craftily used outside interference as a justification for their own unwillingness to come to grips with their political problems.

Before the war, the Lebanese played a series of sophisticated games that succeeded in preserving Lebanon's sovereignty. One such game might have been called "The Lion and the Unicorn." According to the rules the Unicorn, which represented the Muslims and the Druze, repeatedly asserted its own identity. If the game became too serious, the Lion, representing the Christians, called to its Western protectors to intervene and prevent consequences no one wanted. Everyone was happy. The Unicorn blamed the Lion for forcing its withdrawal from Arabist involvement, and the Lion took pride in reasserting its own identity. Realistically, both sides agreed that neither got the crown, and both were satisfied that Lebanese independence had been preserved. But the game became deadly, because the Lebanese lost their ability to compromise. Both sides fantasized that the foreign powers they called upon for help—the Palestinians, Syrians, Israelis, Americans, and Europeans—would arrive like the cavalry, save one faction from being destroyed by the other, restore order, and then retreat, saving the Lebanese from themselves. Instead, the Lebanese found that these powers had their own agendas. They were there neither to save the

Lebanese formula nor to impose a new order. With some concession given to the MNF, they were there to promote their own interests. And once involved, they refused to leave. The saviors became the masters.

By the beginning of October 1983, Lebanese sovereignty was eclipsed. Syrian influence cast its lengthening shadow over Lebanon. The Gemayel government, controlling the same amount of territory the Maronites held in 1975, was hanging on only with the tolerance of Hafiz Assad. Syria's Palestinian nemeses, Yassir Arafat and Fatah, were all but destroyed in Lebanon, leaving Syria in control of anti-Fatah factions in the Bekaa. Syria was the major arms supplier to the Druze and the Shiites, the new variable in the equation. And the Israelis had withdrawn to a security zone in the south. Everything was ready for Lebanon's final assault on the West.

NINE

THE WAR AGAINST THE WEST: THE HOSTAGES

The soft night enfolded Beirut in an ephemeral peace. In a third-floor apartment just off Rue Hamra, the wide French doors leading out to the balcony stood open, allowing the autumn breeze to fill the high-ceilinged rooms with the briny smell of the ocean. Only sporadically did the menacing turmoil of a country at war invade the serenity. Once a group of noisy Nasserites armed with drums and placards paraded through the street below, shouting their support of the Arab nation. But then they were gone. The quiet returned, broken now and then by the bark of rifle fire on an adjacent street. Once in the distance, a lone rocket blazed across the horizon; the beauty of its light in the inky blackness belied the ugliness of its purpose.

The room was crowded with Westerners, all veterans of the bloody feuds on Lebanese land. Seated on the middle cushion of a worn but comfortable sofa, I listened to one after another zestfully postulate on when or if peace would come. While they talked, a small, bespectacled man in his early fifties sat silently against a far wall. When the discussion passed its crescendo, one of the participants said to me, "If you really want to know about Lebanon, ask Ben. He's been here longer than any of us and speaks Arabic like an

193

Arab." I turned to the quiet man by the far wall. After some
prompting, the Reverend Benjamin Weir, Presbyterian missionary
for twenty-eight years, began to speak modestly about Lebanon.

"We all talk about the Maronites and the Druze and the Sunnis, but no one talks about the Shiites. They are the forgotten ones
in this war." Motioning to his pink-cheeked wife, he continued,
"Carol and I spent five years working in a Shiite village in the
south. The people there have so little, not even roads to move their
produce to market in Beirut. And now they are caught between the
PLO and Israel. Someday we may all feel their anger." Several
years later Benjamin Weir, blindfolded and chained to a radiator in
a bare room in West Beirut, cowered on a thin mattress, a hostage
of the rage of the Shiites.

The Shiites arrived in Lebanon on the heels of the Muslim
armies that had so successfully spread Islam throughout the Middle East during the seventh century. Although some scattered into
the northern Bekaa, most settled in the south, which has remained
not only the geographic center of the sect in Lebanon but its
spiritual heartland. Since those early days, southern Lebanon and
Lebanon's Shiites have been joined in a common destiny.

Throughout the periods of the Ottomans, the French Mandate,
and the Lebanese Republic, the Lebanese Shiites lived on the
fringe of a Christian–Sunni–dominated Lebanese society. But they
were also on the edge of Shiite culture. Although they acted as
intermediaries between Persia (Iran), the home of their religion,
and Lebanon, the home of their birth, they were rejected by the
Persians because they were Arabs and by the Arabs because they
were Shiites.

In 1920, when Greater Lebanon was born, the Shiites comprised 17 percent of the population, enough to give them a role in
the political system but not enough to assure them power. The
French, the Maronites, and the Sunnis allowed the Shiites through
the door of government and then quickly co-opted their leaders. In
return for keeping their community passive, the Shiite clan chieftains and large landowners were allowed to feed with the establishment at the trough of Lebanon while their people languished as a
disinherited subproletariat.

The Shiites essentially played no part in the 1958 miniwar.
The breakdown of the political understanding between the Sunnis
and the Maronites established by the National Pact barely touched

the remote world of the Shiites. Yet when that upheaval ended, Fuad Shihab, the most uncommon of Lebanese presidents, recognized that it was crucial to Lebanon's future as a nation-state to address the inequalities between the Shiites and the rest of the Lebanese population.

In 1959, Shihab commissioned a leading French research group to prepare the first broad study of socioeconomic conditions in Lebanon. Named the *Lebret Report*, the group's findings spelled out just how deplorably the administrations of Bishara Khoury and Camille Chamoun had neglected regional development, especially in the south. Pushed by the report's censure and Shihab's influence, the Chamber of Deputies reluctantly directed a minimal amount of government funds into the neglected south. Limited but meaningful reforms delivered some roads, electrification, and other basic building blocks of a modern infrastructure. But most of all, Shihab opened to the Shiites the promise of an education. It became possible, albeit extremely difficult, for the son of a stooped peasant to earn a university degree with the help of one of a handful of government scholarships. Education, in turn, opened up to the Shiites the chance to compete for better-paying jobs abroad. Thus, hundreds escaped the grinding poverty and toil of the land and found their way into the commerce of West Africa and the automotive factories of Detroit. The remittances they sent back provided education for the next generation. The Shiites had begun to stir.

But when Charles Helou became president in 1964, he quickly caved in to the greed of the Christian-Sunni merchant class and slowed to a trickle the already scant development funds going into Shiite regions. Concurrently, thousands of Shiites were allowed to slip through the cracks of the bureaucracy, leaving them with no national identity cards and hence no access to government services or the right to vote. Nevertheless, the Shiites as a community remained politically docile, seeming to accept their position as second-class citizens. Alienated from their traditional leadership, they possessed no vehicle for revolt. The small minority of Shiites who were politically active followed the left of Lebanese politics. During the 1960s, they gravitated toward a variety of leftist political movements, including the Nasserites, the Baath Party, the PPS, the Popular Front for the Liberation of Palestine, and the communists. But none of these groups addressed the Shiites' particular needs. The left attracted the Shiites because they resented Lebanon's laissez-faire capitalist economy that nurtured the concentration of wealth in the hands of the *zuama* and perpetuated the Shiites' poverty. But the socialist parties contained their own traps. The left, dominated as strongly by pan-Arabism as by socialism, threatened to drown the Shiites in Sunni dominance. Thus the Shiites drifted, waiting for their own political voice—a voice that would come by way of Iran.

Traditionally, the ties between the Shiite communities of Lebanon and the religious establishment of Iran were close. The Lebanese Shiites, in fact, derived much of their religious instruction and many of their leading clerics from Iran. Therefore, in 1960, when Sayyid Abdul Hussein, the religious leader of Tyre, sought his replacement, he naturally turned to the rising young clerics of Iran. From among them, he chose Musa al Sadr.

Born in 1928 in Qom, the Shiite theological center of Iran, Sadr was the scion of a distinguished clerical family and a *sayyid*, one who claims descent from the prophet Muhammed. Sadr was less than enthusiastic about Sayyid Hussein's offer. No ambitious cleric was eager to sacrifice the great ecclesiastical cities of Iran for the backwaters of southern Lebanon. But perhaps even more important in Sadr's hesitation were the conflicting cultures of Iran and Lebanon. Although Arab by descent, Sadr was Iranian by culture. Only the foolhardy ignored the peril of being an Iranian in an Arabic-speaking country caught in the strident Arabism that held sway in the Levant in the 1960s. Nevertheless, Sadr accepted the invitation. Over the next eighteen years, Musa al Sadr became the Lebanese Shiites' political voice and as such achieved extraordinary fame in a country that boasted few contemporary heroes.

Sadr looked like a casting director's vision of a cult figure. In a nation of relatively short men, his six feet, six inches towered over the powerful and the meek. His intense eyes blazed out of a patriarchal visage fringed with a lush, precisely trimmed beard. Heavy black curls escaped rakishly from the raven-black turban that, along with his flowing *abaya*, or gown, completed his outward credentials as a cleric. Yet Sadr's physical appearance was only a prelude to the magnetism of his personality and the grandeur of his oratory, crucial to great leaders in a culture that exalts the spoken word.

From the beginning of his mission in Lebanon, Sadr established himself as different from the moribund clerics who presided over the Shiites' affairs. Throwing aside the tradition of writing exhaustive treatises on obscure points of Islamic law, Sadr assumed for himself as a religious leader political obligations and prerogatives. From the outset, he made it clear that his was a political quest. He shocked the religious community by traveling freely in Europe and defended himself against charges of flirting with the devil by saying, "One partook of the glamorous civilization out there, learned its ways, in order to prepare the realm of Islam for the assault of the West."

In the first phase of his plan to politicize the Shiites, Sadr drew around him young Shiite men in their thirties and forties who possessed money, education, and a determination to elbow their way into Lebanon's rigid confessional hierarchy. These men formed the core of the movement. The second phase of Sadr's plan was to revamp the traditions of Shiism to convert a faith of lament and submission into one of exaltation and rebellion. Shiite history of wallowing in tales of defeat would be neither accepted nor denied by Sadr. The tradition would simply be reworked to cast Shiism in a new, ennobling light. Sadr brought his commanding presence and fiery oratory to mass gatherings at which he transfigured the central symbols of Shiism into vehicles for a Shiite awakening. Ashura, the annual ceremony of mourning and self-flagellation that commemorated the defeated and martyred Hussein, became a celebration of defiance in which the Shiites threw off their subservience and emerged as an "elite minority" who refused to submit to injustice. Sadr exhorted his followers to reject their fatalistic acceptance of deprivation. Transforming Lebanon into a new Kerbala, he charged the followers of the martyred Hussein to shed their fright and silence.

With the cry of resurgent Shiism at the vanguard of political power, Musa al Sadr molded the slum dweller of Beirut, the peasant of the south, and the sometimes wild clansman of the Bekaa into an inclusive communal identity.

Marching in lockstep, Sadr and the Shiites inched toward Lebanon's political core. In 1963 President Fuad Shihab, acting despite his reservations that Sayyid al Sadr was a rabble-rouser, bestowed Lebanese citizenship on the Iranian-born cleric. In 1969, the Chamber of Deputies sanctioned the formation of the Higher Shia Council, a representative body for the Shiites that freed them from the tutelage of the Sunni Muslims. On his installation as president of the council, Musa al Sadr issued the Shiites' battle cry: "O rising generations, if our demands [for political and economic equality] are not met, we will set about taking them by force: if this country is not given, it must be taken."

By 1970, Musa al Sadr was challenging the traditional leaders of southern Lebanon, especially Kamil Asad, who to Sadr epitomized all that was wrong with the Lebanese political system. Sadr organized a massive general strike that forced the Chamber of Deputies to create and fund the "Council of the South." Although imperfect and chaired by the corrupt Kamil Asad, the council was nonetheless the government's first serious attempt to channel development funds into the impoverished Jabal Amil.

Yet fate would intervene to deny the Shiites the opportunity to pursue their own destiny. Before they achieved political power, the Shiites became trapped and enfeebled between the aims of the Palestinians and the resolve of the Israelis.

In 1968, Palestinian commando raids against Israel began from southern Lebanon. In the vicious cycle of blow and counterblow between Palestinians and Israelis, Palestinian commandos scattered, leaving the Shiites as the targets of Israeli bombs. As a result, the image of a woman in a colorful dress squatting on the ground in front of her collapsed house, wailing over her dead husband's body, became the caricature of south Lebanon.

In the wake of the Israelis' low-flying bombing raids, merchants and farmers piled their battered luggage into old Mercedes taxis or on beds of pickup trucks for the desperate flight to Beirut. But many stayed, for there was really nowhere to go. Although Ahmed Hadi Ayub, a farmer, lost his house and two of his nine children in one bombing raid, he remained. The plot of ground on which the rubble of his house stood was all he had. In a voice of resignation, he said, "The Palestinians want back their land. The Israelis don't want to give it up. Both are determined to fight. And we are caught in the middle."

Most of those who did leave dispersed into the squalor of South Beirut. Thousands of proud men, the leaders and providers of families in a powerfully patriarchal society, were reduced to refugee status and stripped of their honor. But the physical burden of the disruption fell on the women. They were the ones who packed the family's belongings when trouble erupted, and they were the ones who established makeshift homes in Beirut among strangers.

The Shiites were experiencing a whole society in upheaval. Since the south was the epicenter for the Shiite community, what happened in Jabal Amil reverberated through the entire Shiite populace of Lebanon. Through the extensive family networks, the plight of the southern Shiites became the symbolic plight of every Shiite in Lebanon. In the confusion and misery, radicalization undermined what little authority traditional political bosses still claimed, and allegiances shifted to the new brand of leader epitomized by Musa al Sadr.

Sadr rallied the Shiites against a government both unable and unwilling to protect the south against the increasingly bloody reprisals of Israel. If Sadr challenged the existing political system, he also challenged the basic, if imprecise, Christian-Muslim and right-left divisions of Lebanon. Sadr was fond of saying, "We are neither of the right nor of the left but we follow the path of the just."

The Shiites fit into neither the largely Christian right nor the overwhelmingly Muslim left. Sadr was a Lebanese nationalist if for no other reason than he saw Lebanon as *al watan nihai*, the final homeland of the Shiites. Economically, Shiite interests lay with the left, but leftist politics and its accompanying pan-Arabism raised for Sadr, as for other Shiites, the specter of their age-old subjugation to the Sunnis. Even more, Sadr resisted the leftist bloc's demand of subservience to the Palestinian movement. In the leftist politics of the time, "[T]o be an Arab meant to be certified by the Palestinians, to accept the prerogatives asserted by armed Palestinian organizations, and to take in stride the reprisals launched by Israel into the ancestral Shia land in the south of Lebanon." While Sadr claimed to support the Palestinian resistance movement, he was unwilling to countenance the actions of the PLO that exposed the Shiites to the wrath of Israel. In a clear break with the Arabs' unquestioning public backing of the Palestinians, Sadr charged that the PLO was a military machine that terrorized the Arab world, extorting money, support, and the sympathy of world opinion.

Combining the Shiites' demand for equality in the political system with their outrage at the government's failure to protect them from the clashes along the border, Sadr launched the Shiites' own political movement, which he called Harakat Mahroomin, the "Movement of the Deprived." Sadr received foreign funding from a variety of sources, including the Shah of Iran and the Baathist government of Iraq. But he was cautious in both his foreign entan-

glements and the degree to which he was willing to push the
Maronites. In the escalating disorder that plunged Lebanon into
civil war, Musa al Sadr became the country's most compelling
figure.

By the early 1970s, Sadr bore the title of *imam*, a distinction
that he never claimed but one that was implied by his followers and
accepted by the clergy. Its significance was its potent symbolism of
Sadr's status among his followers. Shiism recognizes only twelve
imams. The first eleven succumbed to battle, poison, or prison,
perpetrated by what the Shiites regarded as unjust usurpers of
religious authority. In Shiite theology, the twelfth imam vanished
to live in concealment until he returned as the *mahdi*, or savior.
Drawing from the Hadith, Shiite tradition framed the promise of
the hidden imam: "He will fill the earth with equity and justice as
it was filled with oppression and tyranny."

The years 1974 and 1975 were Musa al Sadr's. In March 1974,
seventy-five thousand men turned out in Baalbek to hear the
"imam." He arrived to frenzied shouts of "Allah u-Akbar" (God is
Great) and the shrill ululations of women. In his speech, Sadr
struck his recurrent themes. Thrusting the Shiite economic reality
into the face of those in power, he cried, "Let us look at the ghettoes
of Beirut: Oh men in power, do you not feel ashamed that a few
kilometers away from your homes are houses that are not fit for
human habitation?" And he castigated those who wreaked havoc on
the south: "The PLO is a factor of anarchy in the south. The Shi'ias
are conquering their inferiority complex with respect to the Palestinian organization. We have had enough!"

When the civil war came, Musa al Sadr reluctantly followed
the leftist National Movement. In the 1975–1976 phase of the war
around one-half of the thirty thousand to forty thousand Muslims
killed were Shiites. To Sadr, it appeared that Kamal Jumblatt, the
National Movement's leader, was willing to fight the Christians to
the last Shiite. Consequently, Sadr secretly began to expand his
own Shiite militia. In 1975, when twenty-seven of Sadr's soldiers
were killed in an accident at a military training base in the Bekaa,
knowledge of the militia became public. Confronted with the revelation, Sadr hastily improvised the name *Amal*, meaning "hope,"
an acronym for Afwaj al Muqawamah al Lubnanya (Lebanese
Resistance Battalions). Amal was Sadr's admission that the war
had forced him to shift away from the sermons and fasts that had

sermons and fasts that had worked so well for him in peacetime to the new reality that in Lebanon power came from a gun.

The new arena in which Lebanon's protagonists played out their hands would prove to be one in which Sadr was less successful. Sadr was at his best in contests of moral persuasion. When Lebanon passed the point where persuasion no longer had any relevance, Sadr's influence began to wane. His critics, who either had never approved of the mixing of religion and politics or were simply jealous of his stature, began to whisper that Musa al Sadr was an American agent who had been dropped into Lebanon nearly twenty years before by the CIA.

Sadr, now fifty years old, continued his frenetic travels on behalf of the Shiite cause. On August 25, 1978, he arrived in the Libyan capital of Tripoli accompanied by one of his clerical assistants and a journalist. On August 31, a group of Lebanese acquaintances saw him leave his hotel to attend a meeting with Muammar Qaddafi. No one saw Musa al Sadr again. That night his luggage arrived in Rome on Alitalia flight 881 and was checked into the Holiday Inn by two Libyans. The imam had vanished.

Inquiries, official and unofficial, went out across the world. A month after Sadr's disappearance, four clerics traveled to Damascus to confront Muammar Qaddafi, who was on a state visit to Syria. They appeared at the head of two hundred thousand protesters in a convoy of cars, buses, and tractors that stretched for fifteen kilometers and carried placards with the pointed message "O Arabs, where is the Imam?"

Sadr's disappearance restored any mystique he had lost. For the Shiites of Lebanon he became the vanished imam, the concealed one moving among them who would one day return to preside over a redeemed world. As extraordinarily important as he had been before vanishing, Sadr became even more significant after his mysterious disappearance. Sadr had always dealt in symbols, and no symbol held more meaning for the Shiite community than a leader's—an imam to most—vanishing without a trace. Had he remained, Sadr could well have been destroyed by the civil war as were most of the other political leaders of 1975. But Sadr remains a potent force in the Shiite community. Amal militiamen battle with his picture encased in plastic hanging on cords around their necks. Children playing war in the streets with wooden guns run beneath posters pasted on pockmarked walls celebrating the imam. And on the street corners, his portrait stands alongside those of the latest martyrs, the young men killed fighting for Musa al Sadr's vision of empowered Shiism.

Sadr's disappearance fell between two other events that proved to be powerful mobilizing forces of Shiite politics—Israel's Litani Operation in March 1978 and the January 1979 Islamic revolution that toppled the Shah of Iran.

One of the ironies of the period from 1968 to 1978, when the Israelis were striking south Lebanon with such devastating force, was that the Shiites felt no particular enmity toward Israel for causing their misery. After all, the Shiites were also suffering the arrogance of the Palestinian commandos, and it was they whom the Shiites blamed for exposing their families, homes, and livelihoods to constant danger. While the leadership of Amal bitterly said, "The people of the south . . . have given the Palestinian cause their land, their children, their security, their orchards—everything but their honor and dignity," a villager echoed, "We gave the Palestinians everything and they gave us back insults, corpses, and a lesson in corruption." So angry were the Shiites at the PLO that at one point Amal flirted with the idea of striking a modus vivendi with Israel. After all, both sides shared the goal of dismantling the Palestinian ministate in the south and imposing order along the border. But in March 1978, Israel decided to use its firepower to cleanse south Lebanon of commandos. Coming on the heels of Major Saad Haddad's program of shelling, kidnapping, and extortion to prevent Shiite villagers from supporting the Palestinians, the Litani Operation caused a radical shift in attitude. The Israeli aerial assault on south Lebanon killed two thousand Shiites, destroyed twenty-five hundred houses, and sent another wave of refugees toward Beirut. Israeli army units that followed up the air attacks rounded up Shiites suspected of aiding the PLO and detained them for days or even weeks. The Shiites, no longer entertaining any thought of cooperation with Israel, either joined Amal or identified with it largely out of a desperate need to protect their families and homes.

The politicalization of Lebanon's Shiites under the banner of Islam was already in flower when the Islamic revolution rocked Iran in 1979. The Iranians' revolution did not plant the seeds of revolt in the Shiites of Lebanon; rather, it provided a compelling example of what a well-organized and mobilized Shiite community could accomplish. The revolution of the Ayatollah Khomeini was, in an important sense, a revolution of cultural affirmation. While overlaid with important economic factors, the Iranian revolution was undergirded by an emotional rejection of the pervasive westernization that Shah Muhammad Reza Pahlavi had imposed on Iranian society. Islam's centuries of hostility toward the West erupted in Khomeini's revolutionary rhetoric that branded the West as a "satan" and singled out the United States as the "Great Satan." Khomeini, utilizing the stratagem of symbols so central to the Shiite ethos, paraded fifty-two bound and blindfolded American hostages through the streets of Tehran to the taunts of thousands of chador-draped women and their frenzied men. Retribution was being delivered on those who denigrated Islam.

The traditionally close ties between the two Shiite communities ensured that the events in Iran would reverberate in Lebanon. Psychologically the Shiites of Lebanon were primed for Khomeini's ideology. They had already launched the Movement of the Deprived. In Khomeini's system of values, the concept of the deprived masses is as basic as his implacable enmity toward the West. His ideology promises social justice based on the Koran rather than on some secular, socialist theory concocted by the Sunnis. And it carries with it Islam's message of defiance toward Israel, principally over the Jewish state's possession of Jerusalem, Islam's third holy site. Rejecting failed secular ideologies, the Shiites embraced Islam as their crucible of protest. In Lebanon, where the very essence of politics is the sect, the Shiites had at last found their political rights in a movement that served as a touchstone for their identity as Lebanese Shiites. Amal ripened into a full-blown political movement.

In 1980, Amal acquired a new leader—Nabih Berri, a forty-one-year-old lawyer as unassuming as Musa al Sadr had been flamboyant. Berri possessed none of the traditional credentials for political leadership in Lebanon. He had been born in Freetown, Sierra Leone, the son of a Lebanese Shiite who had emigrated to West Africa and become a successful businessman. Berri graduated from neither St. Joseph nor the American University of Beirut but from the heavily Muslim Beirut University College. He left Beirut after graduating and lived in the United States in the early 1960s and again briefly in the 1970s. Retaining his U.S. "green card" after he returned to Lebanon, Berri is still called "the

American" by some of his colleagues. Quiet and somewhat reserved, Berri represents the Shiite middle class more than he does
those at the bottom of the economic heap. Although a devout
Muslim, Berri is a political man seeking political reform within the
Lebanese system. It is in his political agenda that Berri is the
successor to Musa al Sadr.

When Berri took over Amal, the movement's actual membership relative to the number of its sympathizers was incredibly
small. In one major Shiite village, only ninety men out of an active
male population of fifteen hundred even held membership. When a
villager said he was with "Harakat Amal," he was merely confirm-
ing his acceptance of Amal's message, not claiming membership.
But a new chapter in Shiite politics was about to unfold, and again
the catalyst would be the ill-fated Israeli invasion of 1982. No other
facet of Israel's gross misadventure in Lebanon presents a clearer
case of bad judgment and self-defeating policy than Israel's mis-
handling of the Shiite population of south Lebanon that turned a
confederate against the Palestinians into a formidable adversary of
the State of Israel. Even before Israel moved in 1982, a Shiite
warned Israeli Arabist Moshe Sharon, "Do not join those who
murdered Husain, because if you bring the Shi'is to identify you
with the history of [their] suffering, the enmity that will be directed at you will have no bounds and no limits. You will have
created for yourselves a foe whose hostility will have a mystical
nature and a momentum which you will be unable to arrest."

Initially the Shiites had welcomed the Israelis into south Lebanon. As tank-led columns rolled through the villages, smiling
Shiites tossed flowers to Israeli soldiers and ran alongside the open
personnel carriers offering cold fruit juice while murmuring
words of praise for their deliverance from the PLO. But soon
Israeli arrogance, as had Palestinian arrogance, drove a searing
wedge between the Shiites and their erstwhile saviors. The Israeli
"iron fist" slammed down on the Shiites, turning the south's liberation into occupation. Sweeps through villages gathered up Shiites
suspected of sympathies with the PLO. Some, in violation of the
Geneva Convention, were marched across the border to detention in
Israel. Grieving women clutching their weeping children clustered
in nervous knots watching their houses being systematically blown
apart by demolition teams because the Israelis had accused their
husbands or sons. Whole villages suspected of harboring the PLO

were reduced to pulverized concrete. From June to August, the Shiites of Beirut lived through the merciless siege, and it was they who were massacred along with the Palestinians in Sabra. The words of Musa al Sadr came ringing back: "Israel is the very embodiment of evil."

During that dreadful summer of 1982, Amal began to split. The mainstream, those still seeking equal rights in a secular Lebanon, stayed with Berri. But a growing number rejected the relative moderation of Amal for the promise of an Islamic republic ruled by the tenets of the Ayatollah Khomeini's Iran.

The utter despair that the Israeli invasion had thrust upon the Shiite community gave fundamentalism an appeal that more moderate political leaders were unable to match. In a compelling litany, the militants cried that the Shiites had suffered at the hands of the Ottoman Empire, the Western colonial powers, the Christian and Sunni Lebanese, the Palestinians, and now the Israelis. Reacting with fury at Arab countries for failing to come to their defense against Israel, they posed this penetrating question about the late-twentieth-century Arab world: Is there something fundamentally wrong with Arab society and political institutions that cripples the Arabs vis-à-vis Israel and the West? Out of Iran, the Shiite spiritual heartland, the words of Ayatollah Ruhollah Khomeini washed over Shiite Lebanon: "Thus we have seen that aggression can be repelled only with sacrifices and dignity gained with the sacrifices of blood, and that freedom is not given but regained with sacrifices of both heart and soul." In the complexity and confusion of Lebanon, Shiite fundamentalism offered a simple and comfortable message: The future of the Shiites lay within the distinctive culture of the followers of the martyred Ali and Hussein.

Claiming to draw authority from Shiism itself, a number of fledgling groups that looked to the Iranian revolution as their model and to Khomeini as their leader sprang up under the tutelage of various sheikhs. By the fall of 1982, the groups had coalesced under a fluid organization called Hizbollah, the party of God. Although he claimed no official role in Hizbollah, Sheikh Muhammed Hussein Fadlallah was recognized as its ideological force. Born in Iraq, Fadlallah arrived in Lebanon in 1966 and took up residence in the Naba quarter of East Beirut. Following a typical clerical career, he was radicalized in 1976 when the Maronites drove into his neighborhood and dispossessed him and members of his community. Under Maronite guns, he wrote *Al Islam wa Mantaq al Quwa* (*Islam and the Logic of Force*). In this work, Fadlallah took the Shiites another step beyond the political activism of Musa al Sadr. Persuasion was not enough. The Shiites would free themselves through force and power. Fadlallah argued, "One must face force with equal or superior force. If it is legitimate to defend self and land and destiny, then all means of self-defense are legitimate." Fadlallah also left behind Amal's commitment to Lebanon's secular state. While calling for dialogue and mutual understanding among sects, he planned for the eventual creation of a state ruled by Islam that he insisted was applicable to Lebanon: "When a Muslim lives in a state that does not adopt Islam, his life remains confused because of the dualism [of authority] that he is living under. . . . The Christian, by contrast, does not have this problem living in an Islamic society."

In the summer of 1982, muscle was added to the fundamentalist Islamic movement, which became Hizbollah when Iran dispatched an estimated one thousand of its own Revolutionary Guards to the Bekaa. Ostensibly meant to fight Israel, the guards were really political commissars for the Iranian Revolution. For Iran's revolutionary leaders correctly saw in Lebanon a fertile opportunity to spread the Islamic revolution beyond the borders of Iran. With a large Shiite population historically and emotionally tied to Iran, Lebanon was chosen as the country in which Iran would demonstrate the power of its revolution.

Armed with Fadlallah's militant message and Iran's money and political spearhead, Hizbollah reaped converts in the Bekaa, Jabal Amil, and the southern suburbs of Beirut. If Fadlallah was Hizbollah's spiritual guide, Sheikhs Subhi Tufaili, Ibrahim Amin, Hassan Nasser Allah, and Abbas Musawi were its operatives. Each commanding his own group of followers, they were both colleagues and competitors. With no firm structure, Hizbollah functioned by negotiating and cajoling, which seldom delivered any unified action. Each Hizbollah group essentially set and executed its own agenda. As a result, Hizbollah has never achieved the cohesion of even the most formless political party. It is but a movement, an ideological umbrella under which autonomous groups wage their own versions of the Islamic revolution. Although all of Hizbollah's clerics are fanatically committed to the concepts of the Islamic revolution, few unquestioningly toe the line for Iran. All of the groups can be influenced by Iran, but none is its lackey.

The division of Shiite politics into the relatively moderate Amal and the radical Hizbollah began in 1982 when a former chemistry teacher named Hussein Musawi split with Nabih Berri over Berri's agreement to participate in the American-sponsored negotiations aimed at ending the siege of Beirut. Musawi, distinguished by his slight build and seething black eyes, went to Baalbek, where he linked up with Iran's Revolutionary Guards to found Islamic Amal. It is Hussein Musawi, dubbed "Carlos" in reference to the international terrorist figure, who Western intelligence experts believe is Hizbollah's architect of terror.

Hizbollah did not introduce terrorism into the Lebanese civil war. Acts of terror played an integral part in the war from the very beginning. Camille Chamoun, with a characteristic flick of his well-manicured hand, once said, "Cutting innocent throats to propagate terror is nothing new in the mentality of the Middle East." Karantina, Tel Zaatar, and Damour were all instances of terror directed against communities. Largely unreported were acts of terror against individuals. Kidnapping was rampant. Victims were seized at roadblocks, in their homes, and on the street for no reason other than that they were "suspicious persons." Collective kidnappings of innocent people were at times perpetrated by one group capturing prisoners to exchange them for kidnap victims held by a rival group. Children were abducted simply to extort ransom from their parents. Victims could be exchanged, ransomed, or released at random. Those who were not released either vanished or turned up as cadavers dumped along the side of the road.

Common citizens subjected to wanton acts of terror remained lost in the media coverage of the war. Only noted foreigners and Lebanese celebrities rated mention in the newspapers or on the international wire services. In mid-May 1975, U.S. ambassador Frances Meloy and economic counselor Robert O. Waring were killed at the Museum crossing and thrown in a garbage dump near a beach in West Beirut. Salim al Lowzi, the widely respected Lebanese publisher of *Al Hawadith*, was kidnapped, murdered, and mutilated in 1977. French ambassador Louis Delamare was gunned down like Meloy and Waring at the same location in 1981. Seldom did anyone claim responsibility for the outrages—it was not the thing to do. But in 1982, acts of terror by nameless perpetrators with shadowy motives diminished. Radicalized Shiites proudly laid claim to their own acts of terror, releasing bold statements of political purpose to newspapers and radio stations. The sword was drawn. Terrorism became militant Islam's chosen weapon for driving the last vestiges of the West out of Lebanon.

On July 19, 1982, David Dodge, the acting president of that most Western of Lebanese institutions, the American University of Beirut, was abducted. Transported to Iran, he was held for 366 days, most likely by Musawi's Islamic Amal. Dodge was not the first American kidnapped in Lebanon. In July 1975, a tape-recorded message arrived at the U.S. embassy in Beirut from Colonel Ernest R. Morgan, a black army officer. It began, "My government and people should not abandon me because of my color and my race." Morgan had been missing for several days after being pulled from a taxi in central Beirut. He was released within three weeks by an ultra-leftist Palestinian group seemingly under the good offices of Yassir Arafat. Morgan, dressed in civilian clothes at the time of his capture, had been randomly chosen by his kidnappers, who wanted ransom in the form of relief aid for Maslakh, a slum section of Beirut inhabited by Palestinians. Dodge's abductors, on the other hand, were making a political statement about Western influence in Lebanon. Dodge was taken during the siege of Beirut. The period of his captivity spanned the exile of the PLO from Beirut, the departure of the Multi-National Force, the Sabra and Shatila massacres, the return of the MNF, and the David and Goliath clash at Souq al Gharb between the Muslims and the *U.S.S. New Jersey.*

Of all the miscalculations in America's misadventure in Lebanon, the decision to shell tiny Souq al Gharb was the single act that would keep coming back to haunt the United States. When its military might inflamed the hills of the Shuf, the United States, along with France, created a new symbol for the Shiites. Besieged and embattled Muslims facing the firepower of a mighty battleship fit the Shiites' image of their centuries-old struggle against their enemies. The highly dubious military advantage the United States delivered to the Gemayel government in the operation against Souq al Gharb became lost in the imagery that the action created for the Shiite militants and their followers. And the very nature of their militancy demanded revenge. Hussein Musawi verbalized the emotions of those committed to the radical side of militant Shiism: "If America kills my people, then my people must kill Americans." The militants chose Beirut as their field of battle, striking first at the American embassy on that fateful April afternoon in 1983.

The tragedy of America's operation against the Shuf was that from the viewpoint of the United States the strikes were never intended as an attack on the Shiites. Rather, the United States had meant to send an unmistakable message to all factions in the Lebanese war that the Multi-National Force would protect itself. Ever since it arrived in Lebanon, the MNF had been harassed by the Druze, the Amal, the Palestinians, and even the Israelis and the Lebanese Forces. As a peacekeeping force desperately trying to protect its neutrality, the MNF refused to become involved. All troops were under strict orders to neither initiate nor return fire—in fact, to keep the safety locks on their weapons. Thus cast more in the role of diplomats than soldiers, they were sitting ducks for all of the warring factions. Records of the Marine Amphibious Unit during the summer of 1983 reported that the Lebanese army northeast of Beirut was firing into the east, south, and west of the city; the Progressive Socialist forces in the city were firing east, and those in the hills were firing north; and the Lebanese Forces occupying the northern hills were firing south. Isolated mortars and guns were everywhere, firing in all directions. The Marine command reported to Washington, "The fire support situation was best described by the American Ambassador as being unclear as to who was doing what to whom and why."

The Marines deployed around the airport huddled in tight little units behind layers of sandbags. Volleyball and jogging were struck from the activities list because of the level of sniper fire peppering the troops. A basketball goal backed by a ten-foot sandbag wall with the American flag atop was still usable. Otherwise, the Marines burrowed in their bunkers watching the dirt around them kick up where sniper bullets hit. All there was to do was drink the one beer allotment a day, crush scorpions, and wait for orders to go home.

Marine frustrations over their role in Lebanon were summed up in a cartoon by Dwayne Powell for the *Raleigh News and Observer*. It showed a lieutenant standing before a map of Lebanon with a pointer in his hand, telling his helmeted squad, "OK, Marines—We're faced with Druze and Shia Moslems being backed by the Syrians against the Christian Phalangists. The Druze and Shias are divided among themselves, as are the Christians. The Israeli pullout is leaving a gap that the 'Lebanese army' probably can't fill and the PLO is creeping back in. . . . Nobody likes us, and it's all preceded by 2,000 years of bloodshed. Any questions?"

After the Israelis completed their August 1983 pullout from the Shuf, the Marines became even more exposed to hostile fire. The fight among the Druze, Amal, Phalange, and Lebanese Forces for control of the region just evacuated by Israel pinned down the Marines under a barrage of rockets, mortars, and gunfire. This formed the rationale for calling in the *New Jersey*. The big ship succeeded in silencing most of the action in the hills. But the ceased rocket fire from the Shuf was quickly replaced by a new threat— stepped-up attacks from militant Shiites. Sniper fire from the Shiite slums around the airport intensified. On October 13, a grenade was thrown from a passing car at the sentry post of the temporary U.S. embassy quarters. On October 14, a Marine driving a jeep was shot in the forehead on the airport's perimeter. On October 19, a car bomb exploded as a supply convoy passed along the corniche. Every day seemed to deliver a new attack.

On October 20, 1983, two Marines from Bravo company of the U.S. Eighth Marine Battalion furtively poked their heads out of a sandbagged bunker decorated with a red, white, and blue jingoistic banner declaring, "Without the Home of the Brave, There Will Be No Land of the Free." Assured that snipers from "Hooterville," the nearby Shiite hovels bordering the airport, were absent, the taller of the two men handed his M-16 to his buddy. He stooped, placed a small object on the sand, stood, adjusted his helmet, shifted his feet, and blasted a plastic golf ball toward the sea. This was military duty in Lebanon—ill defined, heavily restricted, and dangerous.

Seventy-two hours after that golf ball flew toward the Mediterranean, the Marines assigned quarters in Beirut Airport's Aviation Safety Building were still in their cots, taking advantage of an extra half-hour of sleep on Sunday morning. Only the cooks were up, preparing the eggs, French toast, and Spam for another GI breakfast. At 6:20 A.M., a big yellow Mercedes truck turned toward the parking lot in front of the concrete-and-stucco building. As it reached the guard at the gate, the driver flashed a smile and hit the accelerator. The truck hurled toward the entrance of the four-story building, vaulted a wall of sandbags, lurched into the lobby, and exploded in a deafening roar. The roof momentarily lifted off the "Beirut Hilton" and then collapsed under the force of two thousand pounds of explosives. Minutes later, a building in the seafront neighborhood of Bir Hasan, where the French contingent of the Multi-National Force was housed, erupted in a similar explosion.

At the airport barracks, emergency vehicles rolled across personal photographs and official documents scattered across the ground. The screaming sirens wound down in a descending moan in front of the folds of concrete where Marine and Lebanese rescue workers dug the dead and maimed out of the rubble. Blacks, whites, and Hispanics were indistinguishable under the brownish-gray mud in which the blast had encased their bodies. Some had miraculously escaped. One dazed corporal standing to the side holding the broken parts of a cassette player vacantly muttered, "I was trying to fix my tape player. I spilled ketchup in the batteries at supper last night."

In the two terrorist attacks, the United States lost 241 Marines, the worst disaster for the American military since the Vietnam War, and the French lost 47, a level of casualties not experienced since the Algerian war twenty-two years before. For the militant Shiites, the destruction heralded a new kind of fighter, one who drove to his death repeating the words of the Koran: "Who fighteth in the way of God be he slain or be he victorious, on him we shall bestow a vast reward." A caller to a French news agency who claimed a victory for Shiism in the desolation of the barracks intoned, "We are the soldiers of God who are fond of death." The West had met its new enemy.

The leaders of the MNF countries went on the verbal offensive. U.S. secretary of defense Caspar Weinberger declared, "Our commitment to the cause of Middle East peace still remains," and British prime minister Margaret Thatcher, through an aide, affirmed, "By attempting to bomb the Multi-National Force out of Lebanon, the extremists . . . have in a perverse way confirmed the success of the force in helping stabilize the country." But behind closed doors, the nations of the MNF began to rethink their presence in Lebanon. They were caught in an inescapable bind: To leave would invite charges that the Western powers were deserting their commitments and caving in to terrorism; to stay would expose their troops to further disaster. They decided to stay, the Western prop of Amin Gemayel's marrowless government.

"Consistency" and "stay the course" emerged as the keywords in U.S. State Department press briefings in the days following the attack on the Marine barracks. After all, President Reagan had declared, "Stability in Lebanon is central to [American] credibility on a global scale." By February 3, 1983, while the battle for control of West Beirut raged between the U.S.-backed Lebanese army and forces opposed to the Gemayel government, Ronald Reagan was still insisting that the United States was not prepared to "surrender" in Lebanon. As long as there was "a chance for victory, for peace [in Lebanon], I don't know of any of the multinational forces that are in there . . . that are desirous of leaving."

But on February 6, Berri's Amal, Jumblatt's Druze, and various cells within Hizbollah, joined by assorted leftist factions, drove the last of the Lebanese army out of West Beirut. The U.S.-trained Lebanese army collapsed when the Muslim contingents deserted rather than fight their own people in the name of a Christian-dominated government. Ras Beirut, the heart of Western life in prewar Lebanon, fell to the Muslims, and with it the last shreds of U.S. policy in Lebanon disintegrated. The next day, Ronald Reagan abruptly announced that U.S. Marines in Lebanon would be "redeployed" to ships off the coast. A little less than two-and-a-half years after they had arrived to move the PLO out of Beirut, the Marines struck the battalion flag. The last Beirut saw of the "leathernecks" was the American flag flapping on the back of a landing craft headed out to sea. Militant Islam had taken on the United States and won.

The Americans were followed in stages by French, British, and Italians. On March 5, Amin Gemayel finally killed the May 17 Agreement that George Shultz had been so sure held the key to peace not only in Lebanon but throughout the Middle East. Burned by its encounter with the Levant, the West withdrew diplomatically as well as militarily.

The Shiite resurgence through the conventional military moves of the Amal and the bold terrorist acts of those adhering to the message of Hizbollah had succeeded in removing the Western military presence from Lebanon's political equation. Unlike in 1860, 1920, 1958, and 1982, the Maronites now lacked a Western backer. Amin Gemayel was left exposed to the opposition. But with the Amal, Druze, Maronites, Palestinians, Syrians, and Israelis each occupying a piece of the country, Lebanon was as tangled as ever. No group had completed its political agenda, least of all Hizbollah.

Buoyed by its success against the MNF and inflamed by its

own rhetoric, Hizbollah would be satisfied with nothing short of driving the last Westerner from Lebanon. In January, even before the MNF retreated, Malcolm Kerr was gunned down and a heretofore unknown group calling itself "Islamic Jihad," or "Islamic Holy War," announced, "We are responsible for the assassination of the president of AUB, who was a victim of the American military presence in Lebanon. We also vow that not a single American or French will remain on this soil. We shall take no different course. And we shall not waver."

Westerners still hanging on in Beirut began to disappear off the streets. At first it was Americans. In February Frank Regier, an engineering professor from AUB, vanished. Jeremy Levin, a correspondent for Cable News Network, was reported missing in March. Less than two weeks later, William Buckley, political officer at the U.S. embassy, was stopped on the street in broad daylight and bundled into a white Renault. On May 8, 1984, the kindly Benjamin Weir, walking to work through the ruins of his beloved Beirut, was grabbed by two men, forced into the back of a car, and whisked away.

Two days later, Islamic Jihad telephoned the French news agency Agence France Presse in Beirut to claim responsibility for kidnapping Weir. They claimed the abduction amounted to a direct challenge to President Reagan's statement that the United States would never allow terrorism to drive Americans from Lebanon. If Islamic Jihad's purpose was to rid Lebanon of the hated Westerners, the choice of Weir was ironic. Weir had lived in Lebanon for thirty-one years, spending much of his time doing relief work among the Shiites of the south. He was fluent in Arabic and intensely sensitive to the issues of the Arab world. During his captivity, his wife, Carol, said of him, "He was not an ugly American who came to push others into the narrow confines of his own Western culture." Nonetheless, Benjamin Weir spent sixteen months as a hostage of the shadowy Islamic Jihad.

Americans and other Westerners continued to be picked off the streets by groups no one knew anything about. So little definite was known about the underground groups within Hizbollah and others who were engaging in hostage-taking that even the hostages themselves were unable to definitively pin down who was holding them. Public claims of responsibility for an act of terrorism by an organization meant little, since these groups often were suspected of competing with one another for press coverage. Although the hostage-takers included radical Palestinians, a suspected Sunni Muslim group, and cells with unconfirmed origins and ties, it was those who share the ideology of Hizbollah who became synonymous in Western eyes with the terrorism of captivity. Frustration over the hostage situation mounted as the West realized that the might of its technology had been disemboweled by coteries of Shiites who pursued their vendetta against the West, undaunted by international censure. Powerless, the Western nations waited out the agony of the hostages' suffering.

The captives of Shiite militancy depended daily on their captors for their very survival. In Weir's case, the guards seldom were much more than teenagers warped by the long war. They could be respectful, taunting, or ugly. They could be erratic and bizarre if the drugs flowing so freely through ravaged Beirut passed through the garrison. Many of the nameless men were simply mercenaries, hirelings earning $27 a month. But according to Weir, few of the foot soldiers of the Islamic revolution who were guarding him were inherently cruel. Mostly they acted like bullies playing out the street-tough role that a childhood spent caught up in urban warfare decreed. Yet the psychological abuse was brutal. And hostages did die at the hands of their tormentors. William Buckley, the CIA station chief in Beirut, is believed to have been tortured to death sometime during 1985. The Frenchman Michel Seurat died in captivity, presumably of natural causes. Both were hostages of Islamic Jihad. Peter Kilburn, the brothers Douglas, and Philip Padfield were shot by a pro-Libyan group in retaliation for the American bombing of Libya in April 1986. Alec Collett, a British correspondent for the United Nations, is presumed dead, killed by his unknown captors. A Dutch priest is also among those believed dead.

Weir spent much of his captivity in solitary confinement. Tethered by a short chain to a radiator, he was allowed to see neither sunset nor stars, but only the reflected light of day and the enveloping black of night. His captors threatened him often and periodically moved him within and between Beirut and what Weir believes was the Bekaa Valley. On one of these nighttime transits, his entire head was swathed in wide plastic wrapping tape that covered his eyes, ears, and mouth, leaving open only a small space over his nostrils. Then his arms were strapped to his side and his whole body encased in viscid tape. Wrapped like a mummy, he was laid by his guards in a narrow metal container, and the lid was bolted shut. Weir later said of the time, "Only when it lurched forward did I suddenly realize I was on a truck. To add to my terror, I could now smell heavy exhaust fumes coming up through the floor of the truck body. I must be right over the tailpipe. Already I was breathing heavily through my nose. God, I prayed, don't let the air passages clog!"

Despite his harsh treatment, Weir usually received the basics he requested—a Bible, vitamins, eye ointment, and warmer clothing during winter. And his kidnappers never completely escaped the Arab cultural dictate of hospitality. At New Year's, a jigsaw puzzle arrived. Hamburgers appeared for the evening meals that broke the daytime fast during the Muslim holy month of Ramadan. And on Christmas, a previously unseen man genially delivered a cake shaped like a yule log along with cologne and a pen and paper with which Weir could write his family. Finally, the stranger ceremoniously produced a Christmas card bearing a picture of Mary, Joseph, and the babe in the manger and the words "Wishing you a Merry Christmas."

During this Christmas visit, the messenger, an obviously well-educated man in his late twenties or early thirties, explained Weir's captivity. With great politeness, he expressed how sorry he was that Weir was being held. It seemed important to assure the hostage that the reasons for his captivity were political, not personal. Drawing on the oral traditions of Arab society, the messenger expounded on the Shiites' opposition to America's unflagging support of Israel. He spewed out his anger about the destruction Israeli forces caused during the 1982 invasion, recounting with a bitter sorrow how the Shiites had suffered. Then he lapsed into an emotional soliloquy about the West's centuries-old deprecation of the Muslims. Little that he said was not already part of Hizbollah's political polemic. But then his voice dropped, and he said what is perhaps the most important thing that Westerners need to understand about the Shiites of Lebanon: They want the West to regard them as being as honorable and as worthy of respect as the Christians.

Between the spring of 1984 and early summer of 1985, the list of Western hostages grew. Peter Kilburn, Father Lawrence Jenco, and Terry Anderson were abducted. The Frenchmen Fontaine,

Carton, Kaufmann, and Seurat fell victim to Islamic Jihad. Then two more Americans were snared in the Hizbollah net—David Jacobsen and Tom Sutherland. The dwindling number of Western- ers still in Lebanon either left or spent most of their time barri- caded in their apartments. In June 1985, yet another ill-defined group influenced by the ideology of Hizbollah shifted to even more spectacular tactics against the leader of the Western world.

On June 14, 1985, TWA flight 847 took off from Athens en route to Rome. Just after the plane leveled off, two dark-haired, olive-skinned men jumped from their seats. Waving pistols and hand grenades, they screamed orders for the plane to change course toward the east. Within two hours, the Boeing 727 touched down at Beirut Airport adjacent to the Shiite slums of South Beirut and near the ruins of the Marine barracks leveled the previous October. For the next three days, Captain John Testrake shuttled his aircraft between Beirut and Algiers while the hi- jackers threatened to blow up the plane. In the process of collecting their captives' passports, the hijackers spotted twenty-three-year- old Robert Dean Stethem, a Navy diver attached to the battleship *New Jersey*. Seizing his military identity card, one of the hijackers ran up and down the aisle screaming, "New Jersey! New Jersey!" At the controls of the plane, Testrake lightheartedly asked one of his cockpit crew, "What has he got against New Jersey? It's not my favorite place either, but why is this guy so violent about it?" But the levity faded quickly. While women and children were released in Algiers, Stethem was savagely beaten, the victim of a man whose rage had been inflamed by the monstrous shells the *New Jersey* had slammed into the Shuf. Life was literally escaping from Stethem when, on the second stop in Beirut, he was pulled to the door of the aircraft. A scruffy, shaggy-haired man pulled the trigger of the gun in his hand, and Stethem's battered body tumbled onto the tarmac.

On the third day of the TWA drama, the hijackers read their fourth communiqué to the control tower:

> In the name of God the compassionate and merciful. . . . We would like the world to know that had it not been for Ameri- ca's military and financial assistance to Israel, had it not been for Israel's arrest of our brothers in south Lebanon, and had it not been for Israel's invasion of Lebanese territory, we would not have undertaken this act. . . . We are not war criminals

and we are not air pirates. We have a right that has been robbed by Israel. This right cannot be recovered except by force of arms.

On the final stop in Beirut, the thirty-seven remaining American hostages were moved off the plane under the protection of Amal into the darkness of Beirut's southern suburbs. Nabih Berri, seeking to recapture some of the power he had lost to the militants, had intervened between the United States and Hizbollah. Berri reiterated the hijackers' demand that seven hundred Shiites rounded up during the 1982 Israeli invasion of Lebanon and sent to the Atit prison camp in Israel be released. Ironically, the United States already had accused Israel of violating the Geneva Convention by moving prisoners across the international border from Lebanon to Israel. Israel itself had been planning to release the prisoners before the hijacking. But now both sides were trapped in their respective policies barring negotiations with terrorists. Ronald Reagan, the Washington cowboy who had sworn never to cave in to terrorism, now knew the vicissitudes of power. For seventeen days, the Shiites of Lebanon held the power that Musa al Sadr envisioned for his community. Between them, the hijackers and Nabih Berri, who shuttled back and forth between the parties, represented virtually all the Shiites of Lebanon. Sheikh Abdel Amir Qabalan gloated, "The giant has been let out of the bottle. It will never be bottled up again."

Finally, in a complex six-way deal among the United States, Amal, Hizbollah, Israel, Syria, and Iran, the hostages on flight 847 were freed, and freedom for the Shiite prisoners in Israel followed.

As the plane hijacking faded from the headlines, the random kidnappings of Westerners continued. These included Cornea and Normandin, French; Keenan, Irish; McCarthy and the Padfields, British; Kilburn, American; Reed, Cicippio, and Tracy, American; Auque, French. The victims were not soldiers but professors, reporters, clergymen, diplomats, businessmen, and a hospital administrator.

Of the seventy or so foreigners who have been held hostage in Lebanon, only two are known to have been connected with Western intelligence agencies (Buckley and Seurat), and only one, Lieutenant Colonel William R. Higgins, was a military man, attached to UNIFIL. The wrath of the militant Shiites revisited itself time and time again. Occasionally speculation or claims by abductors themselves identified a specific event, such as the United States' refusal to allow condemnation of Israeli actions in south Lebanon by the United Nations, as having sparked an abduction.

No Westerner was completely safe from the long arm of Hizbollah and others bent on driving Westerners from Lebanon. In the small village of al Hermel in the Maally district of the Akkar, a young American lived with her Shiite Lebanese husband and his family. She had converted to Islam and now communicated comfortably in Arabic. Lebanon was her home. But al Hermel, poor and rural, became a hotbed of Islamic fundamentalism and antiwesternism. Life for an American, even a member of a Lebanese family, grew difficult. She was spat upon in the market. Her husband and his brothers found it increasingly difficult to find work because of the presence of an American in their household. Finally, with the help of her Lebanese family, the young woman fled across the border into Syria on the night the United States took out on Libya its frustrations over terrorism.

Despite the periodic claims of cause, terror in reality took on a life of its own. Hostage-taking became an expression of power, for "it is not in the existence of terrorism, but in the image of impotence and vacillation that terrorist attacks can create; not in the eruption of isolated violence, but in the image of growing and ever-more-militant dissent that the violence suggests." In the scramble for power within the Shiite community, hostages meant prestige. For it was the personal plight of the hostages and the powerlessness of the West's conventional military might to free them that made giants of little men who had spent their lives at the bottom of Lebanon's social order.

The more power the radicals amassed, the less willing was the West, especially the United States, to talk to this new breed of adversary. A strident "antiterrorism" campaign replaced policy in American dialogue with the Lebanese. From the collapse of the May 17 Agreement in 1983 to the Palestinian uprising on the West Bank at the end of 1987, the Reagan administration had no Middle East policy and certainly no coherent policy aimed at rapprochement with the militant Shiites. In its frustration in trying to free the hostages, the Reagan administration, Congress, the Department of State, and the public, egged on by the press, turned Hizbollah into the American version of the "Great Satan." Those dealing with the militants became almost as irrational as the terrorists. In a meeting with hostage families, Secretary of State

George Shultz once pounded a table and accused the Shiites of "being crazy," of claiming to hear voices from God, and of practicing a primitive, pagan ritual called Ashura.

The hostage issue struck some of the basic chords that separate the West culturally from the Arabs, especially the fundamentalist Shiites. The seizure and incarceration of innocents was an unforgivable affront to a culture that prides itself on protecting the rights of the individual. The fanatical Shiites, on the other hand, used the hostages as a noxious statement against westernization, a crude symbol of power that somehow would affirm the force of Islam as a way of life. Terrorism was the tragic symptom of a people long angered and bewildered by the domination of a culture they never understood and its Western propagators, whom they perceived as never extending to them an acknowledgment of the validity of their own society.

On the operational level of the attempt to free the hostages, Western and Arab cultures eyed each other across the minefield of cultural dictates. The United States, bolstered by Britain's Margaret Thatcher, has insisted ever since the hostage ordeal began that it would never cave in to terrorists' demands. Under no circumstances would America "negotiate with terrorists." In Western terminology, negotiation by its very nature implies compromise. And "appeasement" has ranked as the dirtiest word in Western diplomacy since Neville Chamberlain went to Munich in 1938 to declare "peace in our time." But the roots of this policy go much deeper than the painful experience of a calamitous decision. American diplomatic history specifically, and American society generally, has been overburdened with the imagery of "standing tall," of "dealing from strength," of refusing to surrender to "blackmail." Toughness wins respect, and respect wins capitulation.

This is sound policy in dealing with some adversaries, but not the Arabs. Arab culture thrives on negotiation. For centuries, the tribal wars of the desert halted so the antagonists could gather in the tent of the sheikh to partake of his hospitality and engage in endless discussions of their differences. This coming together acknowledged the honor of all those present. And it was in a council of equals that they struck a consensus. No one expressed triumph, no one experienced humiliation, and no one necessarily expected the agreement to last. If it collapsed, the all-important negotiating process would begin again.

The West and its Arab adversaries are akin to the proverbial ships passing in the night. Terrorism is the act of the weak to gain the attention of the powerful. Once that attention is captured, it becomes difficult for the aggrieved party to enter the dialogue the act itself originally demanded. The militant Shiites screamed out to the West by using tactics abhorrent to Western values. The West responded to the acts themselves without attempting to understand what prompted them. Neither side won. The Shiites alienated themselves from the West even further, and the United States continued on its collision course with resurgent Islam. In the meantime, the hostages wound up being the innocent pawns.

While Western governments pursued their tough talk against terrorism, others sought to go outside government to make contact with the Shiite radicals in the hope of securing the hostages' release. Terry Waite, a bearded giant, is a lay minister attached to the staff of Robert Runcie, the Archbishop of Canterbury. Between Christmas of 1980 and January 1987, Waite was credited with winning the release of at least ten political prisoners in Muslim countries—four in Iran, four in Libya, and two in Lebanon (Benjamin Weir and Father Lawrence Jenco). Acting in the capacity of personal representative of the Archbishop of Canterbury, Waite credited his negotiating skills to his ability to distance himself from the diplomatic establishment and to build up personal relationships with the captors. In 1986, Waite said that in dealing with those holding hostages he tried "to establish three very simple attributes of God to which we could both subscribe. God as a God of compassion, mercy, and justice."

In the frustrations of the hostage standoff, Waite became almost a cult figure in Britain. Much to the displeasure of his own government, the image of his six-foot, six-inch frame unfolding from airplanes and jeeps flashed through the media as he shuttled back and forth to Lebanon trying to free the hostages. Waite, known for his gentleness and humor, seemed to be conveying to Lebanon's radical Shiites what they craved: respect and recognition of their cause as one that ultimately sought justice, not terror.

Waite's last trip to Lebanon was in January 1987 amid growing speculation that he would return with the hostages. But by now Waite was tainted. The Reagan administration's Iran-Contra fiasco was out in the open. Benjamin Weir and Father Lawrence Jenco may have been released through U.S. arms sales to Iran rather than through Waite's negotiating skills. Waite's credentials as an honest broker dissolved. Whether out of innocence or conspiracy, he had acted as a minor cog in Oliver North's Iran-Contra network. Suffering from a degree of naïveté and believing that he still enjoyed a relationship of mutual respect with groups holding the hostages, Terry Waite left his Beirut hotel on January 20, 1987, to become yet another hostage. As the months of his captivity extended to a year and beyond, a special candle burned every Sunday at evensong in the massive Canterbury Cathedral. These services included a special prayer for the safe return of Terry Waite, the negotiator who became the captive.

After four professors, three Americans, and one Indian were kidnapped from the offices of Beirut University College a few days after Terry Waite's disappearance, the U.S. Department of State forbade American citizens traveling on U.S. passports to enter Lebanon. For Americans and most other Westerners, all the illusions that surrounded the "jewel of the Levant" had at last ended, and Westerners were no longer safe in Lebanon.

I spent a morning with Ben Weir a year after his release. The beard that had covered his chest when he was a hostage was now neatly trimmed. But he still wore the same old-fashioned eyeglasses he had worn when I met him several years earlier. In his quiet voice, he talked about his captivity—about the fear, anger, and loneliness. He spoke of the other hostages—Terry Anderson, Tom Sutherland, Terry Waite. And then this man, with a wisdom about Lebanon that few possess, talked about the Lebanese, the Syrians, the Palestinians, the Israelis, and, finally, the West—all hostages of the confluence of passion and intolerance that plagues the Levant and those who tread there.

The society has been destroyed. There is nothing in
Lebanon. We are playing in our blood.
                    a Maronite monk to the author, 1988

TEN

CRY, LEBANON

Deep in Mount Lebanon, the Adonis river pours forth out of a
cavern secreted below ragged limestone cliffs, drops, and
then flows into the valley below. For the Phoenicians and
the Romans, the river and its grotto were sacred, the site where the
water ran red as the beautiful Adonis died in the arms of Venus.
Centuries after the ancients, the waters of the river still run red in
the late spring. For scientists, the color is not crimson but rust, the
result of iron ore washing out of the hills on the melting snow. But
for poets, the red of the rushing river has always been the color of
blood, the blood of Adonis, spilled by a wounded boar and mourned
by Venus. Yet now when the river runs red, when the blood is
reborn, it is Lebanon, not Adonis, who is mourned.

Lebanon has been at war for almost a generation. Over those
years, governments, institutions, and individuals have all attempted to quantify the magnitude of the carnage by a variety of
measures. But all the statistics enumerating the dead and
wounded, all the calculations of the physical destruction, and all the
comparisons drawn about the awesome firepower of competing
militias dull in contrast with the stories of what has happened to
individuals. It is only when the war is reduced to the level of the

ordinary people that the scope of its devastation becomes real. For in many respects, the deepest manifestations of the war for the Lebanese are not economic and political, but emotional and psychological.

One among the thousands upon thousands of the nameless victims of the conflict is an Armenian who came to Lebanon in 1939 when the Turks annexed Syrian Alexandretta. He settled in the village of Anjar in the Bekaa Valley near the Syrian border. With the strength of his back and the toil of his own hands, he planted apple trees. While his trees took root, grew, and finally produced, he and his family lived in poverty.

By the time the Golden Age burst upon Lebanon, the Armenian refugee presided over a successful orchard. The groves of broad-boughed trees even survived the first seven years of the Lebanese war. But then during that convulsive summer of 1982, the Syrians, moving tanks and other heavy equipment through to the warfront near Beirut, refused to allow the fruit trees to be irrigated, lest the soggy soil slow down their military columns. When harvesttime came that year, there were no apples. Every tree was dead. The Armenian immigrant, now past middle age, turned aside the help of his sons. With his ax, he felled, one by one, the trees he had so carefully planted forty years earlier. Today, he sits in an apartment in Beirut, a vacant and broken man, as much a victim of the war as those who are physically maimed.

The pain of shattered lives reaches into every group and confessional in Lebanon. Only the particular circumstances of loss divide one family's grief from another's.

George and Nadia, Greek Orthodox Lebanese, were married in Ashrafieh, East Beirut, the day the war began in 1975. The incident at Ain al Rummaneh that Sunday passed with little notice amidst the gaiety of the Lebanese wedding. It was just another clash in a series of conflicts during that spring. George recalls the day: "Guests at the wedding did not want us to leave Beirut for our honeymoon. I thought they were joking. All we were looking for was the future."

But it was no joke. For the next several months, the young couple moved from location to location looking for a place where they felt secure. They finally settled back in Ashrafieh, even though it was as much a target of bombs and rockets as most places in Beirut. In the beginning, the rockets were small. They were even playfully called "birds" by the residents. But they kept getting bigger and bigger. And as the security situation deteriorated, political kidnappings multiplied. In time, every apartment became a prison housing a family afraid to trust anyone outside its own narrow circle. When the Syrian army came in 1976, most people in Ashrafieh thought it signaled the end of the war. Instead, the Syrians turned into an army of occupation, creating fear instead of security.

In 1977, Nadia developed debilitating migraine headaches. In 1978, she was hospitalized for severe depression. After nine months of treatment, she was improved enough to go home. As long as she stayed in the Christian area of Beirut, her anxiety level stayed manageable.

In spite of the war, George and Nadia's wholesale jewelry business thrived. Importing gold from Italy and diamonds from Antwerp, they crafted the florid designs that appealed to the tastes of the wealthy Arabs along the Persian Gulf. Their business even endured Israel's siege of Beirut. Then on the morning of April 2, 1983, three days before Easter, Nadia left her apartment for the factory at around nine o'clock. At 9:45 a barrage of Syrian rockets aimed at an adjacent building housing a Phalange arms cache exploded, engulfing the area in fire and havoc. George raced from the factory to rescue his nephew from his nearby school. Returning with the seven-year-old boy, Sebastian, clutched in his arms, he was in sight of the factory when an incoming rocket hit less than twenty feet ahead of them. The force of the explosion blew Sebastian's head away and severely wounded George.

The factory was leveled. Nadia and the employees, sealed in the basement, frantically clawed their way through the rubble. George lay in the street, his skull broken open across the forehead. Somehow maintaining enough consciousness to seek help, he crawled through blackened bodies to the curb, where an old woman carefully stretched him out on the pavement. She then seated herself and gingerly laid his bloody head in her lap and waited until help could make its way through the burning debris in the streets.

At a hospital overwhelmed by war casualties, a doctor who had never performed neurosurgery relieved the pressure on George's brain. For fifteen days, the wounded man lay in a coma. Nadia, freed from her basement tomb, sat at his side. If he ever recovered from his head wound, he risked amputation of his mangled legs. But then with excruciating slowness, his skull and both of his legs mended.

At the end of 1983, George and Nadia took their four children and left Lebanon. They now live in Cyprus in a bare apartment permeated with sadness. George, sitting on a cheap vinyl couch, smiles easily, his straight white teeth and soulful eyes diverting attention from the large blood vessel that pulsates in a deep indentation in his forehead. Nadia is unable to sit still. She paces the floor, talks rapidly, gestures extravagantly with her hands, and smokes one cigarette after another. They survived because they had built up a sizable foreign bank account before they left Lebanon. But that will not last forever, and there is little work for Lebanese in Cyprus. Unable to secure permission to enter either Europe or the United States, they want to emigrate to Canada. But that is proving difficult. If they fail to win Canadian visas, there is no alternative plan. Throwing her hands once again in the air, Nadia declares, "I don't want to go back to Lebanon. It's a comedy, and I know it—a lot of people know it. I want to escape."

No one knows how many thousands have escaped the horrors of seeing their child lying dead in the street, unable to reach his or her body until rival militias cease fighting; of spending night after night in a dank, overcrowded basement, shuddering every time a rocket explodes overhead; of moving from place to place, seeking a shelter that is habitable; of living with the incessant fear that in the next round of fighting, someone within the family will be killed or will simply disappear. The Lebanese have fled in droves to the West, to the states of the Persian Gulf, to Africa, to South America. Some unable to secure residence visas float between relatives on two or more continents. Others, primarily those with skills or resources, are able to settle, bringing with them their memories and their mementos, often curious reminders tucked here and there of what they left behind.

One such memento is a luminous golden yellow throw pillow propped on the hearth of a small fireplace in the suburban American home of a Lebanese who lived through ten years of the war in West Beirut. Leaping out of its center is the cartoon character Garfield, defiantly clutching a Lebanese flag in one hand and a rifle in the other. The inscription below reads, "I survived Beirut."

Still, for every Lebanese who left the country, hundreds more stayed behind. Some had no choice, but others remained because of a deep love of place and an unshakable faith that this year or next the war would end. Instead, they found themselves over the years besieged and beleaguered by almost every known form of malice and terror, from the one-on-one cruelties inflicted in the name of factional and religious bigotry to the massive devastations of urban areas wrought by militant organizations and state-sponsored armies.

A whole generation has grown up in Lebanon knowing nothing but war. There are children who have never completed a term in school. Roaming the streets as gun-toting adolescents, they have received their education only in the grisly art of killing. Social disorganization is currently so pervasive that a Lebanese psychiatrist laments, "The mental hospitals are not functioning because the patients are on the streets carrying guns." Significantly, those who do not carry guns carry the attitudes guns create. Thus, when a Lebanese clergyman told his family that an elderly woman had just died, it seemed normal that his young daughter casually asked, "Who killed her?"

Yet life goes on in the twilight between death and survival. Throughout much of Lebanon, people live with no boundaries dividing security from danger, no discernible differences between allies and enemies, no logic to random violence. Even the most feeble attempts at normal life are invaded by menacing reality. Thus in a dark, cavelike apartment on the Green Line, friends converse haltingly while bullets ricochet off the heavy steel covers placed over the balcony windows to protect the family from instant and senseless death. A picnic on the Litani River on a fine summer day ends abruptly when rival militias begin firing artillery at each other across the picnic ground. Those who go to the market to buy food for the family's lunch do so knowing they risk becoming victims of random car bombs, a tactic of urban guerrilla warfare that reached its ugly pinnacle in Lebanon. Still, as hardened survivors, the Lebanese continue to marry, procreate, raise their children as best they can, and bury their dead.

Lebanon, which in the mid-1970s was a bustling, thriving monument to the entrepreneur, now sits on the World Bank's list of underdeveloped nations. The Lebanese economy, like the country, declined over the years of the war rather than collapsing at the outset. In fact, Lebanon miraculously lived through the first ten years of the war with its economy intact. The Lebanese pound held firm at an exchange rate of about three pounds to the dollar primarily because of the spin-off effect of the oil boom in the Persian Gulf. From the beginning of the boom in 1973 into the early 1980s, large numbers of Lebanese streamed into the booming economics of the Gulf. Most of their earnings wound their way back to their families in Lebanon. During the late 1970s, well into the Lebanese civil war, the Lebanese-owned Middle East Airlines jumped into the ranks of the world's most profitable carriers by ferrying the goods demanded by the voracious consumer appetites of the Gulf countries. And Lebanese banks continued to attract depositors and clear drafts for the fast-moving trade between East and West.

Even during the Israeli invasion, the Lebanese pound declined only as far as 5.35 to the dollar and then rebounded to 3.8 by the last months of 1982. Neither civil war nor foreign invasion, it seemed, could impede the Lebanese' indefatigable talents as traders. While rival militias and the foreign armies battled each other across Lebanon, merchants in the most nondescript Lebanese villages sat atop their caches of Scotch, imported perfume, and Japanese VCRs, all of which they briskly moved at a profit.

But by the summer of 1985, the economy began to stumble. The cumulative effects of the years of destruction, the progressive erosion of the country's social fabric, and a deeply ingrained sense of despair settled on the economy. Everything that propelled Lebanon's prewar prosperity had either been destroyed or fatally curtailed by the war. Tourism, one of the mainstays of the economy before 1975, no longer existed. Lebanon's transit trade between the Mediterranean and the Arab hinterland essentially had been killed off by the instability produced by the war and by competition from ports in Syria, Turkey, and the Persian Gulf. Lebanese exports of fruits and vegetables declined to 20 percent of their prewar levels. The all-important service sector had almost ceased to function. And few were any longer willing to put their money in a Lebanese bank. Even remittances dropped as workers were laid off in the declining Gulf economies hit by the worldwide oil glut. The Lebanese finally had nothing to trade.

A dead economy and high inflation followed. In December 1987, the exchange rate soared to 700 Lebanese pounds to the dollar before dropping back. By the end of 1988, the pound was tottering at a little over 500 to the dollar, still catastrophic for a country that lives on imports.

Inflation has been devastating. Coffee prices have risen 312 percent over 1986 levels, cheese 463 percent, meat 500 percent, soap 600 percent, eggs 723 percent, and rice 805 percent. As a result, the stress of putting food on the table now often exceeds the stress of violence.

There is still plenty to buy in Lebanon, but it is all priced in dollars. Those with access to foreign currency flourish; those without suffer. The rich, living from their foreign bank accounts, cruise the streets in their Mercedes and feast at French restaurants on memorable meals that cost about $4 apiece.

The militias also are thriving. They meet their payrolls and keep themselves supplied with arms through their various racketeering activities and by drawing on the resources of their foreign sponsors. Iran, for instance, pays foot soldiers affiliated with Hizbollah as much as $60 a month and employs women in Baalbek to drape themselves in the black folds of the chador. Members of the Israeli-sponsored South Lebanon Army earn $100 a month and permission for their families to cross the border into Israel to work at good wages. Every foreign adventurer in Lebanon similarly seeds money to its clients.

The poorest people, already living as squatters and thus avoiding rent payments, are not measurably affected by the economic crisis. As they did through much of the war, they depend on charity, much of it administered by international relief agencies.

It is the middle class that has been wiped out by the economic crisis. With a fixed salary going only far enough to buy milk and bread for the family, doctors, teachers, and civil servants have no choice but to try to emigrate or to fall back on the support of family networks abroad. With roughly $100 a month in hard currency, an average-size family can survive. Thus, Lebanese who have emigrated dispatch money back to Lebanon literally to feed family members. As a result, remittances are once again the mainstay of the economy.

The only growth industry in war-ravaged Lebanon is the illicit drug trade. As one of the world's major suppliers of hashish, Lebanon has always earned money from the drug trade. But hashish never constituted a major source of national income nor involved such a diversity of groups and individuals as it now does.

Before the war, hashish cultivation was largely limited to the Hermel region of the northern Bekaa. Then, during the early years of the war, it gradually extended southward, eventually reaching all the way to the Beirut-Damascus road. By the mid-1980s, drug organizations were paying farmers to convert croplands to poppy cultivation for the production of heroin. At the same time, these organizations also began importing coca leaves from South America to process into cocaine. From raw material to finished product, the drug economy was complete. With no government to interfere, production has been prodigious. In 1987, Lebanon exported an estimated thirty thousand pounds of marijuana and four tons of heroin as well as the cocaine processed in an unknown number of underground laboratories. By March 1988, international drug enforcement authorities estimated that 20 percent of Lebanon's gross national product was being generated by the narcotics trade.

Militias from all sides participate in the lucrative drug business. Rival militias collaborate in moving illicit shipments across each other's checkpoints and to the various ports each controls. From these ports, Lebanese drug dealers run highly organized operations employing resources that range from the sophisticated marketing networks used for the prewar trade of legal goods to grandmotherly couriers shuttling between Lebanon and major airports in Europe and the United States. Even factions of the hyperreligious Hizbollah are believed to be involved in heroin production and transit. According to Western intelligence sources, the Shiite Muslim religious hierarchy issued a *fatwa* (religious decree) sometime in 1986 that legitimized opium and heroin production as long as its sale was limited to "infidels." The Shiite clerics reportedly reasoned that drug sales furthered the Shiites' holy war against the West by undermining decadent Western society.

Tragically, the Lebanese themselves have become victims of their own felonious industry. Traditionally hashish was strictly an export item. Drug abuse existed, but it never ranked as a major social problem in Lebanese society until the war. Now, out of a population of perhaps three million, an estimated quarter of a million people swallow, smoke, and sniff anything that helps them make it through the anxiety of one more day. Among the militias responsible for much of the trade, the rate of drug use may outrank that of the general population. Many militiamen receive as compensation a cut of the drugs that the militia handles. This they can either sell or use themselves. Tragically, young boys who originally entered a militia for identity, pay, or glamour are now captives of the drugs their militia trades.

Drug abuse in Lebanon, as many would argue about drug abuse in the West, is a symptom of a society in disarray. The toll of years of animosity, widespread fear, chronic trauma, and the frenzy of hatred have damaged Lebanon's social fabric as much as the bombs and shells have damaged its physical infrastructure. The lines between justice and injustice, moderation and excess, legitimate concerns and illogical claims have all merged. And the most basic elements that normally hold a society together—trust, loyalty, confidence, compassion, and decency—have all been fatally eroded by the cavalcade of violence and brutality. Although the people have exhibited remarkable resilience for over a decade, the long-term trauma has finally so muted their sensibilities that they are unable even to feel outrage. Consequently, during recurring outbreaks of fighting among rival factions, people retreat with grim resignation to their airless, windowless basements, knowing that organized society is powerless to stop the acts of the few. For Lebanese society is hostage to those who control guns.

Fatigue-clad men who draw arms from private arsenals now define Lebanon. Often nameless, they patrol the streets without anyone necessarily knowing what cause they represent or to whom they answer. Many of those on the fringes of the violence are nothing more than freelance thugs who for a few dollars will shatter a kneecap or for $100 will become assassins. They terrorize; they do not control.

Control is left to the open and arrogant masters of power—the major militias of the Maronites, the Druze, and the Shiites augmented by the Palestinians and their leftist allies. These are not just bands of citizen-soldiers who rush from their shops and their jobs to defend their community under attack. The leading militias command armories stocked with tanks and heavy artillery. They control ports. They generate huge profits by trading arms and smuggling drugs. Like sovereign powers, they conduct their affairs with foreign sponsors. These private armies are so powerful because they face no opposing force except rival militias motivated by the same drive for power and dedicated to the same tactics.

In mid-1987, Prime Minister Selim Hoss concluded:

Lebanon's crisis has become self-perpetuating. It has formed into an entity all its own. It has its institutions, its generation, its manners and values. There are the militias, the illegal radio stations, illegal television stations, illegal taxes—these are the institutions of crisis. When I grew up . . . , it was unimaginable that someone who liked your car would simply take it, that someone who liked your apartment would break in and squat in it. That happens all the time now.

The violence in Lebanon has endured so long that it generates its own justification. Those who continue to wage war with such passion have little time or inclination to reflect on their collective future. And perhaps this is the real calamity. Caught between the Western and Arab worlds, belonging to neither, the Lebanese seem to have embraced the most base trait of both cultures—killing. In doing so, they have all but dismembered their already fragile society. Charles Malik, foreign minister and president of the General Assembly of the United Nations, once prophetically said, "The flaw of crossroads of culture is that they breed decadence. The complexity and multiplicity of life overwhelm the soul. . . . It [the society] is distracted. It is easily tempted, and that pulverizes it into bits and pieces, and in the end it is extinguished." Speaking less eloquently but far more graphically, one of those militant Maronite monks who backed the 1975 war for Maronite supremacy says, "The society has been destroyed. There is nothing in Lebanon. We are playing in our blood."

Lebanon, crowned by glittering Beirut, disintegrated in a generation from the standard by which heterogeneous societies are measured to a cesspool of viciously hostile groups in league with avaricious foreign sponsors all claiming sovereignty of their interests. With their rivalries, ambitions, and weapons, the Lebanese along with the foreigners—sometimes as allies, sometimes as conquerors—threw assault after assault against the Lebanese state. Together they turned Lebanon from what was once little more sinister than a fractured and fragile republic into a scarred and repugnant symbol of hatred and self-interest. In the process, they left Lebanon physically crippled, its economy ruined, its society corrupted, its very soul wasted. Finally, all that was left to destroy was the fragile illusion of the state itself.

Just when Beirut thought life couldn't worsen . . .
                                    Christian Science Monitor
                                    October 4, 1988

ELEVEN
A HOUSE DIVIDED

O n November 22, 1988, the forty-fifth anniversary of Lebanon's independence, rats and wild cats operating like allies
prowled through the uncollected garbage on the corners of
Beirut's once most fashionable streets. In the old hotel district, the
grubby facades of damaged buildings and the rusting debris of
battle testified to the years of neglect. In this fourteenth year of the
war, there were no celebrations marking Lebanon's passage from
colony to independent state. Instead, Amal and Hizbollah militiamen engaged in fierce street combat for control of Beirut's southern suburbs. From East Beirut, the Lebanese Forces issued
threats to shell the central bank located in West Beirut if funds
were not released for the use of Christian military forces. Everywhere there was talk of shutting the Museum crossing point on the
Green Line, the only mutually recognized contact point between
Christian and Muslim Lebanon. The words that Kamal Jumblatt
wrote just before his death had come to fruition: "People lied to
themselves in this country, even about the 1943 National Pact and
independence. . . . Our leaders had been vaunting the Lebanese
formula at the four corners of the earth, but this formula was it
seems just one more myth about our country. . . . In Lebanon the

232

precarious adhesion around a lie was doomed eventually to dissolve and disappear."

In spite of Lebanon's collapse into anarchy and violence between April 1975 and the early autumn of 1988, a semblance of constitutional legitimacy had been somehow retained in the presidency. It was one of the many ironies of the war that, regardless of the reality of the situation, all the factions acknowledged that as long as there was a president installed by common consent, Lebanon could still claim to be a nation.

Yet Lebanon was a truculent parody of a nation. The Chamber of Deputies, the sitting parliament, had not been elected since 1972. Twenty-three of its ninety-nine seats stood vacant, abdicated by death or emigration. The Maronite president and the Sunni prime minister were so bitterly split that the full cabinet had been unable to convene since early 1986. The president, barricaded within the sanctuary of the Mountain, was forced to conduct the business of state through written notes carried by messengers between ministers, while the prime minister executed his duties from self-imposed imprisonment in a West Beirut apartment that was encased in steel mesh designed to deflect shells and equipped with windows made of one-way glass to prevent potential assassins from taking aim from neighboring buildings.

The national army, bisected into its Christian and Muslim factions, was outnumbered by the heavily armed Lebanese militias that occupied enclaves within the various parts of Lebanon, which they controlled like fiefdoms. In addition, a twenty-five-thousand-man Syrian army of occupation spread out over northern and eastern Lebanon; Israel claimed its "security zone" in south Lebanon; and Iran directed cadres of Revolutionary Guards, scattered through the Bekaa Valley, which plotted the destruction of Lebanon as a secular state. Lebanon remained a country only through the symbolism of a sitting president whose claim to office was recognized by all the major factions of the multifarious Lebanese mosaic.

But on September 22, 1988, the term of Amin Gemayel, elected in 1982 to fill the place of the assassinated Bashir, expired. Once more Lebanon faced the hazardous task of choosing a new president. And once again the choice was fraught with symbolism. Even though the civil war had shorn the presidency of most of its power, it was still the prize the Maronites required as the emblem of their continued existence in Lebanon and the laurel the Muslims demanded as the affirmation of their equal status with the Christians.

Nevertheless, in the year before the election, the Lebanese' flagging confidence had been buoyed, if only slightly, by the possibility of a political rapprochement that would end the war. Walid Jumblatt, as much a master of the declaratory statement as his father Kamal had been, affirmed his faith in the Lebanese' ability to forge an agreement: "Reconciliation can be attained through finding a settlement which conflicting parties in Lebanon find acceptable."

But reconciliation was doomed because the political system on which the election was predicated was dead. The mechanisms in place were structured by the reigning *zuama* forty-five years before to accommodate a unique political system. But these crafty men among the Maronites, the Sunnis, and the Shiites were no longer there to make the mechanisms work. During the course of the war, Kamal Jumblatt and Rashid Karami fell to assassins. Camille Chamoun and Pierre Gemayel surrendered to Father Time. Gemayel's son, Bashir, groomed to succeed his father, died before him. The Solhs and the Salams lost their authority when their confessional became irrelevant in terms of power. Other *zuama* as well as their descendants were dead, in exile, or dethroned by the militias. Of the lions of prewar politics, only the aged Suleiman Franjieh remained.

The traditional *zaim* fell because he lost his constituency. In a grim paradox, the chaotic bloodletting of the civil war vastly broadened the Lebanese political base, altering forever the power configuration that existed before the war. From the beginning of the conflict, young men with guns contested the authority of the old political leaders, and eventually, in a crumbling social order, it was they who harvested the power.

By the summer of 1988, these new kingmakers were ready for the end of Amin Gemayel's term, their militias were in place, and their foreign allies were alerted. As if Lebanon had somehow moved back to 1974, the last election before the war, the root issue in the 1988 election was still the distribution of political power as established by the National Pact. The war, it seemed, had settled nothing except to destroy the existing power structure and realign the Muslim opposition to Christian dominance. Nabih Berri, representing the Shiite Amal, the largest Muslim faction, pronounced

the National Pact dead and called for the election of a constituent
assembly to lay the foundation for "a new republic for Lebanon."
But the Maronites stood firmly behind the National Pact, or at
least the portion that reserved the presidency for a Maronite. In
defense of their stand, a member of the Lebanese Forces delivered
the same argument the Maronites had voiced since Lebanese independence: "The presidency gives Maronites moral security."

But in a change from 1974, the validity of the National Pact
could no longer be determined by the Lebanese themselves. Any
president, Christian or Muslim, had to satisfy Syria's Hafiz Assad.
Assad, himself reaching to the past, determined that the tottering,
seventy-eight-year-old Suleiman Franjieh should become president. In choosing Franjieh, who had been president when the war
began, Assad did politically what he could not do militarily—he
united the Lebanese if only in opposition. Franjieh was an affront
to the Muslims because he was a Maronite; to the new generation of
Lebanese leaders because he was of the old order; and to the
Maronites because he was a puppet of Syria, an icon of the Syrian
presence in Lebanon that the Maronites so hated. On August 18,
the Maronite hard-liners in the Chamber of Deputies, the body
charged with choosing the president, blocked the election of Franjieh.

A new election was set. The deputies were to assemble in the
old parliament building in West Beirut on September 22, the day
before Gemayel's term was to expire. On the appointed day, Prime
Minister Selim Hoss, surrounded by bodyguards, cautiously
emerged from his apartment fortress to undertake the nostalgic
journey to the once sparkling center of Beirut. Elsewhere in the
Muslim sector of the city, Hussein al Husseini, the speaker who in
1974 tried to deny the election of Suleiman Franjieh, left his office
and climbed into his car surrounded by his retinue and a covey of
bodyguards nervously holding their fingers on the triggers of their
automatic weapons. Other deputies representing the Sunnis,
Shiites, and Druze came from across Lebanon.

But the Chamber of Deputies did not convene that day either.
The Maronite deputies refused to leave the security of the Mountain. Without them, there was no quorum. And without a quorum,
there was no election. Hussein al Husseini adjourned the session.
Lebanon's attempt to elect a new president ended fittingly in a
barrage of artillery shells laid around the parliament building and
an explosion of gunfire across the Green Line. And so the clock

ticked away the remainder of Amin Gemayel's term.

At the stroke of midnight on September 22, Lebanon was without a president, the last symbol of its unity. Drawing on the precedent established by the twelve-day vacancy created by the resignation of Bishara Khoury in 1952, Amin Gemayel named an interim government headed by Michel Aoun, commander of the Lebanese army. Lebanon's Muslim factions immediately denounced the move, claiming that in the absence of an elected president, the interim government should be headed by the Sunni prime minister, Selim Hoss. Thus, as the sun rose on the morning of September 23, Lebanon had two governments—the Christian government of Aoun defended by the Christian half of the Lebanese army and, for the time at least, the Lebanese Forces; and the Muslim government of Hoss condoned by the Muslim militias and allowed to claim power by Syria. Lebanon was broken politically as well as socially and geographically. With the militias barricaded in their own self-declared territories, the wisdom of Selim Hoss's words uttered in 1980 was confirmed: "I am not afraid for the Lebanese, but I am afraid for Lebanon."

In the twentieth century, the conflict over Lebanon has revolved around four rival concepts of the Lebanese state: a small Christian Lebanon, a greater Christian Lebanon, a greater pluralistic Lebanon, and an Arab Lebanon. The small Christian Lebanon existed at the sufferance of the Ottoman Empire and with the support of the European powers during the period of the autonomous *mutassarifate*. Greater Christian Lebanon lived under the French. Pluralistic Lebanon, 1946–1975, was the uneasy Christian-Muslim partnership under Christian hegemony. Then came 1975 and the rupture of the old order. From that rupture, the Muslims vowed they would strip away Lebanon's Western patina and expose, at last, its Arab soul. But before the Muslims could claim their legacy, Lebanon split. If it is to be bandaged together again, the various factions in Lebanon must reach some accommodation on just what each wants Lebanon to be. That task is daunting. In reality, the perception of Lebanon among the leading confessionals—the Maronites, Druze, Sunnis, and the Shiites divided between Amal and Hizbollah—is vastly different, defined by the self-interest of each.

From the eastern side of Beirut west to the Anti-Lebanon mountains, from the Shuf north to just beyond Ehdene stands

Christian Lebanon. Crowned by the seaport city of Jounieh, it is strikingly free of the scars of war. Pleasure boats ply the waters of the bay and dock at a marina dotted with bright umbrellas and colorful chaise longues reminiscent of Beirut's Bay of St. George before the war. Little girls in black patent leather shoes and white anklets play in the parks, their laughing eyes free of the desolate pain of children caught in war. Along the oceanfront, sporty Fiat convertibles driven by the sons and daughters of the elite wearing immense designer sunglasses dart through the traffic. Although hit hard by the economic collapse, Jounieh is a fading reminder of the Lebanon that once was.

With its somewhat uniform population, the Christian sector of Lebanon has escaped much of the rancor that boils in West Beirut and south between the Druze, the Sunnis, the Shiites of Amal, the Shiites of Hizbollah, and the Palestinians. It has also been spared much of the devastation of the proxy wars that foreigners continue to wage in Lebanon. Much of the reason is that Christian Lebanon has actually stood as a garrison state since 1976. Dug into the hills, the Lebanese Forces and the Christian elements of the Lebanese army have fended off most assaults on its territory and have internally maintained public order. Increasingly referred to as "Marounistan," this is Maronite land. Outnumbered roughly two to one, the Greek Orthodox and the Greek Catholics living in the region have buckled under Maronite domination to become part of Christian Lebanon.

Christian Lebanon's strength lies in its geographic position within the Mountain. The Maronites' strength lies in the military power of the Christian elements of the thirty-seven-thousand-man Lebanese army and the estimated twenty-thousand-man Lebanese Forces, the largest unified armed force in Lebanon after Syria. The Lebanese Forces is, in fact, the most viable institution in Lebanon. It controls a tax-collection mechanism that is far more efficient than that of the government, allowing it to fund its own multimillion-dollar budget. The Forces also run a sophisticated system of kickbacks and payoffs, replacement for the old patronage system that oiled Lebanese politics before the war. Short of a massive military intervention by Syria, no one can overpower the Lebanese Forces.

But the Lebanese Forces represent only one faction of the Maronites, for the Maronites are no more a monolith now than they were before the war. Personal ambitions and rivalries, as well as the ever-present family vendettas, characterize the divisions. But the primary philosophical cleavage is between the burning ideology of the Lebanese Forces and the more pragmatic attitudes evidenced by others. Although virtually all the Maronites publicly uphold the philosophy of an independent Lebanon in which their Christian identity would be protected, they are bitterly divided over just what "independent Lebanon" actually means. Once again they divide over the same question that has tormented the Maronites for so many centuries—what is Lebanon's relationship with the Arab world?

The Lebanese Forces are the zealous guardians of Maronite culture. It is they who wield the shield against all the polities that they judge to be "anti-Lebanese." Continuing to draw their ideology from the militant Maronite monks, they are, to themselves, the incarnation of the Crusaders, the defenders of Christianity against the tide of the mythical Arab nation.

Through most of the war, the Lebanese Forces' price for accommodation with the Muslims was essentially an affirmation within the antebellum political sphere of the status quo. Most Maronites exuded confidence that somehow they could escape Muslim ascendancy. And many among them continued to play their games of pseudodemography in order to defend their claims to their political prerogatives in Lebanon. A Maronite prominent in the affairs of his community, for example, still insists that the Maronites are the majority in Lebanon if all the emigrant Lebanese around the world are counted: "There are three million in Lebanon and four million outside Lebanon. There are a million Lebanese, 60 percent of them Maronite, in Brazil alone."

But reality relentlessly pressed against the Maronites. No longer did it seem that the Maronites could end the war on their own terms. And the time had passed when most Maronites believed that the Muslims were willing to "convince us we can live together." While those reflecting the mentality of the Lebanese Forces publicly affirmed their support for a united Lebanon, they were moving inexorably toward the idea of turning their Christian-held enclave into a ministate protected by foreign guarantors, almost a return to the old *mutassarifate*.

While the Lebanese Forces' perception of the Lebanese state has changed, that of other Maronites has not. Amin Gemayel, representing those who shared his general philosophy, upheld the historic role of Lebanon as the bridge between the East and the West. This faction accepted the territorial composition of Greater Lebanon and expressed a willingness to share a measure of power with the Muslims. Not long before the aborted election of 1988, Gemayel said, "It is in our fundamental interests as Christian Lebanese to be Arabs. The Christian community cannot live in a ghetto."

Remarks like these, aimed at preserving Lebanon's ties with the Arab world, led the Lebanese Forces to brand Gemayel as "Muhammed." Yet he and those of similar persuasion were the realists, if there is such a thing in Lebanon. They seemed to accept that Lebanon as a Christian fief died with the civil war. Their concern was to salvage what they could of their eroded position, to preserve somehow a semblance of Maronite superiority in Lebanon. Their answer was that the Maronites would hold the presidency and certain other prerogatives in a reconstituted Lebanon. The old republic would give way to some form of decentralized government in which each confessional preserved its own identity but one that fell short of a confederation of independent cantons proposed by some of the Maronites. A hardheaded Maronite businessman argued the point for a new government: "The Christians can only survive. They have no future. Lebanon will be Islamized sooner or later. This would at least buy us some time."

Yet when the time came to elect a new president, to risk the possibility of reform of the Lebanese system, Gemayel was unwilling to succumb to the entreaties of the Muslims or the dictates of Syria. Regardless of his attitude toward Lebanon's territorial integrity and its Arab character, Amin Gemayel was responsible for appointing an interim government headed by a Maronite, effectively splitting the country.

At the beginning of the war, the Maronites feared the Palestinians and the Sunnis. Now they fear the Shiites. Yet to the Maronites all these groups coalesce in that word they so dread—*Muslim*. In many respects, the Maronites of today are no different from their ancestors. For centuries the Maronites of the Mountain have perceived Islam as their ultimate menace. Just as St. Maron retreated into the Mountain to save the ethos of his religion, the Maronites of today have pulled into the Mountain as their last bastion against Muslim Lebanon. And like their ancestors, they can only survive with outside help.

Although they have now turned east to the Arab world, to Syria's nemesis, Iraq, for the weapons for their defense, it is to the West that the Maronites continue to look for their definition. They still insist they are Mediterranean, not Arab, in culture. They still claim Greece and Rome as their heritage and France as their ideal. And they still hold the West morally responsible for their survival. The Maronite mystique of separateness and endurance within Lebanon, underwritten by the West's duty toward the Christians of the East, always seems to lead back to the University of Kaslik. Sitting with a slim, erudite priest of less than middle age discussing his disappointment with Western support for the Maronites, one could not keep from being startled when he suddenly leaned forward, looked with piercing eyes, and passionately asked, "Does the West want the Christians in the East?"

To the south of Christian Lebanon, buried within the Shuf, stands another garrison state—that of the Druze. There is little gaiety left in a region oppressively damaged by war, only stark symbols of the Druze' determination to protect themselves. It is thus appropriate that on the beach just outside Beirut, a bulky Druze tank sits behind heavy barbed wire, its menacing gun trained on the Ferris wheel of the old amusement park.

Before the war, the Druze shared with the Maronites an intense interest in an independent Lebanon, a haven for the minorities of the Arab world. But that was all the Druze had in common with a confessional from which they were divided by history and self-interest. Lebanese sovereignty aside, the cardinal points of the Druze' political agenda—the insistence on breaking the Maronites' grip on political power and the insistence on transforming the economic system—both reverted to the Druze' all-consuming passion to foster their communal integrity.

As the war moved along its tortuous path, particularly after 1982, the Druze began to find that some of the issues central to their political stance before the war had come to threaten their existence as a politically relevant community in Lebanon. In helping break the Maronite grip on political and economic power, the Druze had opened the door for the Shiites, who, as the largest community in Lebanon, now threatened their own domination of the Lebanese system.

Shiite plans to restructure the quilt of multiple electoral districts in the existing political system in favor of one-person, one-vote loudly sounded all of the alarm bells in the Druze community. With only 6 percent of the population, the Druze were no match for the Shiites in a contest of demographics. Faced with the loss of any guarantee to elective office, the Druze suddenly found themselves having more in common with the Maronites than with the Shiites. And like the Maronites, the Druze vowed to use their geographic location and mighty militia to stave off Shiite control of Lebanon.

The Druze commitment to Lebanese sovereignty has turned out to be as hollow as that of the Maronites. Like the Maronite Christians, the Druze have seized the idea of regional autonomy in which each confessional is dominant rather than pursuing inter-communal reconciliation. As a result, they have opted to create their own ministate.

The Druze have succeeded in protecting their autonomy because man for man they command the best-trained and best-armed militia in Lebanon. But they have, in effect, created their own prison. Druze communal autonomy lives within its hilly fortress surrounded by the community's warriors. They are secure, but they are trapped. With the Maronites to the north, Amal backed by Syria to the south and east, and the Mediterranean to the West, the Druze are locked in the Shuf. One Druze proud of his community's stand still laments, "I feel like I'm in a cage. I can't go anywhere."

On the edge of Sidon, a small boy of no more than six, dressed in a brown fleece jogging suit and wide-strapped sandals, vacantly watches orange flames and billowing black smoke announce one more battle for his city. The son of a Sunni merchant family, he symbolizes his class and his confessional. Relegated to the edge of events, he can do little but watch the conflagration around him.

The Sunnis, the Maronites' major rival for power before the war, have been destroyed as a major political force by that war. Although Selim Hoss holds the title of prime minister, the Sunnis are the most fragmented of all of Lebanon's confessionals. They are split into competing power centers in Tyre, Sidon, Tripoli, and West Beirut. What power they have in military terms is provided by Tripoli's fundamentalist religious movement Tawhid (Islamic Unity Movement); by Sidon's Muslim Popular Liberation Army, a militia largely composed of leftist Nasserites; and by Fatah, Yassir Arafat's faction of the PLO. Politically, the Sunnis have lost out to

the numbers and armed strength of the Shiites. As a result, the
Sunnis, like the Greek Orthodox and the Greek Catholics, have
been relegated to the margins by the Lebanese conflict.

Within the narrow alleys twisting through the shattered buildings of West Beirut, two militiamen, their feet planted far apart for
balance, blast each other with automatic weapon fire. The flying
bullets ricochet off a buff-colored stucco building and hit a metal
sign that bears the likeness of Musa al Sadr. It is a profane act for
the political descendants of the *imam*. For both men are Shiites,
and both are willing to die for their own vision of Arab Lebanon.

The Shiites are no longer the oppressed of Lebanon. As a
confessional, they are the most dynamic force in Lebanon today.
They hold one-half of Beirut and most of the south outside the
Israeli security zone. As a bloc, they have challenged the political
and economic assumptions on which prewar Lebanon was based,
thwarted the Israelis, and compelled the United States and its
allies in the Multi-National Force to change a major foreign policy.
By late 1983, they stood poised to launch the final stage of the shift
in political power in Lebanon from the Maronites to the Shiites.
Instead, the Shiites, so carefully coaxed into political action by
Musa al Sadr, ruptured into two movements hostile to each other—
the Amal, committed to a secular Lebanon, and Hizbollah, wedded
to the promise of Lebanon as an Islamic republic, a facsimile of the
Ayatollah Khomeini's Iran.

Amal, headquartered in the unfinished Murr Tower, which
played such an important part in the "war of the hotels," forms the
mainstream of the Shiite political movement. Amal regards itself
as the true embodiment of Harakat Amal, the heirs of Musa al
Sadr. Since the Shiites are the most important piece in Lebanon's
postwar puzzle, neither peace nor reconciliation can come without
Amal's support.

Of all the political groupings in Lebanon, Amal is the most
dedicated to a sovereign Lebanon. Amal's leadership, headed by
Nabih Berri, candidly admits that only as an autonomous state can
Lebanon preserve the social and political integrity of the Shiites
against the immensity and hostility of the Sunnis of the Arab
world.

Yet, in preserving Lebanon, Amal also demands a new political
system that meets its requirements. After ending the Israeli occu-

pation and stripping Lebanon of its Western facade, Amal wants a parliamentary republic, a free economic system, the redress of social inequities, and an abolition of sectarian politics. Anticipating that their numbers would ensure them a majority, Amal insists on a one-person, one-vote political order, an end of the confessional system. But Amal is dealing in its own illusions when it envisions an escape from communal politics, for Amal itself is a sectarian movement.

Like other sectarian groups, Amal is split into factions. Within its ranks, Nabih Berri's position is always in question. As in other confessionals, the competition often has less to do with platforms than with the allure of personal power.

Despite the internal dissention, the one constant theme running through the political literature of Amal is the movement's commitment to Lebanon as a distinct and definitive homeland for the Shiites. It is this dedication to a secular, sovereign state that so distinguishes Amal from its radical Shiite opponents. In the vision of Hizbollah, Lebanon should emerge from war as an Islamic republic, a compartment within the Islamic *umma*.

The strength of Hizbollah among the Lebanese is as difficult to assess as are its membership and organizational structure. Significantly, its weakest link is its central doctrine—the commitment to turning Lebanon into an Islamic republic. As much as 65 percent of the population of Greater Lebanon consists of non-Shiites. Even within the Shiite community, most Lebanese are too Levantine in attitude to succumb to the rigors of a fundamentalist Islamic state. Still, Hizbollah is a potent force.

Principally it promotes an ideology that fires the emotions of the Shiites far more than do the secular political reforms backed by Amal. Hizbollah's power is, in fact, its passion. Its strength rises from the symbols it creates. Hence, helpless Western hostages standing before video cameras are transformed into emblems of Western impotence in the face of a revitalized Islam. Guerrilla raids into Israel's security zone translate into the Muslims' holy war against Zionism.

Because of its symbolism, Israel is a basic component in Hizbollah's strategy to win converts. On the ideological plane, the recapture of Jerusalem, Islam's third holy site, from the Zionists is powerful rhetoric in the Islamic revolution. On the practical level, revenge against those whom the Shiites blame for most of their ills is potent propaganda in support of Hizbollah's operations.

But attacks against the Israeli presence in Lebanon are more than theater. Through its assaults on the South Lebanon Army and units of Israel's Defense Forces, Hizbollah's five thousand fighters made operations north of the Israeli border expensive for Israel, bringing Israeli policy into question among its own people. Israelis were shocked on November 19, 1988, when seven of their soldiers were killed by three hundred pounds of explosives packed into a Toyota idling alongside an Israeli convoy just across the border. Day after day, Hizbollah presses against what Israel regards as a buffer zone and Hizbollah condemns as a zone of occupation.

The campaign against Israel unites Hizbollah with some Palestinian military units in south Lebanon, thereby increasing its potential military strength as long as this compatibility of interests survives. But it is an alliance that also stokes Hizbollah's rivalry with Amal. Lebanon since 1983 has been dominated by Amal's drive to shape the future of Lebanon.

In 1983, when Israel pulled out from all of Lebanon except the southern security zone, Amal moved in what it determined as a final push to control Lebanon. To succeed required neutralizing Druze control of the coast south of Beirut, subduing the Palestinians, and quelling the influence of its rival Shiite organization, Hizbollah. Suddenly a new and potent force faced those who for so long opposed the power of the Maronites.

In 1984 Amal encroached on Druze territory, triggering a renewed alliance between the Druze and the Palestinians. Both had been a part of the contentious Muslim bloc at the beginning of the war. That alliance was against the Maronites. This new alliance was against Amal, for Amal not only had designs on Druze territory but was bent on driving the Palestinians from Lebanese territory—something the Maronites vowed to do in 1976 and the Israelis swore to do in 1982.

In mid-February 1987, during the height of Amal's campaign, its militia, along with Shiite elements of the Lebanese army, clashed with the Druze, elements of the Palestinians, and armed units of the Lebanese Communist Party over control of West Beirut. Hundreds of heavily armed gunmen turned civilian neighborhoods once more into battlegrounds. The Commodore Hotel, long the favorite center of foreign journalists, took a rocket hit, forever silencing the talkative parrot in the lobby. Civilians went back into their basement bomb shelters and pockmarked stairwells to wait out the fighting, the worst since the 1982 Israeli siege of Beirut. Through several days of intense combat, appeals went out over the combatant-controlled radio stations, pleading for people to allow fire trucks through to extinguish the multitude of fires. The International Red Cross issued urgent appeals to the rival militias to allow rescue workers into cordoned-off streets to remove decaying bodies. It was a fight to the finish to determine who would control West Beirut.

Syria watched its Amal and Druze clients pound each other, destroying eleven years of Syrian effort to control Lebanon. After six days of fierce fighting, a column of Syrian T-55 tanks crested a hill east of Beirut. Before them lay the city, as deceptively serene as when the Israelis approached it in 1982. Residents of Muslim West Beirut greeted the Syrians as they had in 1976 and as they did the Multi-National Force in 1982, as liberators. But Syria was not a liberator, only a police force that maintained some order until Amal made its next move against its rivals in West Beirut—this time Hizbollah.

In May 1988 in the south Beirut suburbs, a bearded, curly-headed Amal militiaman carrying a grenade bag and an automatic rifle peered out from behind the corner of a building on which was plastered a picture of Nabih Berri conferring with Hafiz Assad. Across a space littered with burned-out cars and one denuded tree, another militiaman in a ragged shirt and an elastic headband emptied his recoilless rifle into a Hizbollah stronghold.

Once more the Red Cross sent out appeals to both sides in the fighting to let rescue teams in to evacuate the wounded, and refugees gathered their meager possessions to flee the fighting. After sixteen days of intense combat, with at least 250 dead and over 800 wounded, Hizbollah had won as much as anyone wins in Lebanon. The Party of God proved to be more tenacious than the more numerous and better-armed Amal. Equally important, Amal had failed to release Hizbollah's Western hostages, denying to Amal a potent sign of its control over the actions of the Shiites. Syria was called in once more to restore order, and once more Hafiz Assad was forced to pump more men and money into Lebanon.

Common wisdom holds that Hizbollah cannot last long in the Lebanese political equation. To turn Lebanon into an Islamic

republic, Hizbollah's various factions would have to defeat everyone
in Lebanon, including Syria. Nevertheless, the threat of Hizbollah
is real. With the end of the Iraq-Iran war, Hizbollah may actually
experience a resurgence as Iran is freed from the battlefield,
allowing the mullahs to concentrate again on propagating the
Islamic revolution in Lebanon. Even without increased Iranian
interest, no Lebanese or foreign government can take control of
Lebanon without confronting Hizbollah. It is a confrontation that
will be bloody, another in a long series of events that have established carnage as a Lebanese birthright.

Anyone having contact with Lebanon during the war has
heard the Lebanese offer a torrent of explanations for the conflict.
They have laid blame for the war on the French, the Palestinians,
the Syrians, the Israelis, the Arab League, the Americans (principally the CIA), the British, the Iranians, the Russians, and the
United Nations, among others. A Sunni Muslim theorizes that the
war would end if the French Mandate were reestablished. A Melkite is convinced that Lebanon's whole problem arises from a
seventh-century conspiracy among the leadership of Mecca to
conceal the fact that Muhammed was in truth a Christian. And any
number of Lebanese claim the theory that the war is a universal
conspiracy to destroy Lebanon because all nations, east and west,
are jealous of its beauty and frightened by the Lebanese' commercial abilities.

While all of these observations, delivered with burning passion, elicit a certain wry amusement in those who have heard them
often before, they say something profound and deadly about the
Lebanese psyche. In all these scenarios, the Lebanese are refusing
to accept any responsibility for the fate that has befallen Lebanon.
In a 1987 interview with the *Christian Science Monitor*, a Maronite was asked when the war would end. Without a pause, he
replied, "It's God's will. It is not our problem."

Every communal group fervently insists, with the Lebanese'
own particular brand of assurance, "You know the war is not our
fault. The Lebanese have no quarrel with each other." The inescapable truth is that the war germinated in the soil of the Lebanese'
own discord and then expanded as the Palestinian factor was
added and finally peaked with the involvement of Syria, Israel, and
others.

Although an American diplomat claims that "Lebanon is a

Lebanese problem that the Lebanese have to solve for themselves," there is a more accurate assessment. While the resistance of the leading militia leaders to any meaningful form of power-sharing perpetuates the war, the presence of foreign powers on Lebanese territory also precludes the Lebanese from solving their own problems. Since the destiny of every faction in Lebanon depends to some extent on the objectives of the foreign patron or ally to which each is attached, the Lebanese are incapable of determining their destiny in isolation. Thus, there is no greater truism than the one that says all things in the Middle East are interconnected.

Red Cross Quits Lebanon Under Threat
New York Times
December 21, 1988

TWELVE
CLOSING THE CROSSROADS

I n the dry Bekaa Valley, Syrian soldiers hidden within the terrain hurry for cover as a sleek Israeli jet streaks across the southern sky, breaking the stillness of midday. In the next shallow valley, the same noise energizes a ragged coterie of the militant Islamic Amal camped under the soiled green flags of the Islamic revolution. Then it is quiet again except for the occasional military transport that rumbles along the dusty roads past forlorn orchards and farms victimized by the war. Among the half-tended orchards is a deserted chicken farm. Established by a Shiite who invested all his earnings from five years in Saudi Arabia, it had just turned profitable in 1987 when Syria sent additional army units toward Beirut. The chicken farmer's total stock was consumed by a hungry army that paid no compensation. Lebanon the state has been similarly consumed by hungry powers unwilling to pay compensation.

In time measured by war, it seems an eternity since Lebanon basked in its Golden Age and all of the myths about the "jewel of the Levant" were still intact. Within that mythology, perhaps the greatest myth of all was that the conscience of the world would never allow any serious harm to befall such a benign little country

248

as Lebanon. According to the illusion, it was to everyone's interest—that of Lebanon, the West, Israel, the Arab world—to preserve Lebanon as a "window on the West," a cultural gateway between the Western world that lay beyond the Mediterranean and the vastness of the Arab East that lay across the Mountain. Instead, those who supposedly held a special interest in Lebanon contributed to its destruction.

Today Lebanon functions as the playing field for the conflicts of the Middle East, the locale to which everyone comes to settle old scores. Sitting between the Lebanese themselves and the policies and power of state armies are the Palestinians, martyrs and malefactors in the tangle of Lebanon. Fiercely united in their nationalism, bitterly divided among themselves, the Palestinians are as central to events in Lebanon now as they were when the war began.

As always, the Palestinians do not represent the Lebanese dimensions of the war but rather the rivalries of Lebanon's neighbors waged on Lebanon's soil. As such, the Palestinians weave in and out, as enemy or friend, in the power configuration of most of the factions and countries involved in Lebanon. For the Palestinians themselves, however, there is only one issue—the right to utilize Lebanon as a base of operations.

Although they may regard Israel as the adversary, the Palestinians also confront the bitter antagonism of Amal and Syria as well as the factional disputes among themselves. For Amal, the exile of the Palestinians from Lebanon is crucial to Shiite dominance within Lebanon. For Syria, the subjugation of the Palestinians is critical to Hafiz Assad's ambition of attaining dominion over Lebanon. For the rivals of Yassir Arafat and the mainstream of the Palestinian movement, the determination of who speaks for those in Lebanon profoundly influences the terms on which Palestinian nationalists deal with Israel.

The Palestinian camp of Shatila is a chronicle of the Palestinians' history in Lebanon. It was established to house refugees from the 1948 war for Palestine. During the late 1960s, it was fertile recruiting ground for the *fedayeen* who renewed the Palestinians' war with Israel. During the early 1970s, Shatila functioned as part of the Palestinian state within Lebanon, an autonomous area out of reach of the Lebanese government. In 1975-1976, it was caught up in the fighting between the Maronites and the Muslim front. In

1982, it achieved grim notoriety as the site of the Sabra-Shatila massacre. After that tragic drama, Shatila's fate became entwined with Syria's power struggle with PLO leader Yassir Arafat for control over Lebanon's Palestinians.

The evacuation of Yassir Arafat and the PLO from Beirut in 1982 contributed to Syrian as well as Israeli objectives in Lebanon. But it was only a stopgap measure against those who fought in the name of Palestinian nationalism. Within a year, at least five thousand of Arafat's men stole back into Lebanon. Arafat himself eventually returned, upsetting Assad's drive to consolidate his hold over the Palestinians and Lebanon.

Unable to force Arafat to heel to Syrian wishes, Hafiz Assad set out to destroy him within his own organization. Assad had long supported Saiqa among the PLO's amalgam of competing factions. From it, Assad drew his tool: Colonel Saeed Musa, whose nom de guerre is Abu Musa, was the self-styled conscience of the Palestinian armed struggle against Zionism. Declaring, "There must be complete liberation of the whole land of Palestine," Abu Musa raised insurrection against Arafat's most tentative moves toward some form of negotiated settlement with Israel. In November 1983, Abu Musa, armed to the teeth by Syria, drove Arafat and his supporters out of Tripoli:

> The month-long intra-Palestinian battles near Tripoli . . . which resulted in yet another ignominious expulsion from Lebanon for Arafat, was a testimony to Syria's absolute, even brutal, determination to keep the PLO in its grip, so that Syrian control over Palestinian affairs, and beyond over Lebanese affairs, [would] not in any way be undermined.

Although defeated and humiliated, Arafat was not subdued. Small groups of Fatah guerrillas stole back into Lebanon by the back roads and the sea, disappearing into Shatila and the other refugee camps to the south. In response, Syria recruited another powerful ally against the wily Arafat—Amal.

In May 1985, grim fame once again awaited Shatila as Amal began the long siege of Palestinian camps that became known as the "camp wars." Intent on crushing the Palestinians, Amal sealed off areas of heavy Palestinian concentration in southern Beirut and around Sidon. For the next three years, Shatila once again became the site where politics and hatred between the Palestinians and their adversaries were played out. Along with Burj al Barajneh, Shatila became another of those Palestinian "Leningrads" to which Yassir Arafat alludes. Trapped in a living hell, the Palestinians fought the blockade with an inspiration that comes from desperation.

Unable to break free and unwilling to surrender, the Palestinians came to depend for their survival on provisions smuggled in from the sea and food carried through the lines by six- and seven-year-old children. During February 1987, food became so scarce that camp inhabitants were reduced to eating dogs, cats, and rats. At last their plight forced its way into international attention when the starving people asked religious leaders for permission to eat their dead.

Shamed by the international condemnation, Amal reluctantly called a truce. With the guns stilled, shell-shocked people crawled out of their shelters and into the sunlight. As they sat scattered across ruins that lay on top of ruins, their haggard faces showed no emotion, just resignation that they were still alive.

And then it began again. For almost a year, Shatila held out against the Syrian-supplied might of Amal. In December 1987, events outside Lebanon abruptly altered Amal's brutal siege of the camps. The Palestinians living in the Israeli-occupied territories of the West Bank and Gaza unleashed a hail of stones and anger against Israeli rule. The *intifadah*, or Palestinian uprising, notably framed the Palestinian question once again as an "Arab" issue, forcing Amal to end the ordeal. With at least three thousand dead, Nabih Berri announced, "Amal decided to lift its military siege around the camps as a gift to our brothers in the West Bank and Gaza Strip."

Amal had failed to break the Palestinians. At Hafiz Assad's instigation, Abu Musa took up again where Amal left off. Shatila exploded once more, this time caught in the death struggle between Arafat and his ultraistic rival. By mid-July 1988, another 127 people within the camp of Shatila had died before those loyal to Yassir Arafat surrendered.

Nothing that could be called a house was left standing. From Shatila's once teeming population, only seven families were left, living within the remaining corners of shacks and shanties that they covered with battered sheets of corrugated metal. Slaughter and siege had at last destroyed Shatila, but not the Palestinians' resolve to manage their own destiny. As twenty-two-year-old Khalid Bishrawi filed out of Shatila past the guns of Abu Musa, he said, "We've become the football of the Middle East, kicked around by Arabs, Israelis, and by our own kind." From Shatila, the soldiers of Fatah went south to Sidon to continue their struggle for a homeland.

The Palestinians and the Israelis are both mired in Lebanon because of their virulent quarrel with each other. Except for the grand strategy of 1982–1983, Israeli policy in Lebanon has remained remarkably consistent since 1968—to keep the Palestinians from establishing a presence in Lebanon powerful enough to challenge Israel's northern border. Even the tactics stay the same—use of the surrogate South Lebanon Army (SLA) as a buffer between the Israeli border and Palestinian implacements in Lebanon, coupled with punishing retribution against those who attack Israel. Neither has succeeded in winning security for the Israelis.

Since 1968, Israeli fears about the Palestinians in south Lebanon have been real, and their response to those fears predictable. Nothing has changed in twenty years except perhaps the ingenuity and cruelty with which they strike each other. In November 1987, a Palestinian commando in an audacious action crossed the Israeli border swinging from a motorized hang glider, dropped into an Israeli army post, and slaughtered six Israeli soldiers before he himself was gunned down. From the Palestinian perspective, the raid was a spectacular success. A lone gunman using stealth and daring had bared the vulnerability of the Israeli army.

Within weeks, Israel struck back, bombing Palestinian and Lebanese guerrilla bases in south Lebanon. The Palestinians, joined by Hizbollah, launched punishing attacks on the SLA. For the first time, Israel responded to attacks on the security zone rather than on Israel proper. In May, the Israeli army moved roughly ten miles beyond the zone to sweep Lebanese villages as far north as Maydoun. And once again it was the Shiites who paid the price. On suspicion that the occupants were aiding guerrilla forces, Israeli demolition crews leveled more than sixty houses within Maydoun under the gaze of the families who once called them home.

For Israel, the torment of Lebanon is that, as a staging area for the PLO, it cannot be ignored. Yet what Israel regards as legitimate operations carried out in the name of Israeli security simply add to the Shiites' corrosive hatred of Israel. Militant Shiism feeds on Israel's tough tactics against civilian populations. Villages where children cannot go to school because fear of Israeli reprisal raids keeps teachers away and where farmers can work their fields only in sight of soldiers of UNIFIL are the most fertile ground for Hizbollah enlistment. With their recruits pulled from these villages, the militants strike Israeli troops and units of the South Lebanon Army in a passionate mission to drive them out of Lebanon. Periodically they are joined by Amal, forced into action by an alarming loss of support in the south. With the groups as bitterly hostile to each other as ever, the limited cooperation between Amal and Hizbollah rises from the apprehension that the "security zone" is about to be incorporated into Israel.

As if the situation were not chaotic enough, the Israelis use south Lebanon as the dumping site for the Palestinian exiles of the *intifadah*. There they join those driven by a loathing of Israel. Thus grappling with the Palestinians, the Israelis have created new enemies, forging an alliance between radical, fatigue-clad Palestinian commandos and the fighters of Hizbollah often wrapped in the blood-soaked rags of their own martyrdom. Both are dedicated to the destruction of Israel.

But Israel is not the only foreign power bogged down in Lebanon, trapped between goals and realities. Israeli defense minister Yitzhak Rabin once observed, "The Syrians learned the hard way, as everybody who tried to be involved in Lebanon, that whoever sets his foot on the Lebanese mud sinks."

Syria has been in Lebanon since 1976, trying to build its hegemony over the fractious Lebanese. While Israel sees its mission in Lebanon in terms of security, Syria sees its mission in terms of destiny. Hafiz Assad, the originator of Syrian policy in Lebanon, claims that "throughout history, Syria and Lebanon have been one country and one people." Although questionable historically, this philosophy nevertheless undergirds Hafiz Assad's actions in Lebanon and imposes on them a notable consistency.

Since 1976, Hafiz Assad has tried to tame Lebanon, to force the Lebanese to accept Syria's version of the Levant. The cost has been enormous. In 1988, for example, maintaining between twenty-five thousand and forty thousand troops in Lebanon was costing some $1 million a month above Syria's ordinary military budget, a heavy burden considering Syria's own strapped economy. In addition to the direct outlay of money, the allure of fast profits has corrupted the Syrian military in Lebanon, creating a highly organized and vastly profitable smuggling ring that wreaks havoc with Syria's own economy. Along the border, long lines of trucks, most painted orange, line up to cross into Syria carrying the products from Lebanon's ports. With Syrian soldiers acting as both smugglers and police officers, a tidal wave of tax-free goods flows into Syria, swamping local industry and further straining Syria's chronic foreign exchange problem.

The other cost of the long Syrian immersion in Lebanon is social. Raw, naive recruits, often from the countryside, are sent into the Sodom-and-Gomorrah atmosphere of Lebanon. As one high-ranking Syrian close to the military commander of Lebanon bluntly stated, "Syria has paid a big price for its involvement in Lebanon. Not only in terms of money. We send young soldiers there. They spend a year and come back behaving like the Mafia. What do you expect when they are living in a country made up of Mafias?"

Despite the costs and frustrations, Syria is the only foreign power that has dealt realistically with Lebanon. Hafiz Assad, with clear-headed pragmatism, has never sought to merge Lebanon with Syria. Rather, he bolsters the Lebanese elements that serve Syrian interests and possess the power to exercise effective control over parts of Lebanon, and he ruthlessly punishes those who do not.

It could even be said that Assad's Lebanon policy is one of negatives rather than positives. He does not want disorder in Lebanon, Syria's front yard. He does not want an anti-Syrian government to win out. He does not want an Islamic republic. He does not want the Lebanese situation to lead to a confrontation between Syria and Israel. And he does not want Israel, Iran, the United States, France, or the Soviet Union meddling in Lebanon. In short, Assad does not necessarily insist on ruling Lebanon, but at the same time he will not allow anyone else to do so either. Assad's problem is that Lebanon has been easy for Syria to swallow but impossible to digest.

Syria holds the trump card in Lebanon. The Lebanese themselves cannot strike a bargain without Syrian approval. Nor can any foreign power, including the United States, strike a deal without winning Syrian approval. Even Hafiz Assad, after years of trying to piece together a workable coalition in Lebanon that would impose peace on the splintered state while protecting Syrian interests, has never been able to close a deal. Control of the PLO in Lebanon continues to escape him. The Israeli military presence in south Lebanon presents a constant risk of an unwanted war. Within the Lebanese dimension of the war, Assad cannot force his will on the Christians of the Mountain without sustaining enormous cost. And without attacking the anarchy and fragmentation in Muslim Beirut caused by the rivalry of Amal and Hizbollah, he cannot corral the Shiites.

Perhaps no group offers a better example of the limits of Syrian power in Lebanon than the Maronites. In December 1985, Syria managed to broker a power-sharing accord that was actually signed by Muslim, Druze, and Christian militia leaders, including Elie Hobeika, the commander of the strong-willed Lebanese Forces.

As the replacement for the National Pact, the Tripartite Agreement broke the power of the confessionals in the Lebanese political system by adopting the principle of one person, one vote. But it also gave Syria control over Lebanon's internal security, army, schools, information services, and foreign policy. Intended to form the basis for an intercommunal understanding that might end the war, the Tripartite Agreement stirred a hornet's nest among the Maronites. Although opposed by three former presidents and one sitting president, it finally was torpedoed by the opposition of the Lebanese Forces. Since then Syria has applied direct and indirect pressure on those who thwarted the agreement. Amin Gemayel's village of Bikfaya was heavily shelled and is nearly in ruins. Other areas were similarly fired upon, and a series of bombs, strongly rumored to have been planted by Syrian agents, detonated in market areas. In the end, the Syrians only accomplished an infusion of hatred, which fed the Maronites' obduracy and sense of unity as a community under siege.

To end Christian Lebanon's semi-autonomy, Hafiz Assad would have to commit as many as fifty thousand more Syrian soldiers to Lebanon, a price he does not seem willing to pay. As long as Christian Lebanon poses no direct threat to Syria as the preeminent power in Lebanon, and as long as the Maronites' strange-bedfellow alliance with Iraq also does not constitute a direct challenge to Syria, Hafiz Assad can let matters lie. At the point that Christian Lebanon and its foreign alliances are no longer tolerable to Syrian interests, he will have to move.

As the Maronites and Iraq push Syria at one end of the political spectrum, Hizbollah and Iran push from the other end. Hafiz Assad's distaste for Hizbollah rises first from his fears of the might of Islamic fundamentalism germinating in his own country. Secondly, "The Syrians will tolerate no rival for influence and power in Lebanon, including the Iranians. . . . Syria will tolerate these groups [Hizbollah and Islamic Amal] only as long as they serve its interests."

During February 1987, when Syria was forced to intervene to end the battles between Amal and Hizbollah for control of West Beirut, a Syrian unit lined up twenty-two Hizbollah fighters, whom they axed and bayonetted to death. But the Syrian military, as a whole, exercised a degree of restraint toward Hizbollah in order to protect that curious Syrian-Iranian alliance. Yet at some point Syria may have to take on Hizbollah because Hizbollah will not participate in any peace negotiations sponsored by Syria. The creation of an Islamic state is the only thing that interests Hizbollah, and that is the very thing that Syria opposes.

Regardless of its military power and its client militias, Syria has problems controlling the Lebanese of whatever faction. The Lebanese hate the Syrians as they hate all foreigners, only perhaps more so. What Syria has been unable to achieve by military force it has sought through terror and brutal intimidation. Moreover, Syria of all the foreign adventurers in Lebanon poses the greatest threat to Lebanese sovereignty. Politically there are no pro-Syrians in Lebanon. The Lebanese, mostly the Amal, the Druze, and the PSP, all use the Syrians for the military and political support that they imagine they can jettison when it is no longer necessary. But Syria is in Lebanon to stay. For Syria and Israel and the Palestinians, Lebanon is a key to their larger interests, with Iraq joining in for the same reason. As a result, the crisis in Lebanon has become central to Middle East politics.

Contrasted to the goals and actions of Syria and Israel, Iran hovers around the edges of the Lebanese storm, pumping in ideology and money more than arms or troops. The motive propelling the leaders of the Islamic revolution is neither security nor influence over Lebanon. Iran is in Lebanon as part of its ongoing clash with the West and its "Great Satan," the United States.

Those massive, taunting crowds on the streets of Tehran that in the winter of 1979 shouted their vitriolic slogans soon became tied into the mounting passions of Lebanon. The emotion aroused by the Iranian revolution among not just the Shiites but other Muslims stemmed from Iran's dedication to eradicating from the Islamic world the "twin evil," the United States and Israel. Lebanon presented itself as an ideal site on which to pursue that goal. Hojatolislan Fakhr Rouhani, the former Iranian ambassador to Lebanon, spelled out the potential of Lebanon to the revolution:

> If we concentrate on the point that Lebanon is considered the heart of the Arab countries in the Middle East, has been serving as one of the most important information centers of the world for years, and has been serving as a platform from which different ideas have been directed to the rest of the Arab world, we can conclude that the existence of an Islamic movement in that country will result in Islamic movements throughout the Arab world.

Thus, Iran moved into the swirling maelstrom of Lebanon. Iranian strategy was to feed support to the Shiites committed to an Iranian-style Islamic republic. Once these elements gained control of the Shiite community and, by extension, Lebanon, this new Shiite stronghold could serve as the base for additional attacks against moderate Arab governments such as Saudi Arabia, Egypt, and others allied with the West. Iranian policy in Lebanon always was and has remained solely a part of the revolution's war against the West.

Iran's entrance into Lebanon was paved by that curious alliance struck between Iran and Syria at the beginning of the Iraq-Iran war. With Syria's blessing, cadres of Revolutionary Guards stole into Lebanon and linked up with groups subscribing to its ideology. The combination of Iranian support and unfolding events contributed to the flourishing of Hizbollah and the Islamic Amal during the Israeli occupation. The vision of Lebanon as an Islamic republic seemed to crystallize in the realm of the possible. But as the malignant complexities in Lebanon eventually drained the militant Lebanese Shiites of their dream, Iran's already cloudy relationship with Hizbollah became even more murky.

The strength of Iran's influence on Hizbollah depends on the particular group within that shadowy organization. Some leading clerics admit their ideological and financial relationship with Iran. But Sheikh Muhammed Hussein Fadlallah, Hizbollah's spiritual mentor, describes his ties to Iran as "an old relationship with the leaders of Islamic Iran, which started long before the Islamic Republic. It is a relationship of friendship and mutual confidence."

With the organizational link vague, Iran's involvement in terrorism in Lebanon remains equally vague. The one sure thing is that Iran provided the model for holding citizens for ransom by their governments when it kept fifty-two American hostages for more than four hundred days. But while America's frustration was a tremendous boost for the exhilaration of the revolution, Iran's revolutionary leaders soon learned that, while hostages may be good theater, they are not necessarily good policy. So the influence of Iran weaves in and out of the anguish surrounding Hizbollah's hostages.

Iran's highest priority is not the success of Hizbollah's drive to turn Lebanon into an Islamic republic but the survival of its own revolutionary regime. The great threat to that revolution, in the eyes of its leaders, is the United States, which Iran's leaders believe is bent on subverting or destroying it. Therefore, Iran's presence in Lebanon and its vehemence against the "Great Satan" is a matter not only of ideology and the promise of an Islamic world untainted by the West, but of survival itself. For Iran, Lebanon is an incubator in which the revolution hatches its moves against the West. It stops when Tehran reaches some accommodation with Washington.

After many centuries, Lebanon is no longer the bridge between East and West. Rather, it is an arena in which the various powers of the Middle East fight their battles through their Lebanese surrogates. During the long course of the Lebanese war, most causes in the Middle East have assumed some form in Lebanon— the ever-enduring dispute between Israel and the Palestinians, the Palestinians' blood feuds with each other, the fading Nasserite dream of socialism and Arab unity, the assurance of Islamic fundamentalism, the doggedness of Syrian hegemony, the mutual belligerence of Iraq and Iran, the meddling of Muammar Qaddafi and other fringe elements, and the innate desire among Arabs to free themselves from Western influence. Any of these factors erupting singly or in tandem threatens to plunge Lebanon and the Levant into dangerous warfare that the West, with its interests and alliances in the area, could not ignore. Yet the West has no leverage to influence events.

The West has withdrawn from Lebanon, much as the Crusaders withdrew. For a period of time in the twentieth as in the thirteenth century, the forces of Islam—be they religious, cultural, or nationalistic—have defied the presence of the alien West. France, which during the last century came to the Mountain ostensibly to rescue the Christian Maronites from the Muslim Druze and which later came to rule Greater Lebanon, now resists all attempts to be drawn back into the maelstrom that Lebanon has become. The British, who pursued longtime commercial interests in the region, and the West Germans, who plied their own economic agenda in the Levant in the decades after World War II, have largely retreated to the relative serenity of the Arab hinterland and the Arabian Peninsula.

The United States, the Western superpower, the defender of vast global interests, is itself only a peripheral player in the ugly drama in Lebanon, moving between the Maronites and the Syrians seeking to strike an accord, recoiling from the assaults of those who adhere to the ideology of the Iranian revolution, and refusing to exercise power at the only point where American influence is still possible in the Lebanese imbroglio—with Israel. The United States, as most of the other Western nations, hovers like a mourner over the corpse of Lebanon.

Lebanon is dead—or at least the Lebanon of which the myths of the Golden Age were spun. That Lebanon did not die in 1988. It died symbolically in 1984 when Ras Beirut moved out of the shrinking Western sphere in Lebanon. Ras Beirut, a false representation of Lebanon, was all that Lebanon wanted to be, not what Lebanon was. Yet this small area within this small country lying at the end of the Western world and at the beginning of the Arab world portrayed for a painfully short time how rich intercultural life could be. The milieu of Ras Beirut seemed to bridge the wide chasm between the Arabs and the West created by generations of distrust and suspicion. For a few years at the midpoint of the twentieth century, East and West met in its unique life. But the destructiveness of war intervened. Walls once plastered with posters advertising Pepsi Cola and recordings of the popular American song "The Age of Aquarius" are now scrawled with graffiti declaring, "No East Beirut or West Beirut, Only Muslim Beirut."

It seems more than a decade and a half since Westerners flowed in and out of Beirut, when they sat around the pool of the Phoenicia Hotel marveling at the verve and tempo of Beirut. When the American University stood as a proud symbol of the West's commitment to the Arab world. And when Rue Hamra vibrated with the languages of the West and of the East, openly welcoming both. Today the Western presence in Lebanon is but a ghost. Gone are the successors of the Europeans who left their names on some of Beirut's streets—Allenby, Clemenceau, Foch, Gourand, Weygard. Gone are the missionaries who more than the diplomats tried to bridge the cleft between Christians and Muslims. Gone are the Western professors who saw in Lebanon's secular universities the conduit through which the technology and ideas of the West and the poetry and zeal of Islam flowed, one to the other. Gone are the international entrepreneurs who established Beirut as the crossroads of commerce between the West and the Arab East. Gone also are the American Marines whose comrades died staving off an enemy their government still does not understand.

Beyond the issue of what political form Lebanon may eventually assume or if Lebanon itself will simply disappear into the geography of the Levant, the West must face the larger issue of what the loss of Lebanon means. Lebanon cannot be measured by the usual criteria of international power politics. It is an exceedingly small country bisected by two mountain ranges. It possesses no great harbor or critical raw materials, or a militarily strategic location. Since the civil war began, the geopoliticians have pondered Lebanon as an explosive piece in the regional politics of the Middle East. Its place as the battleground on which the ambitions and passions of all the major forces in the Middle East are being waged is its obvious significance at present.

But on another level, the importance of Lebanon is in its symbolism as the West's entrance to the Arab world. Particularly after 1948, Lebanon provided the West an entry to the Arab world, not only geographically but intellectually and perhaps emotionally. It was in Lebanon more than any other Arab country that the self-assured, technological West was embraced by Arab life. The liberality of the Levant moderated the Arab reserve toward outsiders, and with the Lebanese in their traditional role of middlemen, the

East and the West came together. Thus, the results of the war in Lebanon for the West extend far beyond Lebanon itself. Lebanon is a complex and dramatic symbol of the West's growing isolation from the Arab world.

The alienation between the Arabs and the West is by no means all one-sided. The West in its dealings with the Arabs confronts exaggerated sensitivity, a level of intolerance, and a measure of xenophobia. But from the Arab point of view, these cultural characteristics, which frustrate Westerners, mean little when compared to Western arrogance toward the Arabs.

Historically, the Western nations have exhibited an almost cavalier attitude toward the Arabs, assuming that the West can dominate the great crossroads between Asia and Europe and that, in spite of the brief oil embargo in 1973, it can depend on unbridled access to the region's resources.

The resentment and mistrust of the West that the Arabs emotionally trace to the Crusades more accurately resides in the technological superiority of the West that flowered during the Industrial Revolution. Industrial and economic strength brought with it a vanity among Westerners as to the preeminence of their own culture. For Westerners, Western culture became the standard by which all other cultures were measured. Lebanon, split between its Western and Arab identities, provided a particularly fertile ground in which the customs and languages of the West could take root.

Politically, Western dominance was affirmed after World War I, when promises of independence made to Arab nationalists evaporated, leaving the Arabs once more subject people, this time to Western powers. While these Western powers pursued their economic and political goals in the Middle East, the product of that imperialism was still cultural. By deliberate policy and sheer example, the might, values, and mores of the West were laid on the Arabs. It was by the standards of the West that they were judged. In certain respects, the West's incognizance about the worth of Arab society was a greater insult to the Arabs than the political and economic burdens of colonialism.

Between the two great world wars, the United States escaped most of the vilification the Arabs directed at Europe. "Prior to World War II, the United States was regarded with good-will, as a benign distant giant, a haven of liberty and wealth represented

altruistically in the area by missionaries, educators and little else."
But after World War II, when the baton of leadership was passed
from an exhausted Britain to the United States, America became
the Arab's Western police officer. All innocence was lost as the
United States allowed the Arab world to be further dismantled to
fulfill its promise to the Zionists.

The single issue around which all Arab feelings of inferiority,
hostility, and injustice against the West coalesce is Israel. Israel,
the child of the West, technologically advanced and esteemed by
the West, is an enraging symbol of the West's past denigration of
the Arabs. And Israel is every bit as much of an occupying and
colonizing power as the West ever was. To the Arabs, Israel simply
took up where the West left off. The settlement of Palestine by
Jewish settlers replayed the flawed imagery of the Crusader states.
The defeat of the Arabs in 1948, 1956, and 1967 humbled the
Arabs' pride, detracting from their honor. Israeli hunger for land,
presented under the guise of security, resulted in the colonization
of one Arab territory after another. The 1948 war that filled out the
borders of the territory designated for the Jews by the United
Nations; occupation of the West Bank, Gaza, and Jerusalem; the
annexation of the Golan Heights; and the de facto extension of
Israel's northern border into the "security zone" of south Lebanon—all brand Israel in Arab eyes as a colonial monster.

Even more than the West, the Israelis condemn the Arabs to an
inferior status. For years, the powerful Israeli propaganda machine succeeded in portraying the Arabs to the West first as rough,
semi-educated zealots and later as inhuman "terrorists." Within
Israel itself, a kind of apartheid exists between the Jewish and
Arab populations. And even before the 1987 Palestinian uprising
or *intifadah*, Israeli policy in the occupied territories ground the
Arabs into a distinct underclass.

The whole Palestinian issue created by the 1948 war for Palestine fits what the Arabs see as the pattern of Western exploitation
of the Arabs. The West, principally the United States, has never
addressed the moral issue of the Palestinian diaspora. By refusing
to acknowledge the Palestinian cause as represented by the PLO
until late 1988, U.S. policy contributed to the process by which an
increasingly angry population was dumped on its neighbors, who
themselves often lacked the political stability or the financial
resources to cope with the nationalistic passions and simple physi-

cal needs of a people dispossessed for forty years. Lebanon was the least able of all the countries in the region to absorb the Palestinians. Yet they came, and from Lebanese territory they struck Israel. And Israel struck back with such force that it speeded Lebanon's demise, all at the sufferance of the West.

Regardless of the nature of Israeli actions, American support for Israel never seemed to flinch. Step by step Israel and the United States marched together until it appeared they stood as one against the Arabs. When Israel dropped its deadly bombs on Lebanon, the United States restocked the Israeli arsenal. When Israeli raids into Lebanon were condemned by the United Nations, the United States vetoed the resolution. While the Israelis ruled southern Lebanon with their "iron fists," the United States signed an agreement formalizing its strategic alliance with Israel. None of this was lost on the Arabs, especially those of Lebanon, who had suffered the brunt of the Israelis' harsh deeds. It all came to rest in the virulent anti-Western campaign of the Hizbollah.

Hizbollah has melded the Arabs' deep hostility to the West and the Shiites' fury against Israel into a powerful weapon. While Amal, the Druze, and what is left of the Sunni establishment sit at the hand of Syria, it is Hizbollah and those who subscribe to the ideology of the Islamic revolution who hurl the Arabs' wrath against Israel and by extension against the United States. Israel's "security zone" in south Lebanon has become an arena where the zeal of the Shiites and the anger of the Palestinians push against the Western-armed military might of Israel. It is a conflict Israel may pay a high price to contain, one that may call into question once again the wisdom of building American strategic concerns in the Middle East almost exclusively around Israel.

As important as Israel is in defining Arab anger, the hatred that the Islamic militants direct against the United States and certain of its Western allies is linked as much to the West's long-term relations with Islam as it is to the forty-year-old Arab-Israeli dispute. The symbolism of the militants' armed struggle against the West appeals to people across the Arab world who for too long have felt themselves diminished by the West. The boldness and sacrifice of Hizbollah's warriors inflame those from the Nile to the Arabian Peninsula who yearn to restore the glory of Islam. And in all Arab countries, political movements dedicated to returning to the basic teachings of Islam are on the rise. As Lebanon was symbolically the synthesis of East and West, it is now symbolically the center of a highly emotional crusade to rid the Muslim world of its Western taint. Southern Lebanon has become the citadel of that cause.

On the fifth anniversary of the bombing of the U.S. Marine barracks, crowds of angry, chador-clad women stood before the burned-out shell of the U.S. embassy in Beirut, waving placards with "Death to America" emblazoned upon them in blood red. It was a far cry from 1946, when a patron at a restaurant in Zahle called out to a passing American military column, "Please give our best wishes to President Truman. We love America too much."

The war in Lebanon is far from over. Yet, for the West, it has already ended. A broken Lebanon has established its Arab identity and in so doing has closed the West's gateway to the Arab world. The tragedy of Lebanon is also a tragedy for the West.

Notes

CHAPTER 1
BEIRUT: PARIS OF THE EAST

Page 4. **In 1966,** *Life* **magazine:** "The West Went Thataway—East" *Life*, January 7, 1966.

Page 8. **And the Lebanese themselves . . . :** The Lebanese thrived in the role of "expediter," that unique creature of the oil boom. In countries where multi-million-dollar contracts were endangered by rudimentary infrastructures, embryonic economic systems, and bureaucracies packed with untrained or corrupt employees, the expediter, armed with cash, scurried to pull everything together at a sizable profit to himself.

Page 9. **Ras Beirut was a safe haven:** Beirut was always a favorite refuge for political exiles. Following the Russian Revolution, the best-known waiter in one of Beirut's finer restaurants was a former admiral in the czar's navy.

Page 12. **The Christians:** The Greek Catholics recognize the authority of the Roman pope but use the Greek Orthodox liturgy.

CHAPTER 2
THE LEVANT

Page 19. **Yet of the three:** Lebanon, within its present boundaries, was not created until 1920, when the French Mandate combined "The Mountain" with parts of Syrian territory to create Greater Lebanon. Prior to that time, the portion of the Levant now called Lebanon passed through a series of administrative forms ranging from the city-states of the Phoenicians to a fragment within the Ottoman Empire. For the sake of clarity, the term *Lebanon* will be used for the part of the Levant that now lies within the borders of present-day Lebanon.

Page 23. **On the stones:** The Crusaders' castles survived for centuries to be fought over by Lebanon's modern-day antagonists. Frederick II's picture-book castle at Sidon has served as a Syrian guard post through much of the current war, keeping Palestinian arms out of Lebanon. Belfort, within sight of the Israel border, was finally destroyed in Israel's 1982 invasion of Lebanon.

Page 24. **The Maronites:** A Christian group allied to the French Crusaders who in 1180 recognized the Pope and became part of the Roman Catholic Church (see Chapter 3).

Page 25. **"This college is . . .":** David C. Gordon, *Lebanon: The Fragmented Nation* (London: Croom Helm, 1980), 180.

Chapter 3
The Christians

Page 29. **"[H]istory evoked in ballads"**: Maronite tract.

Page 30. **They broadly divide**: The term *Greek Orthodox* is misleading in that it infers that the Greek Orthodox of Lebanon are part of the Church of Greece. In fact, they are a self-governing group within the Eastern or Byzantine Orthodox churches, which centers on the patriarch of Antioch.

Page 30. **In 1975, when the war began**: There is also a sizable Armenian population that is Christian. The Armenians actually outnumber the Melkites with roughly 12 percent of Lebanon's Christian population. But the Armenians must be considered an immigrant group rather than Lebanese. They arrived in Lebanon as fugitives from Turkish territory in three waves—at the end of the nineteenth century, in 1920–1921, and in 1939.

Although the French granted them Lebanese citizenship in 1924, the Armenians have never merged into Lebanese society. They remain segregated from the Lebanese population both culturally and linguistically. Living largely in the huge Armenian quarter beyond the harbor of Beirut, they generally avoid the controversy and partisanship of Lebanese politics, preferring their status as a "nation in exile" to absorption into a Christian Arab majority.

Page 31. **Jesus himself preached**: Mark 15:24–31.

Page 31. **The most renowned**: St. George was introduced into Europe by the Crusaders. Although he had no connection to England, he became its patron saint in the fourteenth century and has graced the kingdom's gold coinage ever since.

Page 32. **"[T]he victory of Moslem arms . . ."**: Philip K. Hitti, *Lebanon in History: From the Earliest Times to the Present* (London: Macmillan and Company, Ltd., 1957).

Page 33. **By the middle**: Robert Brenton Betts, *Christians in the Arab East* (Atlanta: John Knox Press, 1978), 10.

Page 34. **"Lebanon set out on . . ."**: Hitti, *Lebanon in History*, 246.

Page 34. **"[S]ettled . . . on the outskirts"**: Maronite tract.

Page 36. **While recognizing the authority**: The Maronites also differ from the Roman Catholic Church in that they do not insist on the celibacy of their priests.

Page 36. **In 1717**: *Melkites* was the original name of the Greek Orthodox.

Page 39. **And after 1946**: The PPS retained a following into the 1950s but began to weaken after the allure of Gamal Abdel Nasser's pan-Arabism started to undercut the appeal of Greater Syria. The party still survives in tightly knit cells in a cross-section of communal groups whose members represent left-wing economic philosophy and a dedication to Syrian nationalism.

Page 39. **The idea of a Syrian nation**: See Chapter 6.

Page 39. **It also gave Lebanon**: In the 1940s, Michel Aflaq, a French-educated writer and teacher of Greek Orthodox background living in Damascus, became the ideologue for a new Arab political movement called the Baath Party. Although a Christian, Aflaq gave voice to post–World War II Arab nationalism. The Baath Party drew support from the Lebanese Greek Orthodox community, but it never became a politically potent movement in Lebanon. Its strength was in Syria and Iraq, where today the military governments of both countries represent the bitterly divided Syrian and Iraqi branches of the Baath.

Page 40. **Twelve thousand Druze**: Charles H. S. Churchill, *The Druzes and the Maronites under Turkish Rule from 1840 to 1860* (London: Bernard Quaritch, 1862), 137.

Page 41. **Herding Dayr al Qamar's**: The accounts of the war that reached the West were all written from the Christian perspective. The ruthlessness with which the Maronites have waged the current war leads one to suspect that the Druze in 1860 were not necessarily more vicious than the Maronites.

Page 41. **"[T]he events of 1860 . . .":** David McDowall, *Lebanon: A Conflict of Minorities* (London: Minority Rights Group, Ltd., 1983), 9.

Page 43. **"So successful was *[France's] la mission civilisatrice* . . .":** McDowall, *Lebanon: A Conflict of Minorities*, 7.

Page 44. **"They wanted to be . . .":** Raphael Patai, *The Arab Mind* (New York: Charles Scribner's Sons, 1976), 192.

Page 45. **And a Frenchman**: Gordon, *Lebanon: The Fragmented Nation*, 123.

Page 45. **Though accused by other Lebanese**: The French bestowed a number of privileges on the Maronites. These were confirmed in the National Pact of 1943, a scheme Lebanese political leaders adopted both to accommodate the interests of the Muslims and to ensure the Maronites' political superiority. See Chapter 6.

Page 45. **Maronite ideologue**: Jonathan C. Randal, *Going All the Way: Christian Warlords, Israeli Adventurers, and the War in Lebanon* (New York: Viking Press, 1983), 57.

Page 48. **During the crisis of 1958**: See Chapter 6.

Page 49. **Under threat of arrest**: While in exile, Franjieh developed a close friendship with a twenty-nine-year-old Air Force colonel, Hafiz Assad, who became president of Syria in 1970. The Franjiehs incorporated Assad and his brother Rifaat in their lucrative black market business deals involving both Lebanese and Syrian markets. The heavy Syrian presence in Lebanon since 1976 protects the profits, and Suleiman Franjieh protects the partnership with frequent trips to Damascus, where he publicly praises the Syrian intervention in Lebanon.

Page 50. **Gemayel returned**: The party was founded under the names al Kataib al Lubnaniyah and the Phalange Libanaise (Lebanese Phalanx), a term borrowed from Spain's right-wing Phalange party.

Page 52. **"While some party ideologues . . ."**: Itamar Rabinovich, *The War for Lebanon, 1970–1985* (Ithaca, N.Y.: Cornell University Press, 1985), 63.

Page 53. **In 1964, more than ten years**: Randal, *Going All the Way*, 51.

CHAPTER 4
THE MUSLIMS

Page 57. **To be Sunni means**: At different times and places, various groups within the Sunni sect of Islam did incorporate elements of mysticism into the faith. But mysticism never constituted an essential element of the overall faith as it did in Shiism.

Page 57. **The only thing different:** The Shiites outnumbered the Greek Orthodox and Greek Catholics combined.

Page 58. **"That day they fought . . .":** M. Husayn Tahatahi, quoted in Thomas W. Lippman, *Understanding Islam: An Introduction to the Moslem World* (New York: New American Library, 1982), 143.

Page 59. **Iran, Persian rather than Arab:** The Shiites are a slight majority in Iraq, but the Sunni-dominated Baath Party holds political power.

Page 59. **Besides the doctrine of self-sacrifice:** Orthodox Muslims recognize no formal clergy; in fact, they regard the idea as an obstruction to the believer's direct contact to God.

Page 59. **In Shiism, *imams* are divinely inspired:** In Shiism, the *imam* applies to two different concepts. Regarding the Twelve Imams of Shiism, an *imam* is a divinely inspired successor to the Prophet. In general terms, an *imam* can also be simply the spiritual leader of the community, not unlike the village priest in Catholicism.

Page 64. **An impresario who caused:** Gordon, *Lebanon: The Fragmented Nation*, 156.

Page 64. **On her deathbed:** Gordon, *Lebanon: The Fragmented Nation*, 156–57.

Page 64. **During Lebanon's 1958 political crisis:** Wade R. Goria, . *Sovereignty and Leadership in Lebanon, 1943–1976* (London: Ithaca Press, 1985), 54.

Page 65. **"Community sectarianism was a poison . . .":** Goria, *Sovereignty and Leadership*, 32.

Page 67. **"The very circumstance that . . .":** Patai, *The Arab Mind*, 302.

Page 68. **In the 1950s:** Wilfred Cantwell Smith as quoted in Patai, *The Arab Mind*, 296.

Page 68. **They opted instead:** This is the same philosophy to which segments of the Greek Orthodox subscribed.

Page 69. **Since Lebanese politics:** See Chapter 5.

Page 71. **When Solh became:** Goria, *Sovereignty and Leadership*, 25.

Page 72. **The two assassins:** Four days later, King Abdullah was assassinated in Jerusalem in an unrelated incident.

Page 76. **State schools were poor**: Before the war, only 40 percent of Shiite children between the ages of six and ten attended school. The Shiites, who claimed one-quarter of Lebanon's population, comprised only 8 percent of the university population.

Page 79. **A former prime minister said**: Randal, *Going All the Way*, 282.

CHAPTER 5
CULTURE AND CONFLICT

Page 82. **The Lebanese civil war**: See Chapters 7 and 8.

Page 82. **"This society is not . . ."**: Halim Barakat, "Social and Political Integration in Lebanon: A Case of Social Mosaic," *Middle East Journal* 48 (Fall 1982), 304.

Page 83. **The Lebanese were torn apart**: Added to this primary division were groups such as the Armenians and Kurds who identified with neither the West nor the Arabs but with their ancestral lands in Soviet Russia and Kurdistan, divided among Iran, Iraq, and Turkey.

Page 83. **As a result**: Barakat, "Social and Political Integration," 304.

Page 84. **Honor, to Arabs . . .**: Honor is discussed in terms of males because a female derives her honor almost exclusively through her family or husband.

Page 85. **A long-time resident**: Gordon, *Lebanon: The Fragmented Nation*, 117.

Page 86. **The Lebanese divided**: A communal group is composed of individuals who possess a common identity determined by shared goals and norms. In Lebanon, communality was particularly intense due to the Lebanese' traditional divisions into intimate, egocentric groups.

Page 89. **But this same phenomenon**: The distribution of the population in Lebanon before the civil war was such that while particular sects predominated in certain areas, few sections of Lebanon's provinces or districts were peopled exclusively by one sect. Yet within the village, communal identity still bound one group of people together to the exclusion of others.

Page 89. **In its simplest terms**: Albion Ross as quoted in *Aramco World*, September-October 1982, 17.

Page 89. **Historically, confessionals**: In Lebanon a religious group is a form of communal group. The term *confessional* is intended to distinguish a religious communal group from a family communal group.

Page 92. **When war finally came**: Fouad Ajami, *The Arab Predicament: Arab Political Thought and Practice Since 1967* (Cambridge: Cambridge University Press, 1981), 4.

Page 93. **Nabih Berri**: David Lamb, *The Arabs: Journeys Beyond the Mirage* (New York: Random House, 1987), 186.

Page 95. **A *zaim* was to Lebanese society**: *Zaim* is the singular form, *zuama* the plural.

Page 95. **A *zaim*, with some exceptions**: The position of the *zuama* is presently cloudy. The power of many of the old traditional *zuama* was destroyed by the war. Some continue to command power, but their influence rests primarily on the control of a militia. See Chapter 10.

Page 95. **He was either the oldest son**: As a group, the *zuama* were as eclectic as the rest of Lebanese society. For every traditional *zaim*, there was at some time a *zaim* who achieved power outside the rigid confines of communal politics. But the latter seldom lasted long. Most of the *zuama* represented old families or built political machines within a confessional. It is they who established the pattern by which the *zuama* gained and retained power.

Page 96. **"Sabri Hamadeh, the traditional political *zaim* ...":** Samir Khalaf, *Lebanon's Predicament* (New York: Columbia University Press, 1987), 73.

Page 97. **Bashir Gemayel summed it up**: Randal, *Going All the Way*, 4.

Page 98. **Behind every public debate**: Michael Johnson, "Fractional Politics in Lebanon: The Case of the 'Islamic Society of Benevolent Intentions (al-Maqasid)' in Beirut," *Middle East Studies* (January 1978), 72.

Page 99. **Father Yussef Yamin**: Randal, *Going All the Way*, 131.

Page 101. **When Bishara Khoury was president**: Habib J. Awal, "Threat to Lebanon," *Commonweal*, August 8, 1947, 398.

Page 102. **The president's reply was**: "Exit 'Father of Belly,' " *Time*, September 29, 1952, 24.

Page 104. **"Such a culture ...":** Edouard Saab as quoted in Goria, *Sovereignty and Leadership*, 138.

CHAPTER 6
THE FRENCH LEGACY

Page 106. **But France, as a result of**: The Sykes-Picot agreement essentially divided up the Ottoman territories between Britain and France, with some concessions to other Allied powers. The agreement was secret because at the same time correspondence was underway between Britain and Hussein, the Sherif of Mecca, that led the Arabs to believe that an independent Arab state would be created after the war out of a portion of the Ottoman Empire. Instead, the Ottoman territories were divided among the Europeans, who concluded their agreements on oil, pipelines, and mandates in the Treaty of San Remo signed April 24, 1920.

Page 107. **And now has ...:** Quoted in Robert Brenton Betts, *Christians in the Arab East* (Atlanta: John Knox Press, 1978).

Page 108. **For these Muslims**: The Greek Orthodox community generally shared the Muslims' distaste for the mandate. Having no close ties with the West, they resented the Maronites' and Melkites' pseudowesternization and shared the Muslims' suspicions toward the other Christians' motives.

Page 111. **Alawites**: A sect of Islam found almost exclusively in Syria.

Page 111. **Baha'is**: The Baha'i faith, which originated in the nineteenth century, believes that despite their differences all the great religions teach identical truths. The Baha'is strive to overcome the disunity of religion and teach a universal faith.

Page 111. **Of these, 50 percent**: In 1939, when the practice ended, 159,571 nonresident Lebanese were registered voters in Lebanon. Of this number, 84 percent were Christian, 60 percent Maronite.

Page 111. **As a result**: Sydney Nettleton Fisher, *The Middle East: A History*, 2d ed. (New York: Alfred Knopf, 1969).

Page 113. **When France fell**: DeGaulle's Free French forces, as part of the larger British effort, invaded Lebanon through Palestine and Transjordan in June 1941. For a brief moment, Lebanon became the site of the struggle for France when the Free French and the forces of Vichy France battled on the banks of the Damour River.

Page 114. **Khoury and Solh**: McDowall, *Lebanon: A Conflict of Minorities*, 10.

Page 114. **Nabih Berri, in another of his sagacious comments**: Augustus Richard Norton, *Amal and the Shi'a: Struggle for the Soul of Lebanon* (Austin, Tex.: University of Texas Press, 1987), 80.

Page 115. **One American soldier**: Maynard Owen Williams, "Syria and Lebanon Taste Freedom," *National Geographic*, vol. XC, no. 6, December 1946, 729.

Page 122. **Chamoun backed up**: The PPS was the most powerful nonsectarian party in Lebanon during the 1950s. It revered the concept of a "Syrian" nation composed of Syria, Lebanon, Jordan, Israel, Iraq, Cyprus, and parts of Turkey. The PPS was forced into alliance with Chamoun because of the perceived threat to "Greater Syria" from the pan-Arabism of Nasser and his Muslim followers within Lebanon.

Page 122. **"The Lebanon's function is . . .":** "Struggle for Lebanon: A Christian Israel," *New Statesman*, July 6, 1957, 21.

Page 124. **This would destroy**: The Air Force did go into action once during the war. It bombed forces loyal to the government by mistake.

Page 126. **But it is probably just as accurate**: Among the long-range ramifications of the 1958 upheaval was the Phalangists' taking their militia to the streets. Long ostracized by the Christian establishment because of their ruffian ways, the Kaitab (the political parent of the Phalange) entered the government for the first time as part of the settlement.

Page 126. **In the end**: Betts, *Christians in the Arab East*, 194.

Page 127. **"The great creeds and philosophies . . .":** Emory S. Bogardus, "Social Change in Lebanon," *Sociology and Social Research* 39 (March-April 1955), 259.

Chapter 7
Outsiders, Insiders—The Palestinians

Page 131. Most Palestinians held: Palestinians with ties to the power structure held both citizenship and a passport. Economic status and personal contacts mitigated all the conditions under which the Palestinians in Lebanon lived.

Page 131. Therefore, the fate of most Palestinians: With the exception of Jordan, during the period following the 1948 war, the legal status of the Palestinians in most Arab countries was no better than in Lebanon.

Page 134. This revenue was derived: Lack of capital seldom deterred Lebanon's aggressive entrepreneurs. During its infancy, the cash-strapped Middle East Airlines tried to barter Lebanese apples for British aircraft.

Page 134. One Western economist: William S. Ellis, "Lebanon: Little Bible Land in the Crossfire of History," *National Geographic*, February 1970, 251.

Page 134. If too many questions: Fouad Ajami as quoted in Gordon, *Lebanon: The Fragmented Nation*, 264.

Page 135. His eyes, ears, and muscle: The only serious challenge to Shihab came in January 1962 from the Parti Populaire Syrien (PPS), which was opposed to the president's internal and external politics that threatened to strengthen the Lebanese government and national sovereignty. Forty soldiers of the Lebanese army and several hundred armed civilians took over army headquarters and the post office and laid siege to the ministry of defense. Arriving at the scene, Defense Minister Antoine Saad casually stopped a boy on a bicycle and sent him to summon a nearby armored unit. Within minutes, three Centurion tanks rumbled through the street. Their passengers took aim, fired, and killed five rebels. The revolt collapsed.

Page 138. According to sociologist Halim Barakat: Halim Barakat as quoted in Rabinovich, *The War for Lebanon*, 32.

Page 140. As one shopkeeper said: "Caught in the Middle," *Time*, January 17, 1969, 28.

Page 140. Between 1948 and 1967: The Arab League was formed in 1945 to strengthen the political clout of the Arab countries. Its original members included Egypt, Syria, Lebanon, Iraq, Transjordan (Jordan), Saudi Arabia, and Yemen. Lebanon's participation was a concession the Maronites made to the pan-Arabists in the afterglow of the National Pact.

Page 141. Yassir Arafat's Fatah: *Fatah* stands for *Harakat Tahreer Falasteen*, the Movement for the Liberation of Palestine.

Page 141. George Habash's Popular Front: Habash is a physician and a Christian whose background is in the Greek Orthodox faith.

Page 141. Yassir Arafat spoke: Dana Adams Schmidt, *Armageddon in the Middle East* (New York: John Day, 1974), 6

Page 142. **On December 28, 1968**: Ironically, Israel paid part of the $18
million in insurance that MEA collected for the loss of its planes.
Through Lloyd's of London, Israeli insurance firms were underwriters
of $50,000 of policies held by the carrier.

Page 144. **In 1960, Fuad Shihab had prophetically said**: Goria,
Sovereignty and Leadership, 72.

Page 146. **"While some [Phalange] party ideologues . . ."**: Rabinovich,
The War for Lebanon, 63.

Page 146. **Continuing Israel reprisals**: Nineteen-seventy was also the
year Gamal Abdel Nasser died. When Nasser's death from a heart
attack was announced on September 28, 1970, public order in Muslim
Beirut virtually collapsed. Strikes, mass demonstrations, and a
widespread outpouring of grief disrupted normal life for days, although
the political effect was minimal. Nasser's real influence on Lebanon had
ended with the Six Day War in 1967.

Page 147. **Interior Minister Kamal Jumblatt**: "If It Happens Here, It
Will Happen There," *Time*, May 25, 1970, 35

Page 148. **Fear that Israel would annex**: From its birth Israel has been
interested in the water resources of southern Lebanon. Any Israeli
incursion into Lebanon always sparks speculation as to intent.

Page 149. **Eight hours later**: Not long afterward, Dany Chamoun, son of
Camille, was kidnapped by Fatah in what appears to have been more of
an extortion plot than a political move. He was held hostage in the
Intercontinental Hotel in Amman and released unharmed after the
payment of an undisclosed amount by his wealthy father.

Page 150. **"Instead of wasting our energies . . ."**: "Almond-Blossom
Battles," *Time*, March 13, 1972.

Page 152. **"In the world that existed . . ."**: Fouad Ajami, "The Shadows of
Hell," *Foreign Policy* 48 (Fall 1982), 106.

Page 154. **A weary Lebanese summed it up**: "High Stakes in Lebanon's
Mini-war," *Newsweek*, May 21, 1973.

Page 154. **Outnumbering any other single group**: Population figures are
from McDowall, *Lebanon: A Conflict of Minorities*, 3.

Page 155. **"Older politicians were incapable . . ."**: R. K. Ramazani,
Revolutionary Iran: Challenge and Response in the Middle East
(Baltimore: Johns Hopkins University Press, 1986), 40.

Page 155. **President Franjieh**: Gordon, *Lebanon: The Fragmented Nation*,
263.

Page 155. **And sociologists David and Audrey Smock**: Gordon, *Lebanon:
The Fragmented Nation*, 261.

Page 157. **And Kamal Jumblatt, accompanied**: Jumblatt had just
returned from a trip to India, where he offered condolences on the death
of his guru.

Page 157. **Four people, including one of Gemayel's bodyguards**: It was
speculated that the suspected Palestinian attack at Ain al Rummaneh
was retaliation for the shooting of a Palestinian at a Maronite roadblock
the preceding week.

Page 158. **"They have been good men . . .":** "Widows and Warlords," BBC.

CHAPTER 8
THE FOREIGN POWERS

Page 161. **In August, the American magazine** *Travel*: "Lebanon: Land of Milk and Honey," *Travel*, August 1975, 38.

Page 161. **But in reality:** Rabinovich, *The War for Lebanon*, 45.

Page 161. **Known as the National Movement:** Although in the war neither side was ever entirely Christian or entirely Muslim, each was overwhelmingly of one or the other religion. In the interest of brevity, the Lebanese Front will sometimes be referred to as "the Christians" and the National Movement plus the Palestinians as "the Muslims."

Page 162. **After the eruption:** Goria, *Sovereignty and Leadership*, 258.

Page 162. **They fought for a percentage:** It is rumored that the Phalange defeated the NLP for the privilege of cleaning out the safe deposit boxes at the British Bank of the Middle East.

Page 164. **The Druze of the Mountain:** Pursuing their own grievances, the Armenians fired two rockets at the Turkish embassy.

Page 165. **In the event that Israel:** Rabinovich, *The War for Lebanon*, 48.

Page 168. **But when Hafiz Assad sent:** Rabinovich, *The War for Lebanon*, 53.

Page 168. **Although the Christians:** The Shiites also shared this concern for an independent Lebanon. Syrian control was perhaps more acceptable to a portion of the Shiites than control by another Arab country would have been because the Shiites acknowledged the politically dominant Alawite sect of Syria as part of Shiism. Because their political voice and their militia were still relatively weak, any position the Shiites might have taken in 1976 was irritating but not fatal to Syrian designs.

Page 168. **At first, Kamal Jumblatt saw the Syrian-Maronite alliance:** Goria, *Sovereignty and Leadership*, 226.

Page 169. **Determined, ruthless, and aflame with ambition:** The more radical Maronites had begun to champion "Marounistan," the portion of Lebanon under Christian control, as a ministate.

Page 169. **The Phalange was:** Fouad Ajami, *The Vanished Imam: Musa al Sadr and the Shia of Lebanon* (Ithaca, N.Y.: Cornell University Press, 1986), 161.

Page 170. **Declaring the Christians:** Rabinovich, *The War for Lebanon*, 91.

Page 171. **"Israel was always second best . . .":** Randal, *Going All the Way*, 7.

Page 171. **"The leaders in the Christian community . . .":** Fouad Ajami, "The Shadows of Hell," 110.

Page 174. **In unveiling his bold plan:** Ze'ev Schiff and Ehud Ya'ari, *Israel's Lebanon War* (New York: Simon and Schuster, 1984), 42.

Page 175. **The PLO, operating from Lebanon**: It was later discovered that Argov was assassinated by the Abu Nidal group, which had been expelled from the PLO.

Page 176. **Israel, in effect, would become**: Rabinovich, *The War for Lebanon*, 106.

Page 176. **A gnarled farmer**: "Suffer the Children," *Newsweek*, June 28, 1982, 25.

Page 177. **As Israeli forces closed**: "Agony of the Innocents," *Time*, June 28, 1982, 20.

Page 177. **A PLO major manning a gun**: "Agony of the Innocents," 20.

Page 178. **"In a war whose purpose . . .":** Schiff and Ya'ari, *Israel's Lebanon War*, 220.

Page 180. **No one doubted Ariel Sharon's warning**: "Looking for a Way Out," *Newsweek*, July 19, 1982, 16–17.

Page 180. **On August 8, Habib assured all sides**: France, Italy, Britain, and the United States sent troops into Lebanon at the request of Lebanese foreign minister Elie Salem. Known as the Multi-National Force, it had no unified mission or command. Each contingent functioned independently both militarily and politically. Of the four, the United States assumed the major political role.

Page 180. **One Reagan administration aide conceded**: *Newsweek*, July 19, 1982, 17.

Page 181. **A State Department official worried**: *Newsweek*, July 19, 1982, 17.

Page 181. **"I'll tell you what this war . . .":** Lamb, *The Arabs*, 189.

Page 182. **"We must remain on good terms . . .":** Schiff and Ya'ari, *Israel's Lebanon War*, 50.

Page 183. **At the funeral**: The culprit behind Bashir Gemayel's assassination has never been proven. The suspects are Hafiz Assad, because Gemayel threatened Syrian hegemony in Lebanon; Israel, because Gemayel backed out on the Lebanon-Israel treaty; and the Franjiehs, because they had never satisfactorily avenged the death of Tony Franjieh.

Page 183. **A hardened Phalangist militiaman**: Randal, *Going All the Way*, 23.

Page 184. **The militiaman shouted back**: Schiff and Ya'ari, *Israel's Lebanon War*, 267.

Page 185. **And he claims the Maronites**: "Fighting for Western Values," *Time*, October 3, 1983, 37.

Page 185. **"To Muslims, Amin Gemayel represented . . .":** Randal, *Going All the Way*, 149.

Page 185. **"The American formula for success . . .":** William B. Quandt, "Reagan's Lebanon Policy: Trial and Error," *Middle East Journal* 38 (Spring 1984), 241.

Page 187. **On the eve of the Israeli invasion**: "Druze Find a Leader," *Economist*, April 10, 1982.

Page 188. **Suddenly the United States stood face to face**: Schiff and Ya'ari, *Israel's Lebanon War*, 298.

Page 188. **In the months following**: Nine months later, Gemayel himself would repudiate his only political achievement in a desperate effort to save his beleaguered regime.

Page 189. **And twelve hundred U.S. Marines**: There was also a token force of one hundred British troops, members of the Queen's Dragoon Guards.

Page 189. **George Ball's words came back**: Lamb, *The Arabs*, 189.

Page 191. **"The compulsion to buy . . .":** Khalaf, *Lebanon's Predicament*, 242.

CHAPTER 9
THE WAR AGAINST THE WEST: THE HOSTAGES

Page 194. **Although they acted as intermediaries**: For centuries, a bitter enmity arising from cultural, religious, and ethnic differences has existed between the Persians (now Iranians) and the Arabs.

Page 197. **He shocked the religious community**: Fouad Ajami, *The Vanished Imam*, 96.

Page 198. **"O rising generations . . .":** Rabinovich, *The War for Lebanon*, 39.

Page 198. **In a voice of resignation**: "Two Views from the Lebanon Border," *Newsweek*, June 8, 1970, 40.

Page 199. **Sadr was fond of saying**: Norton, *Amal and the Shi'a*, 42.

Page 199. **In the leftist politics**: Ajami, *The Vanished Imam*, 158.

Page 200. **Thrusting the Shiite economic reality**: Ajami, *The Vanished Imam*, 146.

Page 200. **"The PLO is a factor . . .":** Juan R. I. Cole and Nikki R. Keddie, eds., *Shiism and Social Protest* (New Haven, Conn.: Yale University Press, 1986), 165.

Page 202. **While the leadership of Amal**: Norton, *Amal and the Shi'a*, 60.

Page 203. **He left Beirut after graduating**: As of this writing, Berri's former wife and two of his six children live in Dearborn, Michigan.

Page 204. **Even before Israel moved**: Norton, *Amal and the Shi'a*, 113.

Page 205. **The words of Musa al Sadr**: Cole and Keddie, *Shiism and Social Protest*, 149.

Page 205. **Out of Iran**: Norton, *Amal and the Shi'a*, 105.

Page 205. **By the fall of 1982**: Hizbollah originally was founded in 1979 in the wake of Khomeini's triumph in Iran. After foundering, it was revitalized in the Bekaa valley in 1982 following the Israeli invasion.

Page 206. **Fadlallah argued**: Ajami, *The Vanished Imam*, 217.

Page 206. **"When a Muslim . . .":** Cole and Keddie, *Shiism and Social Protest*, 172–73.

Page 207. **Camille Chamoun**: Randal, *Going All the Way*, 132.

Page 208. **"If America kills . . .":** Robin Wright, *Sacred Rage: The Wrath of Militant Islam* (New York: Simon and Schuster, 1985), 83.

Page 209. **The Marine command reported**: Official communiqué of the Marine Amphibious Unit quoted in Benis M. Frank, *U.S. Marines in Lebanon, 1982–1984* (Washington, D.C.: History and Museums Division, U.S. Marine Corps, 1987), 81.

Page 209. **It showed a lieutenant**: Frank, *U.S. Marines in Lebanon*, 23.

Page 211. **One dazed corporal**: "Carnage in Lebanon," *Time*, October 31, 1983, 16.

Page 211. **In the two terrorist attacks**: Two days later, a third bomb-laden truck hit Israeli army headquarters in Tyre, killing twenty-nine Israeli military personnel.

Page 211. **A caller to a French news agency**: "The Lebanon Massacre," *The Economist*, October 29, 1983, 25.

Page 211. **The West had met its new enemy**: American intelligence agencies hold Musawi's Islamic Amal responsible for the attacks on the Marine barracks and the French and Israeli headquarters as well as for the bombing of the U.S. embassy in April 1983.

Page 211. **U.S. secretary of defense**: "Carnage in Lebanon," 18.

Page 211. **After all, President Reagan had declared**: "Lebanon Massacre," 25.

Page 211. **By February 3, 1983,**: William B. Quandt, "Reagan's Lebanon Policy: Trial and Error," *Middle East Journal* (Spring 1984), 249.

Page 212. **In January, even before the MNF retreated**: Wright, *Sacred Rage*, 102.

Page 213. **They claimed the abduction amounted**: Weir himself says that his kidnapping was linked to demands to free seventeen Shiites jailed in Kuwait for bombing the American and French embassies along with other Kuwaiti and foreign installations in December 1983. The same demand has surfaced in other kidnappings as well as in the hijacking of a Kuwaiti airliner in December 1984, when two officials of the U.S. Agency for International Development were shot, and again in the subsequent hijacking of another Kuwaiti airliner in April 1988.

Page 213. **During his captivity his wife, Carol, said of him**: Ben Weir and Carol Weir, *Hostage Bound, Hostage Free* (Philadelphia: Westminster Press, 1987), 34.

Page 214. **Weir later said**: Weir, *Hostage Bound*, Foreword.

Page 216. **At the controls of the plane**: "Two Who Triumphed over Terror," *Christian Science Monitor*, May 20, 1987, 17.

Page 216. **A scruffy, shaggy-haired man**: The group believed responsible for the hijacking is called the "Organization of the Oppressed of the Earth," a cell identified with the philosophy of the Hizbollah that is run by the Hamadei family. In August 1988, Muhammed Ali Hamadei, on trial in Germany for air piracy, admitted his involvement in the TWA hijacking. In September 1988, at the same trial, John Testrake identified Hamadei as the man who shot Robert Stethem.

Page 216. **In the name of God**: Wright, *Sacred Rage*, 274.

Page 217. **Sheikh Abdel Amir Qabalan gloated**: "We Eat, We Sleep, We Pray," *Newsweek*, July 1, 1985, 17.

Page 217. **As the plane hijacking faded**: Two Saudis and a Korean were among those taken hostage. Their abductors have never been identified, and it is suspected that their motive was ransom more than politics. In October 1985, four Russians also became victims of a fundamentalist Sunni group in Tripoli. The consular secretary was killed and the others released, but not before one hundred of the Soviet Union's diplomatic staff and dependents escaped to Damascus by bus.

Page 218. **Hostage-taking became an expression of power**: Mazher A. Hameed, *Arabia Imperiled: The Security Imperatives of the Arab Gulf States* (Washington, D.C.: Middle East Assessments Group, 1986), 51.

Page 220. **In 1986, Waite said**: "Waite: the Man, the Methods, the Mixed Reactions to His Plight," *Christian Science Monitor*, February 5, 1987, 7.

CHAPTER 10
CRY, LEBANON

Page 229. **[U]ndermining decadent Western society**: E. A. Wayne, "Militias cooperate on drug trade to pay for war—against each other," *Christian Science Monitor*, March 9, 1988.

Page 231. **"Lebanon's crisis has become self-perpetuating"**: Mary Curtius, "Lebanon's Reluctant but Dutiful Premier," *Christian Science Monitor*, June 19, 1987.

Page 231. **"The flaw of crossroads of culture"**: Gordon, *Lebanon: The Fragmented Nation*, 228.

CHAPTER 11
A HOUSE DIVIDED

Page 232. **"People lied to themselves in this country"**: Goria, *Sovereignty and Leadership*, 49.

Page 234. **"Reconciliation can be attained"**: "Lebanese Leaders Meet President Assad," *Syrian Times*, May 12, 1987.

Page 235. **[T]he day before Gemayel's term was to expire**: Between August 18 and September 22, the United States and Syria, each protecting its own interests, attempted to forge an agreement between the warring factions before the imminent end of Amin Gemayel's term. The new candidate that the bizarre Washington-Damascus axis put forth for president was Mikhail Daher, an all but unknown Maronite member of the Chamber of Deputies from northern Lebanon. The nomination went nowhere as the Maronites steadfastly refused to confirm the choice.

Page 235. **Other deputies . . . came**: At about the same time, four leading officials of Amal were in a car driving through the seaside district of Ouzai on their way to Beirut to await the outcome on the vote. Without warning, their limousine was hit by three rocket-propelled grenades and set afire. All died, along with their bodyguard. Two days earlier, a car laden with TNT had blown up, wounding Joseph Skaf, a Christian member of parliament.

Page 239. **"It is in our fundamental interests"**: Milton Viorst, "A Reporter at Large: The Christian Enclave," *New Yorker*, October 8, 1988, 66.

Page 241. **[T]he Druze vowed to use their geographic location and mighty militia**: In early 1989, Walid Jumblatt invited the estimated three hundred thousand Christians who were driven out of the Shuf during the war to return under the protection of the Druze militia.

Page 241. **They are split into competing power centers**: The Sunnis' armed strength in Tripoli lies with the fundamentalist religious movement Tawhid (Islamic Unity Movement) and in Sidon with the Muslim Popular Liberation Army, a militia largely composed of Nasserites and Fatah, Yassir Arafat's faction of the PLO. Prime Minister Rashid Karami, the Sunnis' most effective politician during the war, was assassinated in June 1987 by a bomb planted in the helicopter taking him on the twenty-five-minute trip from Tripoli to Beirut.

Page 244. **In mid-February 1987**: Another of Amal's rivals is the Lebanese Communist Party. Commanding a membership of approximately three thousand, it also competes with Amal for power among the poor Shiites. The party is one of the oldest political parties in Lebanon and draws members from both the Muslim and Christian communities. It fields a militia, which receives most of its arms and money from the Soviet Union.

Page 245. **"It was a fight to the finish"**: Ihsan A. Hijazi, "Unrivaled Clashes Raging in Streets of Western Beirut," *New York Times*, February 19, 1987.

Page 246. **"It's God's will"**: Mary Curtius, "While Beirut Burns, Skiing and Style Survive," *Christian Science Monitor*, March 3, 1987.

CHAPTER 12
CLOSING THE CROSSROADS

Page 249. **[T]he right to utilize Lebanon as a base of operations**: How Lebanon is to be used varies between Palestinian moderates and radicals. In early 1989, the Israeli government confirmed that since the United States announced its decision to open a dialogue with the PLO, Fatah, the Arafat-led faction of the Palestinian movement, had ceased raids against Israeli territory.

Page 250. **"The month long intra-Palestinian battles"**: Adeed Dawisha, "The Motives of Syria's Involvement in Lebanon," *Middle East Journal* 38 (Spring 1984), 235.

Page 251. **"[A] gift to our brothers"**: "Lebanese Militia Lifts 3-Year Siege," *International Herald Tribune*, January 18, 1988.

Page 252. **"[T]he football of the Middle East"**: Ihsan A. Hyazi, "To P.L.O., Base Is Not Home for Long," *New York Times*, July 5, 1988.

Page 253. **"The Syrians learned the hard way"**: *Christian Science Monitor*, June 18, 1986.

Page 253. **"[O]ne country and one people"**: Dawisha, "The Motives of Syria's Involvement in Lebanon," 229.

Page 256. **"The Syrians will tolerate no rival"**: R. K. Ramazani, *Revolutionary Iran: Challenge and Response in the Middle East* (Baltimore, Md.: The Johns Hopkins University Press, 1986), 195. Syrian response to Lebanon's Islamic fundamentalists is complicated by its alliance with Iran which began at the beginning of the Iraq-Iran war. The only reason for the existence of the relationship between a secular, socialist state and a quasi-theocracy is the common hatred of Iraq's Saddam Hussein shared by Hafiz Assad and Iran's revolutionary leaders. Although weak, the alliance hobbles Syria's drive to wipe out Hizbollah and its ambition of building an Islamic state free of Syrian control.

Page 257. **"Islamic movements throughout the Arab world"**: Ibid., 1683.

Page 258. **"[A]n old relationship"**: Ibid., 185.

Page 258. **So the influence of Iran weaves in and out of the anguish surrounding Hizbollah's hostages**: In early 1989, evidence began to surface of terrorist links between Hizbollah and radical factions of the PLO, specifically the Abu Nidal Group and the Popular Front for the Liberation of Palestine—General Command. Some evidence points to a link between these two groups in the bombing of Pan Am flight 103 in December 1988.

Page 261. **"Prior to World War II"**: Gordon, *Lebanon: The Fragmented Nation*, 14.

SELECTED BIBLIOGRAPHY

Ajami, Fouad. *The Arab Predicament: Arab Political Thought and Practice Since 1967.* Cambridge: Cambridge University Press, 1981.

——. "The Shadows of Hell." *Foreign Policy* 48 (Fall 1982).

——. *The Vanished Imam: Musa al Sadr and the Shia of Lebanon.* Ithaca, N.Y.: Cornell University Press, 1986.

Awal, Habib J. "Threat to Lebanon." *Commonweal,* August 8, 1947.

Bailey, Clinton. "Facing a Wounded Tiger." *Jerusalem Post Magazine,* March 15, 1985.

Barakat, Halim. "Social and Political Integration in Lebanon: A Case of Social Mosaic." *Middle East Journal* 27 (Summer 1973).

Betts, Robert Brenton. *Christians in the Arab East.* Atlanta: John Knox Press, 1978.

Bill, James A., and Carl Leiden. *Politics in the Middle East.* Boston: Little, Brown, 1984.

Bogardus, Emory S. "Social Change in Lebanon." *Sociology and Social Research* 39 (March-April 1955).

Bulloch, John. *Final Conflict: The War in Lebanon.* London: Century Publishing, 1983.

Churchill, Charles H. *The Druzes and the Maronites under Turkish Rule from 1840 to 1860.* London: Bernard Quaritch, 1862.

Cobban, Helena. *The Making of Modern Lebanon.* Boulder, Colo.: Westview Press, 1985.

Cole, Juan R. I., and Nikki R. Keddie. *Shi'ism and Social Protest.* New Haven, Conn.: Yale University Press, 1986.

Dawisha, Adeed. "The Motives of Syria's Involvement in Lebanon." *Middle East Journal* 38 (Spring 1984).

Deeb, Marius. "Lebanon's Continuing Conflict." *Current History* 34 (January 1985).

Eveland, Wilbur Crane. *Ropes of Sand: America's Failure in the Middle East*. New York: W. W. Norton, 1980.

Fadlallah, Sheikh Mohammed Hussein. *Islam and the Logic of Force*. Beirut: Al Dar al Islamiya, 1981.

Fisher, Sydney Nettleton. *The Middle East: A History*, 2d ed. New York: Alfred Knopf, 1969.

Frank, Benis M. *U.S. Marines in Lebanon, 1982–1984*. (monograph) Washington, D.C.: History and Museums Division, U.S. Marine Corps, 1987.

Frye, Richard N. *Islam and the West*. The Hague: Mouton and Company, 1957.

Fuller, Anne H. *Buarij: Portrait of a Lebanese Muslim Village*. Cambridge, Mass.: Harvard University Press, 1970.

Gilmour, David. *Lebanon: The Fractured Country*. New York: St. Martin's Press, 1984.

Gordon, David C. *Lebanon: The Fragmented Nation*. London: Croom Helm, 1980.

Goria, Wade R. *Sovereignty and Leadership in Lebanon, 1943–1976*. London: Ithaca Press, 1985.

Gubser, Peter. "The Politics of Economic Interest Groups in a Lebanese Town." *Middle East Studies* 11 (October 1975).

Hameed, Mazher A. *Arabia Imperilled: The Security Imperatives of the Arab Gulf States*. Washington, D.C.: Middle East Assessments Group, 1986.

Hitti, Philip K. *Lebanon in History: From the Earliest Times to the Present*. London: Macmillan and Company, Ltd., 1957.

———. *The Origins of the Druze People and Religion*. New York: Ams Press, 1966.

Hudson, Michael C. *The Precarious Republic: Political Modernization of Lebanon*. New York: Random House, 1968.

———. "Democracy and Social Mobilization in Lebanese Politics." *Comparative Politics* I (January 1969).

———. "The Palestine Factor in the Lebanese Civil War," *Middle East Journal* 32 (Summer 1978).

Jabbra, Joseph G., and Nancy W. Jabbra. "Local Political Dynamics in Lebanon: The Case of Ain al-Qasis." *Anthropological Quarterly* 51 (April 1978).

Jansen, Michael. *The Battle of Beirut*. London: Zed Press, 1982.

Johnson, Michael. "Factional Politics in Lebanon: The Case of the

'Islamic Society of Benevolent Intentions (al-Maqasid)' in Beirut." *Middle Eastern Studies* 14 (January 1978).

Khalaf, Samir. *Lebanon's Predicament*. New York: Columbia University Press, 1987.

Khalidi, Walid. *Conflict and Violence in Lebanon*. Cambridge, Mass.: Harvard University for International Affairs, 1979.

Khuri, Fuad. *From Village to Suburb: Order and Change in Greater Beirut*. Chicago: University of Chicago Press, 1975.

Lamb, David. *The Arabs: Journeys Beyond the Mirage*. New York: Random House, 1987.

"Lebanon: Land of Milk and Honey." *Travel*, August 1975.

Leibling, A. J. "Along the Visa Via." *The New Yorker*, August 23, 1958.

Lewis, Bernard. *The Political Language of Islam*. Chicago: University of Chicago Press, 1988.

McDowall, David. *Lebanon: A Conflict of Minorities*. London: Minority Rights Group, Ltd., 1983.

Meo, Leila M. T. *Lebanon: Improbable Nation: A Study in Political Development*. Bloomington, Ind.: Indiana University Press, 1965.

Morris, Benny. *The Birth of the Palestinian Refugee Problem, 1947–1949*. Cambridge: Cambridge University Press, 1987.

Muir, Jim. "Lebanon: Arena of Conflict, Crucible of Peace." *Middle East Journal* 38 (Spring 1984).

Nasr, Nafhat, and Monte Palmer. "Alienation and Political Participation in Lebanon." *International Journal of Middle East Studies* 8 (October 1977).

Nazir-Ali, Michael. *Islam: A Christian Perspective*. Philadelphia: Westminster Press, 1983.

Norton, Augustus Richard. *External Intervention and the Politics of Lebanon*. Washington, D.C.: Washington Institute for Values in Public Policy, 1984.

———. *Amal and the Shi'a: Struggle for the Soul of Lebanon*. Austin, Tex.: University of Texas Press, 1987.

Owen, Roger, ed. *Essays on the Crisis in Lebanon*. London: Ithaca Press, 1976.

Patai, Raphael. *The Arab Mind*, rev. ed. New York: Charles Scribner's Sons, 1983.

Quandt, William B. "Reagan's Lebanon Policy: Trial and Error." *Middle East Journal* 38 (Spring 1984).

Rabinovich, Itamar. *The War for Lebanon, 1970–1985*. Ithaca, N.Y.: Cornell University Press, 1985.

Ramazani, R. K. *Revolutionary Iran: Challenge and Response in the Middle East*. Baltimore, Md.: The Johns Hopkins University Press, 1986.

Randal, Jonathan C. *Going All the Way: Christian Warlords, Israeli Adventurers, and the War in Lebanon*. New York: Viking Press, 1983.

Salibi, Kamal S. *Crossroads to Civil War: Lebanon 1958–76*. New York: Caravan Books, 1976.

Schiff, Ze'ev, and Ehud Ya'ari. *Israel's Lebanon War*. New York: Simon and Schuster, 1984.

Schmidt, Dana Adams. *Armageddon in the Middle East*. New York: John Day, 1974.

Snider, Lewis A. "The Lebanese Forces: Their Origins and Role in Lebanon's Politics." *Middle East Journal* 38 (Winter 1984).

Soffer, Aron. "Lebanon—Where Demography Is the Core of Politics and Life." *Middle East Studies* 22 (April 1986).

"Struggle for Lebanon: A Christian Israel." *New Statesman*, July 6, 1957.

Urquhart, David. *The Mountain: Mt. Souria: A History and a Diary*. London: Thomas Cautley Newby, 1860.

Vocke, Harold. *The Lebanese War: Its Origins and Political Dimensions*. New York: St. Martin's Press, 1978.

Wechsberg, Joseph. "Letter from Lebanon." *The New Yorker*, November 8, 1952.

Weinberger, Naomi Joy. *Syrian Intervention in Lebanon*. New York: Oxford, 1986.

Weir, Ben, and Carol Weir. *Hostage Bound, Hostage Free*. Philadelphia: Westminster Press, 1987.

"West Went Thataway, East!" *Life*, January 7, 1966.

Wolfe, Gayle, and Alia Mounribi. "A Comparison of the Value System of Lebanese Christian and Muslim Men and Women." *Journal of Social Psychology* 125 (December 1985).

Wright, Robin. *Sacred Rage: The Wrath of Militant Islam*. New York: Simon and Schuster, 1985.

INDEX

Edde family, 97
Education, 7, 8, 13, 71, 109, 137
  Palestinians and, 131, 132
  Shiites and, 195, 253
Egypt, 123, 129. *See also* Nasser,
  Gamal Abdel
  1952 military coup in, 7
  Phoenicians and, 19-20
  Shiites vs., 257
Ehdene massacre, 99, 100
Ein al Hilweh, 129, 131, 142
Eisenhower Doctrine, 123, 125
Elections after independence,
  117-18
Emigre remittances, 8, 88, 134, 195,
  228
Excelsior Hotel, 163

Fadlallah, Sheikh Muhammed
  Hussein, 205-6, 258
Faisal, King, 71
  oil embargo and, 151
  overthrow of, 124-25
Families of power, 95-98. *See also*
  Zuama
Family, primacy of in Arab culture,
  84, 87-89, 103
Fatah, 181, 192, 241, 250. *See also*
  Arafat, Yassir; Palestine
  Liberation Organization
  origin of, 141
Fatahland, 145
Fatima, 57
Fayrauz, 22
Fear of shame in Arab culture,
  84-85
Franjieh family, 95, 97, 98
  vs. Gemayel family (vendetta),
  98-100, 182, 170
Franjieh, Hamid, 49
Franjieh, Suleiman, 47-48, 49-50,
  99, 136, 150, 155, 158, 162, 166,
  170, 234, 235
  administration of, 148
  election of, 147-48
Franjieh, Tony, 50, 99
Freedom of the press, 9
French Foreign Legion, 189
French Mandate, 27, 43, 47, 70, 246
  colonial government of, 109-10
  Lebanon under, 105-13
French, 48, 123, 254
  Lebanese blame of, 246
  Lebanese policy today, 259

Maronites' attachment to, 43-44
  Shiites and, 76
  Sunnis' attachment to, 71
Fundamentalism, 29, 205-8. *See
  also* Hizbollah; Maronites;
  Shiites

Gemayel, Amin, 3, 169, 186, 189,
  211, 212, 233, 234, 235, 236,
  238-39, 255. *See also* Maronite
  Christians
  election of, 185
Gemayel, Bashir, 97, 192, 208
  assassination of, 100, 183
  election of, 182
  image of in the West, 170
  Israel and, 174-75, 176, 178
  kidnapping of, 149
  manifesto of, 170-71
  rise of, 169
Gemayel family vs. Franjieh family
  (vendetta), 98-100, 170, 182
Gemayel, Pierre, 47, 50-53, 91, 98,
  99, 100, 135, 136, 145-46, 157,
  162, 169, 182, 234
Ghanem, General Iskander, 157
Golden Age of Lebanon, 4-16, 94,
  223, 248-49, 259-60
  American University of Beirut
  during, 25-27
  Arab nationalists' suspicion
  toward, 69
  Christian-Muslim rivalry during,
  90
  Shiites and, 75
  divisions during, 138
  homicide rate during, 93
  Muslims and, 67
  political corruption during, 101-4
  under Charles Helou, 136-40
Gouraud, General Henri, 105
Government structure, Lebanese,
  11, 12-13, 65, 65
  Nasser's threat to, 121
  under the National Pact, 113,
  118-19
Great Britain, 219, 246, 262. *See
  also* Thatcher, Margaret
Greater Lebanon, 163, 194, 243, 259
  creation of, 106-7
Greater Syria, 38-39, 165
  Muslim enthusiasm for, 110, 120
Greek Catholics, 12, 41, 237, 241

National Movement, 161–62, 173
  collapse of, 168
  composition of, 161
  Palestinians' joining of, 164–65
  Shiites and, 200
  vs. Lebanese Front, 161
National Pact, the, 51, 65, 116, 126,
    138, 145, 152, 162, 170, 185, 194
  establishment of, 113–14
  political system under, 118–19
  replacement of, 255
  validity of, 234–35
National Salvation Front, 188, 189
Nationalism, Lebanese
  Shiites and, 199
  weakness of, 103
Nazi Germany, 113, 115
Nazira, Sitt (Lady), 64
Nestorians, 30
Nixon, Richard, 145
Normandy Hotel, 6, 159
North, Oliver, 221

Oil boom, 8, 16, 151–52
Oil embargo, 151
Oil, Arab, 4, 6, 7
Oil, Lebanese, 134
Olympics (1972), 150
Operation Big Pines, 174–82
Ottomans, 18, 63, 70, 109

Padfield, Douglas, 214
Padfield, Philip, 214
Pahlavi, Shah Muhammad Reza,
    199, 201, 202
Pakistan, 125
Palestine. See Israel
Palestine Liberation Army, 241. See
  also Fatah
Palestine Liberation Organization
  (PLO), 2, 82, 141, 170, 202, 212,
  255. See also Arafat, Yassir;
  Fatah; Palestinians
  birth of, 141
  commando raids of, 142, 147, 148,
    198, 252
  evacuation of from Beirut, 178–82,
    250
  Jordan and, 146, 147
  Lebanon as base of operations of,
    153
  Shiites and, 198–2, 204–5
  sovereignty over Fatahland, 145
  Syria vs., 146–47
  terrorism of, 208

U.S. recognition of, 262
vs. Israel, 173–79
Palestinian Red Crescent, 2, 184
Palestinian refugee camps, 11, 129,
  131–32, 142, 250. See also
  Massacre at Sabra and
  Palestinian refugees
Palestinians, 11, 15–16, 27, 128–32,
  139–58, 164, 191, 209, 230, 237,
  239, 246. See also Intifadah;
  Palestine Liberation
  Organization; Arafat, Yassir
  as catalyst for civil war, 12
  hostage-taking and, 213
  policy of in Lebanon, 249–53
  upper-class, 7
Pan-Arabism, 9, 26, 45, 66
  Baath Party and, 165
  Druze resistance to, 63
  Nasser and, 120–21
  Palestinian identity distinct from,
    141
  Rashid Karami and, 73–74
  Saeb Salam and, 73
  Shiites and, 79, 199
  Sunnis and, 138
  defined, 69
Parliament, 233, 235
Parti Populaire Syrien (PPS)
  (Syrian National Party), 38–39,
  72, 122, 161, 183, 195
Pasha, Jamal, 106
Persia. See Iran
Persians, 21
Phalange, the, 145–46, 161, 171, 182,
  186, 210. See also Sabra and
  Shatila massacre
  alliance with Arafat, 188
  Ehdene massacre and, 99
  elimination of Maronite rivals,
    169–70
  emergence of, 157–58
  origin of, 50–53
  vs. the PLO, 148–49
Phalange militia, 122
Pharon, Henri, 102
Phoenicia Hotel, 4–6, 84, 117, 151,
  163, 260
Phoenicians, 7, 19–22, 23, 222
  Maronite identification with, 20,
    42–43, 46, 51
Political bosses. See Zuama
Popular Front for the Liberation of
  Palestine (PFLP), 141, 150, 195
Powell, Dwayne, 209

Tigers, the, 161, 170
Tripartite Agreement, 255
Turkey, 124, 125
TWA flight 847 hijacking, 216-17

United Arab Republic (UAR),
   122-23
United Nations Interim Force in
   Lebanon (UNIFIL), 173, 175,
   217, 253
United Nations Relief and Works
   Agency (UNRWA), 129, 131
United States, 2-3, 48, 123, 124,
   134, 143, 242, 246, 254
   Arab attitude toward, 261-62
   as ally of Maronites, 115, 166
   hostages of in Iran, 258
   intervention in civil war of 1958,
      125-26
   Israel and, 217
   Israel's 1982 invasion of Lebanon
      and, 179-82, 190-91
   Litani Operation and, 173
   Marines in Lebanon, 2-3, 125-26,
      181, 184, 189, 209-12, 260,
      264
   Shiites and, 215
   recognition of PLO, 262
   support for Israel, 262-64
   support of Bashir Gemayel, 182
   terrorism and, 217, 218-21
Urban II, Pope, 23, 35
Urquhart, David, 78, 93
Usairan family, 76

Vendettas, 12
   as part of Arab culture, 93-100
   elections and, 117-18
   Gemayel family vs. Franjieh
      family, 98-100, 170, 182
Vietnam War, 185, 211

Village, importance of in Arab
   culture, 89
Violence, as part of Arab culture,
   92-94

Waite, Terry, 220-21
Waring, Robert O., 207
Weinberger, Caspar, 211
Weir, Carol, 194, 213
Weir, Reverend Benjamin, 194, 213,
   214, 220, 221
Weizmann, Chaim, 115
West Germany, 259
Westernization, Maronites and,
   41-42
Westernization, Muslim vs.
   Christian attitude toward, 67-68

Yamin, Father Yussef, 99

Zain family, 76
Zghorta Liberation Army, 50, 161
Zionism, 130, 243, 250, 262
   Maronite support of, 115
Zuama (political bosses), 95-101,
   155, 182
   after independence, 115-19
   the civil war of 1958 and, 125-26
   decline of, 234
   economy and, 196
   failure of to strike final
      compromise, 162
   impotence of, 157, 167
   Israeli attacks and, 151
   Nasserism and, 121
   the National Pact and, 113
   Palestinians and, 130-31, 144
   private militias of, 119
   Shihab vs., 133-36
   under French Mandate, 109